Fig. 86. Maze at Hatfield House, Herts.

MAZES
AND LABYRINTHS
THEIR HISTORY AND
DEVELOPMENT

BY

W. H. MATTHEWS

DOVER PUBLICATIONS, INC.

NEW YORK

This Dover edition, first published in 1970, is an
unabridged and unaltered republication of the work
originally published by Longmans, Green and Co.
in London in 1922, under the title *Mazes and Labyrinths: A General Account of Their History and
Developments.*

Standard Book Number: 486-22614-X
Library of Congress Catalog Card Number: 70-107665

Manufactured in the United States of America
Dover Publications, Inc.
180 Varick Street
New York, N.Y. 10014

To

ZETA

whose innocent prattlings on the
summer sands of Sussex
inspired its conception
this book
is most affectionately
dedicated

PREFACE

ADVANTAGES out of all proportion to the importance of the immediate aim in view are apt to accrue whenever an honest endeavour is made to find an answer to one of those awkward questions which are constantly arising from the natural working of a child's mind. It was an endeavour of this kind which formed the nucleus of the inquiries resulting in the following little essay.

It is true that the effort in this case has not led to complete success in so far as that word denotes the formulation of an exact answer to the original question, which, being one of a number evoked by parental experiments in seaside sand-maze construction, was: "Father, who made mazes first of all?" On the other hand, one hesitates to apply so harsh a term as "failure" when bearing in mind the many delightful excursions, rural as well as literary, which have been involved and the alluring vistas of possible future research that have been opened up from time to time in the course of such excursions.

By no means the least of the adventitious benefits enjoyed by the explorer has been the acquisition of a keener sense of appreciation of the labours of the archaeologist, the anthropologist, and other, more special, types of investigator, any one of whom would naturally be far better qualified to discuss the theme under consideration —at any rate from the standpoint of his particular branch of learning—than the present author can hope to be.

The special thanks of the writer are due to Professor W. M. Flinders Petrie for permission to make use of his diagram of the conjectural restoration of the

Labyrinth of Egypt, Fig. 4, and the view of the shrine of Amenemhat III, Fig. 2, also for facilities to sketch the Egyptian plaque in his collection which is shown in Fig. 19 and for drawing the writer's attention thereto; to Sir Arthur Evans for the use of his illustrations of double axes and of the Tomb of the Double Axe which appear as Figs. 9, 10, 11 and 12 respectively (Fig. 8 is also based on one of his drawings); to M. Picard (of the *Librairie A. Picard*) for leave to reproduce the drawing of the Susa mosaic, Fig. 37; to Mr. J. H. Craw, F.S.A. (Scot.), Secretary of the Berwickshire Naturalists' Club, for the use of the illustrations of sculptured rocks, Figs. 128 and 129; to the Rev. E. A. Irons for the photograph of the Wing maze, Fig. 60, and to the Rev. G. Yorke for the figure of the Alkborough "Julian's Bower," Fig. 59.

The many kind-hearted persons who have earned the gratitude of the writer by acceding to his requests for local information, or by bringing useful references to his notice, will perhaps take no offence if he thanks them collectively, though very heartily, in this place. In most cases where they are not mentioned individually in the text they will be found quoted as authorities in the bibliographical appendix. The present is, however, the most fitting place in which to express a cordial acknowledgment of the assistance rendered by the writer's friend, Mr. G. F. Green, whose skill and experience in the photographic art has been of very great value.

Grateful recognition must also be made of the help and courtesy extended to the writer by the officials of several libraries, museums, and other institutions, notably the British Museum, the Society of Antiquaries, Sion College, and the Royal Horticultural Society.

W. H. M.

Ruislip, Middlesex.
   1922.

CONTENTS

CHAPTER I

INTRODUCTION

CHAPTER II

THE EGYPTIAN LABYRINTH

(i) *Accounts of the Ancient Writers*

CHAPTER III

THE EGYPTIAN LABYRINTH (*continued*)

(ii) *Accounts of Later Explorers*

CHAPTER VIII

THE LABYRINTH IN ANCIENT ART

CHAPTER IX

CHURCH LABYRINTHS

CHAPTER X

TURF LABYRINTHS

CHAPTER XI

TURF LABYRINTHS (*continued*)

CHAPTER XII
The Origin of Turf Mazes

CHAPTER XIII
The Floral Labyrinth and the Dwarf-Shrub Maze

CHAPTER XIV
The Topiary Labyrinth, or Hedge Maze

CHAPTER XV
The Topiary Labyrinth, or Hedge Maze (continued)

CHAPTER XX

Maze Etymology

CHAPTER XXI

Labyrinth Design and the Solution of Mazes

CHAPTER XXII

The Labyrinth in Literature

CHAPTER XXIII

Miscellanea and Conclusion

xiv

LIST OF ILLUSTRATIONS

MAZES AND LABYRINTHS

CHAPTER I

INTRODUCTION

A DELIGHTFUL air of romance and mystery surrounds the whole subject of Labyrinths and Mazes.

The hedge-maze, which is the only type with which most of us have a first-hand acquaintance, is generally felt to be a survival of a romantic age, even though we esteem its function as nothing higher than that of a playground for children. Many a tender intrigue has been woven around its dark yew alleys. Mr. Compton Mackenzie, for example, introduces it most effectively as a lovers' rendezvous in "The Passionate Elopement," and no doubt the readers of romantic literature will recall other instances of a like nature. The story of fair Rosamond's Bower is one which will leap to the mind in this connection.

This type of maze alone is worth more than a passing thought, but it is far from being the only, or even the most interesting, development of the labyrinth idea.

What is the difference, it may be asked, between a *maze* and a *labyrinth?* The answer is, little or none. Some writers seem to prefer to apply the word "maze" to hedge-mazes only, using the word "labyrinth" to denote the structures described by the writers of antiquity, or as a general term for any confusing arrangement of paths. Others, again, show a tendency to restrict the application of the term "maze" to cases in which the idea of a puzzle is involved.

It would certainly seem somewhat inappropriate to talk of "the Cretan Maze" or "the Hampton Court Labyrinth," but, generally speaking, we may use the words interchangeably, regarding "maze" as merely the northern equivalent of the classic "labyrinth." Both words have come to signify a complex path of some kind, but when we press for a closer definition we encounter difficulties. We cannot, for instance, say that it is "a tortuous branched path designed to baffle or deceive those who attempt to find the goal to which it leads," for, though that description holds good in some cases, it ignores the many cases in which there is only one path, without branches, and therefore no intent to baffle or mislead, and others again in which there is no definite "goal." We cannot say that it is a winding path "bounded by walls or hedges," for in many instances there are neither walls nor hedges. One of the most famous labyrinths, for example, consisted chiefly of a vast and complicated series of rooms and columns. In fact, we shall find it convenient to leave the question of the definition of the words, and also that of their origin, until we have examined the various examples that exist or are known to have existed.

It may be necessary, here and there, to make reference to various archæological or antiquarian books and other writings, but the outlook of the general reader, rather than that of the professed student, has been mainly borne in mind.

The object of this book is simply to provide a readable survey of a subject which, in view of the lure it has exercised throughout many ages and under a variety of forms, has been almost entirely neglected in our literature—the subject of mazes and labyrinths treated from

2

a general and not a purely archæological, horticultural, mathematical, or artistic point of view.

Such references as have been made have therefore been accompanied in most cases by some explanatory or descriptive phrase, a provision which might be considered unnecessary or out of place in a book written for the trained student.

For the benefit of such as may wish to verify, or to investigate more fully, any of the matters dealt with, a classified list of references has been compiled and will be found at the end of the book.

The first summary of any importance to be published in this country on the subject was a paper by the Venerable Edward Trollope, F.S.A., Archdeacon of Stow, which appeared in the *Archaeological Journal* and in the "Proceedings" of a provincial archaeological society in 1858. Nearly all subsequent writers on the subject—in this country at any rate—have drawn largely upon the paper in question and have made little advance upon it.

The "Encyclopaedia Britannica" contains an illustrated article, written originally by a botanist and chiefly concerned with hedge-mazes. Such books as Rouse Ball's "Mathematical Recreations," Andrews' "Ecclesiastical Curiosities," and Dudeney's "Amusements in Mathematics" devote each a chapter or so to the matter, and from time to time there have been brief displays of interest in some aspect or other of the topic in popular periodicals, the most notable being a pair of richly illustrated articles in *Country Life* in 1903. A condensed and scholarly review of the subject, in so far as it is relevant to his main *thesis*, is contained in the first volume of Mr. A. B. Cook's ponderous work on "Zeus" (1914). A similar remark applies to the recently published (1921) Volume I of Sir Arthur Evans's magnificent summary of his Cretan researches, "The Palace of Minos at Knossos." There is a characteristically Ruskinian discourse on Labyrinths in "Fors Clavigera"

(Fors No. 23); and an interesting, if not convincing, section of Mr. E. O. Gordon's "Prehistoric London" adduces a certain amount of labyrinth lore in support of the Trojan origin of the metropolis. So far as the writer has been able to ascertain, no book dealing solely with the subject has hitherto appeared in our language.

In 1915–16 there appeared posthumously in the *Revue Archéologique* a very remarkable series of articles on "Les Fallacieux Détours du Labyrinthe" by a brilliant young French archaeologist, M. Robert de Launay, who was killed on the field of honour at Neuville-St.-Vaast in May 1915. The articles are characterised by great boldness and enthusiasm and show a wide range of knowledge, but it is probable that, if the author had lived, mature consideration would have led him to modify some of his conclusions. This is the most recent work of importance on the subject, though the new work by Sir A. Evans mentioned above contains much interesting and valuable information on certain aspects.

In the following chapters an attempt is made to set forth, as readably as may be, an account of the various devices in which the labyrinth-idea has been embodied, to indicate where examples may be found, to give some notion of the speculations which have been made regarding their origins, and to consider the possibilities of the idea from the point of view of amusement and recreation.

The earliest labyrinths of which mention is made by the classic writers are those of Egypt and Crete, and we shall find it convenient to consider these first of all. We will then notice the other labyrinths alluded to by the writers of antiquity, and pass on to a consideration of labyrinthine designs introduced by way of ornament or symbolism in various objects of later classic art. We shall see that the labyrinth-idea was adopted and developed by the Christian Church in the Middle Ages, and will note its progress as a medium of horticultural embellishment. It will be interesting to examine the mathematical prin-

4

ciples, such as they are, which underlie the construction or solution of mazes, also to see in what a number of ways these principles may be applied.

We shall find that our inquiry will bring us into contact with a greater variety of subjects than one would at first be inclined to imagine, 'and that labyrinths and mazes need not by any means be considered as exclusively a concern of archaeologists and children.

Incidentally we may help to rescue from threatened oblivion a certain class of native antiquities, small and diminishing in number, but surely worth sufficient attention to ensure their preservation, namely, the *turf-labyrinths*.

As to the actual origin and primary purpose of these devices we cannot be dogmatic on the evidence before us, and herein, perhaps, lies a good deal of their charm. When we can classify and date with precision any object which is not of a utilitarian nature we relegate it at once to our mental museum, and a museum is only too apt to become an *oubliette*. But when there is a considerable margin for speculation, or, as we usually say, a certain amount of "mystery" in the case, we are more likely to find pleasure in rehandling it, looking at it from different points of view and wondering about it. Let us grant, by all means, that there are quite sufficient unsolved riddles in nature and life without raising up artificial mysteries. Let us even admit that when evidence is available (which, by the way, is not the same thing as *existent*) it is better to settle a question straight away than to leave it open to further argument. At the same time, let us not be too hasty in accepting speculations, however shrewd, as proved facts. Antiquarian books should naturally be as free as possible from actual misstatements, but they have lost all their charm when they become collections of bald dogmatic statements or mere descriptive catalogues.

CHAPTER II

(i) *Accounts of the Ancient Writers*

THE earliest structure of any kind to which we find the word *labyrinth* applied was a huge building situated in the North of Egypt, a land always noted for its stupendous monuments, and was probably constructed more than 2000 years before the commencement of the Christian era.

We live in an age when the use of constructional steel enables the dreams of the architect to materialise in many ways that would astonish the builders of old; nevertheless, the modern citizen, whatever his nationality, can rarely resist a feeling akin to awe when making his first acquaintance with such works as the Pyramids of Egypt. One can imagine, then, what a profound effect these massive edifices must have exerted on the minds of travellers in earlier ages.

We find, as we might expect, many wild exaggerations in individual descriptions and corresponding discrepancies between the various accounts of any particular monument, and this is to some extent the case with regard to the Egyptian Labyrinth.

A fairly detailed and circumstantial account has come down to us from the Greek writer Herodotus.

Herodotus, who is rightly spoken of as the Father of History, was born about 484 B.C. and lived about sixty

6

years, of which he spent a considerable number in travelling about over most of the then known world. Those who are fortunate enough to be able to read his works in their original tongue are charmed by their freshness, simplicity, and harmonious rhythm, but those who look to him for accurate information on any but contemporary events or matters with which he was personally acquainted are apt to find a rather too credulous acceptance of the wonderful. No doubt the poetical instinct in Herodotus was stronger than the critical spirit of the true historian, but, so far as the records of his personal observations are concerned, there seems to be no reason to accuse him of gross exaggeration.

The Labyrinth of Egypt he himself visited, as he tells us in his second book, and seems to have been considerably impressed by it. After describing how the Egyptians divided the land into twelve parts, or *nomes*, and set a king over each, he says that they agreed to combine together to leave a memorial of themselves. They then constructed the Labyrinth, just above Lake Moeris, and nearly opposite the city of crocodiles (Crocodilopolis). "I found it," he says, "greater than words could tell, for, although the temple at Ephesus and that at Samos are celebrated works, yet all of the works and buildings of the Greeks put together would certainly be inferior to this labyrinth as regards labour and expense." Even the pyramids, he tells us, were surpassed by the Labyrinth. "It has twelve covered courts, with opposite doors, six courts on the North side and six on the South, all communicating with one another and with one wall surrounding them all. There are two sorts of rooms, one sort above, the other sort below ground, fifteen hundred of each sort, or three thousand in all." He says that he was allowed to pass through the upper rooms only, the lower range being strictly guarded from visitors, as they contained the tombs of the kings who had built the Labyrinth, also the tombs of the sacred crocodiles.

The upper rooms he describes as being of super-human size, and the system of passages through the courts, rooms, and colonnades very intricate and bewildering. The roof of the whole affair, he says, is of stone and the walls are covered with carvings. Each of the courts is surrounded by columns of white stone, perfectly joined. Outside the Labyrinth, and at one corner of it, is a pyramid about 240 feet in height, with huge figures carved upon it and approached by an underground passage.

Herodotus expresses even greater admiration, however, for the lake beside the Labyrinth, which he describes as being of vast size and artificially constructed, having two pyramids arising from its bed, each supporting a colossal seated statue. The water for the lake, he says, is brought from the Nile by a canal.

The Labyrinth and the lake are also described at some length by another great traveller, Strabo, who lived about four centuries after Herodotus. He wrote, amongst other works, a Geography of the World in seventeen volumes, the last of which treats of Egypt and other parts of Africa. Like Herodotus, he speaks of the Labyrinth from personal observation. After referring to the lake and the manner in which it is used as a storage reservoir for the water of the Nile, he proceeds to describe the Labyrinth, "a work equal to the Pyramids." He says it is "a large palace composed of as many palaces as there were formerly *nomes*. There are an equal number of courts, surrounded by columns and adjoining one another, all in a row and constituting one building, like a long wall with the courts in front of it. The entrances to the courts are opposite the wall; in front of these entrances are many long covered alleys with winding intercommunicating passages, so that a stranger could not find his way in or out unless with a guide. Each of these structures is roofed with a single slab of stone, as are also the covered alleys, no timber or any other material being used." If one

8

ascends to the roof, he says, one looks over "a field of stone." The courts were in a line, supported by a row of twenty-seven monolithic columns, the walls also being constructed of stones of as great a size.

"At the end of the building is the royal tomb, consisting of a square pyramid and containing the body of *Imandes.*"

Strabo says that it was the custom of the twelve *nomes* of Egypt to assemble, with their priests and priestesses, each *nome* in its own court, for the purpose of sacrificing to the gods and administering justice in important matters.

He mentions that the inhabitants of the particular *nome* in the vicinity worshipped the crocodile which was kept in the lake and answered to the name of Suchus (Sebek). This animal was apparently quite tame and used to be presented by visitors with offerings of bread, flesh, wine, honey, and milk.

In certain parts of his works Strabo speaks rather disrespectfully of Herodotus as a writer, classing him as a marvel-monger, but it will be seen that in several important respects these two accounts of the Egyptian Labyrinth are in fair agreement.

Another writer of about the same period as Strabo, known as Diodorus the Sicilian, wrote a long, rambling compilation which he called a "Historical Library" and in which he describes the Egyptian Labyrinth and Lake Moeris. He says the latter was constructed by King Moeris, who left a place in the middle where he built himself a sepulchre and two pyramids—one for himself and one for his queen—surmounted by colossal seated statues. Diodorus says that the king gave the money resulting from the sale of the fish caught in the lake, amounting to a silver talent a day, to his wife "to buy her pins."

A generation or so later the Roman writer Pomponius Mela gives a short account of this labyrinth, probably at second-hand, and early in the first century of the

9

Christian era Pliny, in his "Natural History," has a good deal to say on the subject. He refers to labyrinths generally as "the most stupendous works on which mankind has expended its labours."

Regarding the Egyptian Labyrinth he says, "there exists still, in the *nome* of Heracleopolites, a labyrinth first built, it is said, three thousand six hundred years ago, by King Petesuchis or Tithoës," but he goes on to quote Herodotus, to the effect that it was built by twelve kings, the last of whom was Psammetichus, and two other writers who give the king's name as Moiris and Moteris respectively, "whilst others, again, assert that it was a building dedicated to the Sun-god, an opinion which is generally accepted."

He also refers to the fact that the roof was of stone, and notes as a surprising point that the parts around the entrance were constructed of Parian marble, whilst the columns of the other parts were of syenite. "This great mass is so solidly built that the lapse of time has been quite unable to destroy it, but it has been badly ravaged by the people of Heracleopolites, who have always detested it. To describe the whole of it in detail would be quite impossible, as it is divided up into regions and prefectures, called *nomes*, thirty in number, with a great palace to each; in addition it must contain temples of all the gods of Egypt and forty statues of Nemesis in the same number of sacred shrines, as well as numerous pyramids." He describes it further as having "banquet halls reached by steep ascents, flights of ninety steps leading down from the porticoes, porphyritic columns, figures of gods and hideous monsters, and statues of kings. Some of the palaces are so made that the opening of a door makes a terrifying sound as of thunder. Most of the buildings are in total darkness. Outside the labyrinth there is another great heap of buildings, called the 'Pteron,' under which are passages leading to other subterranean palaces."

CHAPTER III

(ii) *Accounts of Later Explorers*

A STRUCTURE which evoked so much wonder and admiration in ancient times can hardly fail to have aroused the curiosity of later generations, but no serious attempts to locate it seem to have been made by Europeans until several centuries later. It was then far too late to observe any of its glories, for it was all but destroyed in Roman times, and a village sprang up on its site, largely constructed from its debris.

The Italian traveller Gemelli-Careri, who visited Egypt in 1693, refers to a subterranean labyrinth which he saw in the neighbourhood of the Pyramids. In the English version of his account we read: ". . . the Arabs conducted us to see a Labyrinth, where the Ancients bury'd Birds. We went down a narrow Passage into a Room out of which we crept on our Bellies through a Hole to certain ways where a man may walk well enough upright. On both sides of these there are Urns, in which the Birds were bury'd; there is now nothing in them but a little dust. These Ways are cut out of a *nitrous* Stone, and run several miles like a City under ground, which they call a Labyrinth." There is nothing in this description, however, to suggest that these works had any connection with the Labyrinth of the ancients.

In 1700 Paul Lucas, the Antiquary to Louis XIV,

11

went on a voyage to Egypt, and, in the book in which he subsequently published the account of his travels, gives us some idea of the state of the remains in his time, but his account is very rambling and unreliable. Fig. 1 is a view which he gives of part of the ruins of the alleged labyrinth.

Lucas states that an old Arab who accompanied his party professed to have explored the interior of the ruins many years before, and to have penetrated into its subterranean passages to a large chamber surrounded by several niches, "like little shops," whence endless alleys and other rooms branched off. By the time of Lucas's visit, however, these passages could not be traced, and he concluded that they had become blocked up by debris.

The next explorer to visit the spot seems to have been Dr. Richard Pococke, whose "Description of the East" appeared in 1743. "We observed at a great distance," he says, "the temple of the Labyrinth, and being about a league from it, I observed several heaps as of ruins, covered with sand, and many stones all round as if there had been some great building there: they call it the town of Caroon (Bellet Caroon). It seemed to have been of a considerable breadth from east to west, and the buildings extended on each side towards the north to the Lake Moeris and the temple. This without doubt is the spot of the famous Labyrinth which Herodotus says was built by the twelve kings of Egypt." He describes what he takes to be the pyramid of the Labyrinth as a building about 165 feet long by 80 broad, very much ruined, and says it is called the "Castle of Caroon."

The neighbourhood was also explored by the archaeologists who accompanied that remarkable expedition sent out by Napoleon at the end of the eighteenth century, and one of them, Jomard, believed that he had discovered the ruins of the Labyrinth.

In 1843 a Prussian expedition, under K. R. Lepsius, carried out considerable excavations in the locality and

12

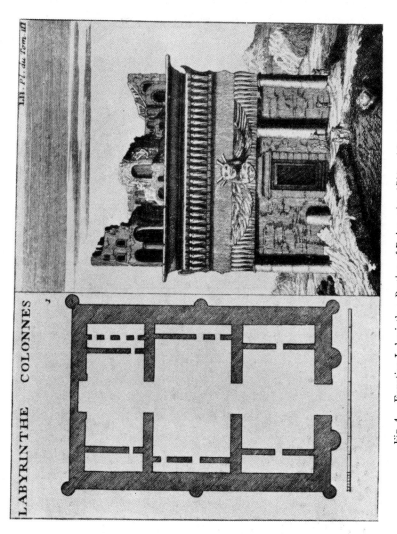

LABYRINTHE COLONNES

LIII. Pl. du Tom. III

Fig. 1. Egyptian Labyrinth. Portion of Ruins, *circ.* 1700. (*Paul Lucas*)

Fig. 2.   Egyptian Labyrinth   Shrine of Amenemhat III.   (*Flinders Petrie*)

claimed to have established the actual site of the Labyrinth, attaching great importance to a series of brick chambers which they unearthed. The data furnished by this party, however, were not altogether of a convincing character, and it was felt that further evidence was required before their conclusions could be accepted.

G. M. Ebers, a pupil of Lepsius, and one who did much to popularise the study of Egyptology by a series of novels, said that, if one climbed the pyramid hard by, one could see that the ruins of the Labyrinth had a horseshoe shape, but that was all.

The actual site of the Egyptian Labyrinth was finally identified by Professor Flinders Petrie in 1888. He found that the brick chambers which Lepsius took to be part of the Labyrinth were only remains of the Roman town built by its destroyers, the Labyrinth itself being so thoroughly demolished that only a great bed of fragments remained. Even from this dreary waste of stone chips, however, a few items of interest were discovered, including scattered bits of foundations, a great well, two door-jambs—one to the north and one to the south—two granite shrines and part of another, several fragments of statues and a large granite seated figure of the king who is now generally recognised to have been the builder of the Labyrinth, namely Amenemhat (or Amenemhe) III of the XIIth Dynasty (also known as Lampares), who reigned about twenty-three centuries B.C. Fig. 2, which, like the diagram shown in Fig. 4, is reproduced by the kind permission of Professor Petrie from his book "The Labyrinth, Gerzeh and Mazghuneh" (1912), represents one of the shrines dedicated to the founder. Sufficient of the original foundations remained to enable the size and orientation of the building to be roughly determined.

The Labyrinth must have covered an area of about 1000 feet from east to west by 800 feet from north to south, and was situated to the east of Lake Moeris, opposite the ancient town of Arsinoë (Crocodilopolis), and just to the south of the pyramid of Hawara, in the district known nowadays as the Fayûm.

The mummified remains of the builder of the Labyrinth, King Amenemhat III, and of his daughter Sebekneferu, have been discovered in this pyramid, which is symmetrical about the same N.–S. meridian as the Labyrinth.

Professor Petrie reviewed all that the classic writers had reported concerning the Labyrinth, and concluded that, in spite of their differences, each had contributed some item of value. The discrepancies between the descriptions of Herodotus and Strabo he attributes to the probable decay or destruction of the upper storey in the intervening centuries.

Many attempts have been made to visualise the Labyrinth as it existed in the time of Herodotus. Fig. 3 shows, in plan, one such reconstruction, according to the Italian archaeologist Canina. The actual plan of the Labyrinth would appear to have differed from this in many respects, judging by the indications found by Professor Petrie. The latter drew up a tentative restoration based upon the descriptions of Herodotus and Strabo so far as these tallied with the remains discovered by him.

He suggests that the shrines which he found formed part of a series of nine, ranged along the foot of the pryamid, each attached to a columned court, the whole series of courts opening opposite a series of twenty-seven columns arranged down the length of a great hall running east and west; on the other side of this hall would be another series of columned courts, six in number and larger than the others, separated by another long hall from a further series of six (Fig. 4).

In spite of the scantiness of the present remains and the discrepancies between the various reports that have reached us from ancient times, we can at least be reasonably certain that this, the earliest structure to which the term "labyrinth" ($\lambda\alpha\beta\acute{\upsilon}\rho\iota\nu\theta\circ\varsigma$) is known to have been applied, did actually exist; that it was of the nature of a

14

stupendous architectural monument, that it is of great antiquity—having been built over 4000 years ago at any rate—and that its site is definitely known.

Its original object is still a matter of conjecture. It is quite possible that it was used as a meeting-place for the

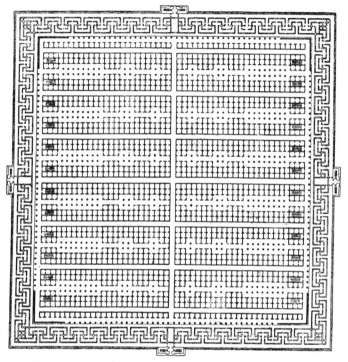

Fig. 3.—Egyptian Labyrinth. Restored Plan. (*Canina.*)

nomes, which would have been about twenty-two in number at the time of the XIIth Dynasty, but it is perhaps more probable that it was intended as a sepulchral monument. In any case it is plain, from the fragments of various gods and goddesses found on the site, that it was a centre of worship of a great variety of deities.

From an almost illegible inscription on a great weather-beaten block of granite, deciphered, with great difficulty,

15

as a dedication by a King Ptolemy to a Queen Cleopatra, Professor Petrie concluded that as late as the beginning of the second century B.C. the building was still in royal

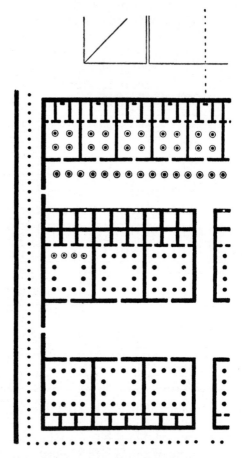

Fig. 4.—Egyptian Labyrinth.
Restored Plan of Western Half.   (*Flinders Petrie.*)

care, but not very long afterwards it was considerably despoiled. Whatever may have been its original object, it afforded several generations the advantages of a most convenient stone-quarry.

16

CHAPTER IV

THE CRETAN LABYRINTH

(i) *The Story of Theseus and the Minotaur*

CHARLES KINGSLEY in "The Heroes" and Nathaniel
Hawthorne in "Tanglewood Tales" have familiarised
most English-speaking people with the story of the exploits of Theseus, and doubtless most folk have some
acquaintance with the first volume of Plutarch's "Lives,"
but it will not be out of place here to recall the portions
of the legend which are associated with our particular
theme, the parts, that is to say, which concern the Labyrinth of Crete. In doing so we will follow the version
given by Plutarch.

This Greco-Roman historian flourished in the latter
half of the first century of our era. His information as to
the deeds of Theseus, already for many centuries a staple
ingredient in popular legendry, was drawn from the accounts of the early Greek writers Bacchylides (fifth century B.C.), Cleidemus (circ. 420–350 B.C.), Philochorus
(circ. 306–260 B.C.), and others.

The Cretan exploit was perhaps the most romantic of
the long series of heroic acts attributed to Theseus. Let
us briefly recall it.

Aegeus, the father of Theseus, was King of Athens.
At that time there reigned at Knossos, in Crete, a monarch called Minos, who held sway over what was then

the most powerful maritime state in the Mediterranean. Minos had a son named Androgeos, who, during his travels in Attica, was treacherously set upon and slain, or so his father was informed. In consequence of this Minos imposed a penalty on the Athenians in the form of a tribute to be paid once every nine years, such tribute to consist of seven youths and seven maidens, who were to be shipped to Knossos at the appointed periods.

There was at the court of Minos an exceedingly clever and renowned artificer or engineer, Daedalus by name, to whom all sorts of miraculous inventions are ascribed. This Daedalus had devised an ingenious structure, the "Labyrinth," so contrived that if anybody were placed therein he would find it practically impossible to discover the exit without a guide.

The Labyrinth was designed as a dwelling for, or at any rate was inhabited by, a hideous and cruel being called the Minotaur, a monstrous offspring of Queen Pasiphaë, wife of Minos. The Minotaur is described as being half man and half bull, or a man with a bull's head, a ferocious creature that destroyed any unfortunate human beings who might come within its power. According to report, the youths and maidens of the Athenian tribute were periodically, one by one, thrust into the Labyrinth, where, after futile wanderings in the endeavour to find an exit, they were finally caught and slain by the Minotaur.

When Theseus arrived at the court of Aegeus, having been brought up hitherto by his mother in a distant seclusion, he was distressed to find that his father's joy in the reunion was overcast by a deepening sadness. On inquiring the reason for this, he learned of the vindictive tribute laid upon the kingdom, and that the time for the third payment was approaching.

"Let me make one of the fourteen," said the valiant youth. "I will find a way to slay this Minotaur, and then there will be no further need for the tribute."

Fig. 5. Cretan Labyrinth. (*Florentine Picture Chronicle.*)

After various attempts to dissuade him, Aegeus at length consented, but stipulated that if Theseus were successful in his design the tribute ship should, on its return voyage, hoist a white sail in place of the black one which it customarily bore.

In due course Theseus came to Knossos, where, shortly after his arrival, he attracted the attention of Ariadne, the fair-haired daughter of Minos. Youth and love conspired against age and rancour, and the fair damsel arranged to provide the hero with a clue of thread and a sword before he was cast into the Labyrinth. One end of this thread was to be fastened at the entrance and the rest unrolled as he advanced.

Theseus followed his instructions, met the Minotaur in its lair and, after a terrific combat, overcame and slew it, after which he retraced his steps by means of the thread and made his escape from the Labyrinth.

By some means or other he contrived to liberate the other prisoners and to obtain possession of the tribute ship. Then, with the fair Ariadne on board, they set sail for Athens.

They do not appear to have been too eager to reach their destination, however, for the party found time to celebrate their escape with dance and song on the islands *en route*. It is said that on the island of Delos they performed a peculiar dance called the *Geranos*, or "Crane Dance," in which they went through the motions of threading the Labyrinth, and that this dance was perpetuated by the natives of that island until fairly recent times.

Theseus seems to have marred his home-coming by two little displays of thoughtlessness that might be considered reprehensible in anybody but a Greek hero. In the first place, he left fair Ariadne behind on the island of Naxos; secondly, he entirely overlooked his father's request concerning the change of sail, with the result that poor old Aegeus, on the look-out for the returning ship, saw the black sail in the distance, concluded that his son had failed in his encounter with the Minotaur, threw himself into the sea and was drowned. Hence that sea was called the Aegean, and is so called to this day.

In Fig. 5 we reproduce an early Italian drawing in which the various incidents in the story are seen simultaneously. This picture is one of a remarkable series, attributed to Baccio Baldini and known as the Florentine Picture Chronicle. The collection was for many years the property of John Ruskin, but is now jealously treasured by the British Museum. A contemporary engraving, of the school of Finiguerra, seems to be based on this picture (Fig. 6).

There are many versions of the legend, some of them greatly at variance with others. For instance, Philochorus, an eminent writer on the antiquities of Athens, gives in his "Atthis" a very rationalistic account of the affair, stating that the Labyrinth was nothing but a dungeon where Minos imprisoned the Athenian youths until such time as they were given as prizes to the victors in the sports that were held in honour of his murdered son. He held also that the monster was simply a military officer, whose brutal disposition, in conjunction with his name, Tauros, may have given rise to the Minotaur myth.

The Cretan poet Epimenides, who lived in the sixth century B.C., says that Theseus was aided in his escape from the dark Labyrinth by means of the light radiated by a crown of blazing gems and gold which Bacchus gave to Ariadne.

Aristotle, according to Plutarch, stated in a work which has not come down to us his belief that the Athenian youths were not put to death by Minos but were retained as slaves. Plutarch, moreover, deplores the abuse which Greek tradition had heaped upon the name of Minos, pointing out that Homer and Hesiod had referred to him in very honourable terms, and

20

that he was reputed to have laid down the principles of justice.

According to the classic faith, he was born of Zeus, the supreme God of the Greeks, and Europa, daughter of man, both marriage and birth taking place in the Dictaean Cave, not far from Knossos. He received the

Fig. 6.—Cretan Labyrinth. (Italian Engraving ; School of *Finiguerra.*)

laws, like another Moses, direct from God, and after administering them during his life on earth continued to do so in the underworld after his death.

The probability is, as Professor Murray has suggested, that Minos was a general name, like "Pharaoh" in Egypt, or "Caesar" in Rome, bestowed upon each of a number of Cretan kings of a certain type. A mark either of the respect in which the name was held or of the colonising power of the monarch or monarchs in question is seen in the application of the name Minoa to several towns and villages scattered along the northern shores of the eastern Mediterranean.

The name Daedalus has likewise been thought by some to have been applied indiscriminately to various artificers and inventors of unusual ingenuity. The principal feats associated with this name are, in addition to the planning of the Labyrinth, the construction of a *Choros*, or dancing-place, for Ariadne, the modelling of a great hollow cow for Pasiphaë, wife of Minos, in order that she might interview the great white bull for which she had conceived an unnatural affection (the outcome being, in the words of Euripides, " A form commingled, and a monstrous birth, half man, half bull, in twofold shape combined"), and the invention of wings, wherewith Daedalus escaped from the Labyrinth when imprisoned there by Minos for his share in the Pasiphaë episode. Daedalus was also credited with the invention of the auger, the plumb-line and other tools, and of masts and sails for ships.

The Theseus-Minotaur incident has been often celebrated in ancient and mediaeval art, instances of which we shall later have occasion to mention. Modern artists, also, have not disdained the theme; a particularly fine example is the colossal marble group by Canova (1819), now at the Museum of Art History at Vienna, formerly in the Theseus Temple in the Volksgarten.

The question naturally arises: Was there actually such a thing as the Labyrinth, and, if so, where was it and what was its nature?

CHAPTER V

THE CRETAN LABYRINTH (*continued*)

(ii) *The Caverns of Gortyna*

ACCORDING to the Romano-Greek writer Apollodorus,[1] whose "Bibliotheke" consisted of a history of the world from the fall of Troy onwards, Daedalus built the Labyrinth at Knossos for King Minos on the lines of the Egyptian Labyrinth, but of only one-hundredth part of the magnitude of the latter. This statement, which was repeated by various other ancient writers such as Pliny and Diodorus, caused many subsequent inquirers to look for evidence in Crete of a building similar to, though smaller than, that described by Herodotus and Strabo.

Nothing corresponding to such a description appeared to exist, but at Gortyna, on the south side of Crete, there was a remarkable series of winding passages, opening on the side of Mount Ida. Some authors of antiquity, such as the Roman poets Catullus and Claudian, held the opinion that this cavern, or one of the many other caves or quarries in Crete, was the real Labyrinth, and this view has been largely entertained in recent times, right up to the beginning of the present century.

The first modern traveller of note to explore the cavern was the French botanist, G. P. de Tournefort,

---

[1] Often erroneously alluded to as "the Athenian Grammarian."

23

who spent three years, from 1700 to 1702, travelling about Asia Minor and the Levant.

Tournefort's book, as well as being a mine of information on various subjects, makes delightful reading, whether in the original French or in John Ozell's English translation of 1718, from which we quote.

"This famous place," he says, referring to the Labyrinth, which he visited on July 1, 1700, "is a subterranean Passage in manner of a Street, which by a thousand Intricacies and Windings, as it were by mere Chance, and without the least Regularity, pervades the whole Cavity or Inside of a little Hill at the foot of Mount Ida, southwards, three miles from Gortyna. The Entrance into this Labyrinth is by a natural Opening, seven or eight Paces broad, but so low that even a middle-siz'd Man can't pass through without stooping.

"The Flooring of this Entrance is very rugged and unequal; the Ceiling flat and even, terminated by divers Beds of Stone, laid horizontally one upon another.

"The first thing you come at is a kind of Cavern exceeding rustick, and gently sloping: in this there is nothing extraordinary, but as you move forward the place is perfectly surprizing; nothing but Turnings and crooked By-ways. The principal Alley, which is less perplexing than the rest, in length about 1200 Paces, leads to the further end of the Labyrinth, and concludes in two large beautiful Apartments, where Strangers rest themselves with pleasure. Tho' this Alley divides itself, at its Extremity, into two or three Branches, yet the dangerous part of the Labyrinth is not there, but rather at its Entrance, about some thirty paces from the Cavern on the left hand. If a Man strikes into any other Path, after he has gone a good way, he is so bewildered among a thousand Twistings, Twinings, Sinuosities, Crinkle-Crankles and Turn-again Lanes, that he could scarce ever get out again without the utmost danger of being lost."

24

He refers to various inscriptions in charcoal, mostly names of former visitors, and notes various dates ranging from 1444 to 1699. "We too," he says, "wrote the Year of the Lord 1700 in three different places, with a black stone." "After a thorow Examination of the Structure of this Labyrinth we all concurred in Opinion, that it could never have been what *Belonius* and some other of the Moderns have fancy'd; namely, an antient Quarry, out of which were dug the Stones that built the Towns of Gortyna and Gnossus. Is it likely that they would go for Stone above a thousand paces deep, into a place so full of odd Turnings? . . . Again, how could they draw these Stones through a place so pinch'd in, that we were forc'd to crawl our way out for above a hundred paces together? Besides, the Mountain is so craggy and full of Precipices that we had all the difficulty in the World to ride up it. . . . It is likewise observable, that the Stone of this Labyrinth has neither a good Hue nor a competent Hardness; it is downright dingy, and resembling that of the Mountains near which Gortyna stands.

". . . It is therefore much more probable, that the Labyrinth is a natural Cavity, which in times past some body out of curiosity took a fancy to try what they could make of, by widening most of those Passages that were too much straitened. . . . Doubtless some Shepherds having discovered these subterraneous Conduits, gave occasion to more considerable People to turn it into this marvellous Maze to serve for an Asylum in the Civil Wars or to skreen themselves from the Fury of a Tyrannical Government: at present it is only a Retreat for Bats and the like."

Tournefort stayed for a while with an ignorant priest, "who would have persuaded us in his balderdash Italian that there was an ancient Prophecy wrote on the Walls of the Labyrinth importing that the Czar of Muscovy was very soon to be Master of the Ottoman Empire and deliver the Greeks from the Slavery of the Turks." He

25

adds: "Whatever Scrawlings are made upon the Walls of the Labyrinth by Travellers, these Simpletons swallow down for Prophecies." He mentions also a labyrinth at Candia, but says it must not be confused with the Labyrinth of tradition, "which, from antique Medals, appears to have been in the town of Gnossus."

Dr. Richard Pococke, to whose description of the Egyptian Labyrinth we referred in Chapter III, paid a visit to Gortyna about forty years after Tournefort. He says that the "labyrinth" was shown to him, but that it was evidently nothing more than the quarry out of which the town was built. He points out that the real Labyrinth was at Knossos and that nothing was left of it in Pliny's time.

Another French traveller, C. E. Savary, visited the spot about 1788. He came to the conclusion that this was the Labyrinth of the Minotaur, but regarded it as something distinct from that built by Daedalus at Knossos.

A very interesting account of the Gortyna cavern is that contained in the Journal of C. R. Cockerell, R.A.,[1] who travelled in Southern Europe and the Levant during the years 1810 to 1817. He and his party entered the "labyrinth" by an inconspicuous hole in the rock in a steep part of the hill (Mount Ida) and found themselves in an intricately winding passage. They had taken the precaution to bring with them a great length of string wound upon two sticks, and it was fortunate that they did so, for "the windings," says Cockerell, "bewildered us at once, and, my compass being broken, I was quite ignorant as to where I was. The clearly intentional intricacy and apparently endless number of galleries impressed me with a sense of horror and fascination I cannot describe. At every ten steps one was arrested, and had to turn to right or left, sometimes to choose one of

---

[1] Edited and published by his son, S. P. Cockerell, in 1903.

26

three or four roads. What if one should lose the clue!"
He relates how a poor lunatic had insisted on accompanying them all the way from Candia and following them
into the cavern. This man, together with a boy who had
a lantern, wandered off and caused the rest of the party
—except some Turks, who philosophically remarked
that God takes care of madmen—to feel much alarm on
their account. They were, however, discovered again an
hour later, the boy half dead with fright.

Chambers opened off from the passages, and contained much evidence of former visitors, in the shape
of names scratched on the walls, such as "Spinola,"
"Hawkins, 1794," "Fiott," and many of a Jewish
character. All of the passage ends were infested with
bats, which rose in thousands when one of the party fired
a pistol. Lichens grew here and there, and in one place
arose a spring. There were signs of metallic substances
in the rock, but not sufficient, thought Cockerell, to
warrant the supposition that the place was a mine. The
stone was sandy, stratified and easily cut, and the air
was dry. The surface of the rock appeared to have been
prepared with a chisel.

The passage was 8 or 10 feet wide, and from 4 to 10
feet high; in many places it had fallen in. Cockerell concluded that the excavation was probably made in the
days of Minos as a storehouse for corn and valuables.
He mentions that he was informed by natives that the
cavern extended right through the mountain and was
three miles in length; also that a sow once wandered in
and emerged some years later with a litter of pigs!

About fifty years after Cockerell's visit, the cavern
was explored by Capt. T. A. B. Spratt, R.N., who, in his
"Travels and Researches in Crete" (1865), tells us that
the Cretans "have long since walled and stopped up its
inner and unknown extremes, so as not to be lost in its
inner intricacies." He discusses the probable location of
the traditional Labyrinth and concludes that probably

27

the latter is to be found in some similar cavern in the neighbourhood of Knossos. He mentions that there is, in fact, an excavation in the side of the ridge overlooking Knossos which the natives state to be the entrance to extensive catacombs, but that it is choked up by the falling in of its sides.

He reproduces a sketch by Sieber of the Gortyna Cavern (Fig. 7); this, he says, took the artist three days to make. Capt. Spratt, by the way, points out that the meander pattern, which is so common a feature of Greek ornament, and is associated by some writers with the origin of the labyrinth idea, may very well have been derived from the square-spiral trenches which are commonly constructed by Eastern gardeners for irrigational purposes. (See also Chapter VIII.)

Whatever the original purpose and function of the Gortyna Cavern may have been, it was certainly a "labyrinth" in the extended sense, and no doubt the classic writers themselves would have had no hesitation in admitting the use of that word to describe it, but, as we shall see, discoveries of recent years have considerably diminished its claim to be considered as the original Labyrinth of the Minotaur.

Fig. 7. Cavern of Gortyna. (*Sieber*)

CHAPTER VI

THE CRETAN LABYRINTH (*continued*)

(iii) *Knossos*

A FEW miles to the north-east of Gortyna, and not far
south of the north coast town of Candia, lay, at the base
of the hill of Kephala, a few ruined walls indicating the
site of the ancient city of Knossos. These walls consisted
of large blocks of gypsum and bore curious engraved
marks.

For many years Dr. A. J. Evans (now Sir Arthur
Evans) had been convinced that excavation of this site
would probably bring to light evidence of a system of
writing which might be of interest in connection with
the origin of the Greek system, but it was not until the
year 1900 that he finally obtained a concession enabling
him to explore the spot. The resulting discoveries were
of such an astonishing nature, and of such absorbing
interest, that one is greatly tempted to digress and to
mention them in some detail. However, they have been
summarised and discussed by many able writers (see
Appendix III, ii.), and it must suffice here to refer simply
to the main points in which they bear upon the story of
the Labyrinth.

After about two months' work, with a staff of from
80 to 150 men, about two acres of the remains of a great
prehistoric building, showing strong evidence of having

29

been destroyed by fire, were uncovered, and later excavations showed that it was yet more extensive, covering altogether about five acres. Not only this palace, but the multitude of objects found within it, or associated with it, were of surpassing importance in their bearing on the nature of the ancient civilisation of which they demonstrated the existence, and to which Sir A. Evans has given the name "Minoan." Vast quantities of pottery of widely different designs and workmanship, written tablets, wall paintings—often of great beauty—reliefs, and sculptured figures, shrines, seals, jewellery, a royal gaming-board, and even a throne, were discovered as the work went on, and eventually the whole area was excavated down to the virgin rock, remains of an earlier and smaller palace being found beneath the other, and below this again a great thickness of deposits containing many remains of neolithic man.

By means of occasional discoveries of imported Egyptian objects, by comparison of Minoan pottery and paintings with some found in Egyptian tombs, and by various other indications, it was possible to date the upper remains, say from 1580 B.C. onwards, fairly nearly. The dating of the older remains is much more difficult, chiefly because, although they can often be equated with certain periods of Egyptian culture, the chronology of the latter admits of widely different views, but it seems safe to say that the earliest traces of the Minoan civilisation date from quite 3000 years B.C., and possibly many centuries before that.

The earlier palace and town seem to have been built before 2000 B.C. and destroyed a few centuries after that date. The later palace was begun somewhere in the eighteenth or nineteenth century B.C., was elaborated in succeeding centuries, and was sacked and burned, just as it had attained the height of its glory, about 1400 B.C.

The discovery of this palace was one of the first-class "finds" of archaeology. Those who based their estimates of the architectural capabilities of ancient Crete on their knowledge of the development of the builder's art in classic Greece, a millennium later, were amazed to find that in many respects the product of the older civilisation was superior.

To mention but a few of the most remarkable facts about the palace, it was of *several storeys*, grouped around a central court and pierced by "light-wells"; it contained several staircases, one of them at least being of a very imposing character and composed of *many flights*. Moreover, it possessed a quite modern system of drainage, with *jointed underground pipes* and with inspection manholes to the main drains. Along the west side of the basement ran a long straight gallery flanked by a series of great storage-rooms or magazines. It was near one end of this gallery that Dr. Evans discovered a store of tablets with pictographic inscriptions, in proof of his suspicion that the Phoenician script was not the original parent of European written language.

Not far from this spot was the room containing the throne (or Worshipful Master's Chair, as the masonic Dr. Churchward prefers to call it) which may actually have been occupied by King Minos.

A definite distinction can be recognised between state and domestic apartments and subsidiary offices and workshops.

To the north-west of the palace was a "stepped theatral area" (*orchestra*), which suggests the "dancing ground" of Ariadne.

From the point of view of our subject, however, the most interesting features were the frequent occurrence of the sign of the double axe, which was obviously an object of great importance in Minoan worship, and the profusion of evidence concerning the cult of the bull. On the fallen plaster of one of the walls of a corridor, too, was a repeated meander pattern, painted in red on a white ground, very suggestive of a sort of maze (Fig. 8).

31

The significance of the axe symbol from our point of view lies in its bearing on the derivation of the word "labyrinth," a question that will be referred to in rather more detail in a later chapter.

One room of the palace, a stately hall about 80 ft. in length by 26 ft. in breadth, traversed by a row of square-sectioned pillars, has been named by its discoverer

FIG. 8.—Knossos. Maze-pattern on Wall of Palace. (After *Evans*.)

"the Hall of the Double Axes," from the frequent occurrence of this symbol therein. Not only does the sacred axe occur as a more or less crude engraving on the stone blocks composing certain pillars in the palace, but little models of it were found associated with an altar, and, in the Dictaean cave, some miles distant, several bronze specimens of the axe were discovered in circumstances which show that they were votive offerings. Sometimes the sacred symbol was set up on a socketed pedestal

32

Fig. 9.   Double Axe and Stepped Steatite Socket from
Dictaean Cave.   (Psychro)

(From *Archæologia*, by kind permission of the Society of
Antiquaries, and Sir Arthur Evans)

Fig. 11.   Knossos.   View of Cist, showing shape of Double Axe.
(From *Archæologia*, by kind permission of the Society of Antiquaries and Sir Arthur Evans.)

(Fig. 9). Moreover, in more recent excavations a curious "tomb" was found (Figs. 10 and 11) which was double-

FIG. 10.—Knossos.   Plan of Tomb of Double Axes, showing position in which relics were found.
(From " Archaeologia," by kind permission of the Society of Antiquaries and Sir Arthur Evans.)

axe shaped in plan and was evidently the repository of a giant emblem (Fig. 12. See plate, p. 42).

Long before Dr. Evans' excavations in Crete the great

33

German archaeologist Schliemann, during his researches at Mycenae on the mainland, unearthed from one of the graves an ox-head of gold plate, with a double axe between the upright horns. The double axe was also the sign of the Zeus worshipped at Labraunda in Caria, a country to the north-east of Crete, on the mainland of Asia Minor, where the implement was known as the *labrys*.

The cult of the bull was also much in evidence in the palace remains. Schliemann, in excavating the site of Tiryns in 1884, came across an extraordinary wall-painting depicting a man holding one horn of a great bull whilst he leaps over its back, the animal meanwhile charging at full speed. Several examples of such scenes have since been discovered, painted upon walls, engraved on gems, or stamped on seal-impressions. Amongst the debris of one of the rooms in the palace at Knossos was found a painting of a scene in which two girls are engaged in dodging the charge of a bull, whilst a boy, who has evidently just left hold of its horns, turns a somersault over its back.

Near the main north entrance to the palace was brought to light a large plaster relief of a bull's head, no doubt originally forming part of the complete beast. This relief was a masterpiece of Minoan art. It was of life-size and beautifully coloured, and particular attention had been given to the modelling and colour of the eye, the fierce stare of which, in conjunction with the open mouth, conveys a fine effect of frenzied excitement.

These are only a few examples, amongst many, which go to demonstrate that the sport of "bull-leaping"—or ταυρωκαθαψια, as it was called by the Greeks—was beloved of the Minoans and was probably practised in the precincts of the palace.

In the light of these discoveries Dr. Evans concludes that the palace of Knossos was the Labyrinth, or House of the Labrys, which gave rise to the classic legend, the idea of the Minotaur originating in the practice of training captives to participate in the dangerous sport of bull-leaping. (*Tauros*=bull, hence *Minotaur*=Bull of Minos.) We will refer further to the etymology of "labyrinth" in a later chapter. The palace was certainly of sufficient complexity to render it difficult for the uninitiated to find their way about it, but the plan of its remains exhibits no resemblance to a designed labyrinth of the conventional type. There is, however, a suggestion of the latter in the meander pattern painted on one of the walls, to which reference has been made above. The notion as to the Labyrinth having been a prison from which escape was impossible may also have some connection with two deep pits beneath the palace, whose function was possibly that of dungeons for prisoners.

In considering the origin of the legend, we must remember that a period of several centuries elapsed between the destruction of the Knossian buildings and the first written account of the Labyrinth, and must take into account the probability that the people who in later ages became the dominant race in Crete would be likely to make ample use of their imagination in formulating an explanation of the vast and complicated ruins of the burnt city, with their mysterious frescoes and enigmatic symbols.

It may also be borne in mind that the excavations in Crete have by no means reached a final stage, and that, although no architectural remains of a plan conforming to the usual conception of a formal labyrinth are yet forthcoming, there is a possibility that something of the kind may yet turn up, though indeed the chance seems very remote. Even as this book is going to press appears an article in *The Times* by Sir Arthur Evans announcing yet further enthralling discoveries; he finds abundant signs of a great earthquake, causing ruin over the whole Knossian area, about 1600 B.C., also evidence

—including portable altars and huge ox-skulls— indicating an expiatory sacrifice recalling Homer's words, "in bulls doth the Earthshaker delight"; and finally, on a floor-level about thirty feet down, the opening of an artificial cave with three rough steps leading down to what was apparently the lair of some great beast. "But here, perhaps," says Sir Arthur, "it is better for imagination to draw rein."

CHAPTER VII

In addition to the Egyptian and Cretan labyrinths, a few other structures are referred to as being in the same category, but not until a fairly late period.

Pliny (died A.D. 79) mentions one built by Smilis of Aegina, after the Egyptian model, on the island of Lemnos, and says that it was renowned for the beauty of its 150 columns and that remains of it existed in his time. He also mentions one at Samos, said to have been built by Theodorus, and says that "all of these buildings are covered with arched roofs of polished stone." No other details concerning these edifices have come down to us, but Pliny quotes from Varro (116-27 B.C.) a detailed description of a very extraordinary tomb at Clusium (the modern Chiusi), said to be that of the great Etruscan general Lars Porsena. This is the only Etruscan tomb described by the ancient writers, and is mentioned by Pliny solely because it was alleged to contain a subterranean labyrinth. It must have been a most elaborate, not to say extravagant, monument. Even Pliny feels some qualms about accepting responsibility for the description, and therefore makes it clear that he is simply quoting from information received.

"It is but right that I should mention it," he says, "in order to show that the vanity displayed by foreign princes, great though it is, has been surpassed. But in

37

view of the exceedingly fabulous nature of the story I shall use the words given by M. Varro himself in his account of it: 'Porsena was buried below the city of Clusium in the place where he had built a square monument of dressed stones. Each side was three hundred feet in length and fifty in height, and beneath the base there was an inextricable labyrinth, into which, if anybody entered without a clue of thread, he could never discover his way out. Above this square building there stand five pyramids, one at each corner and one in the centre, seventy-five feet broad at the base and one hundred and fifty feet high. These pyramids so taper in shape that upon the top of all of them together there is supported a brazen globe, and upon that again a *petasus* [1] from which bells are suspended by chains. These make a tinkling sound when blown about by the wind, as was done in bygone times at Dodona. Upon this globe there are four more pyramids, each a hundred feet in height, and above them is a platform on which are five more pyramids.' The height of the latter, Varro is ashamed to add, but, according to the Etruscan stories, it was equal to that of the rest of the building. What utter madness is this, to attempt to seek glory at a great cost which can never be of use to anyone; not to mention the drain upon the resources of the country. And all to the end that the artist may receive the greater share of the praise!"

There have been many discussions as to the possibility of a monument of this nature having existed, and various reconstructions have been attempted, notably one (Fig. 13), based on Varro's account, by a celebrated French scholar of a century ago, M. Quatremère de Quincy.

One enthusiast, a certain Father Angelo Cortenovis, even wrote a treatise to prove that the whole contrivance was nothing more nor less than a huge electrical machine!

[1] A sort of low-crowned round hat with a broad brim.

38

Fig. 13.   Tomb of Lars Porsena at Clusium.
Conjectural restoration by Quatremère de Quincy after Varro's description.

Most writers on the subject have been inclined to look upon Varro's description as at best a gross exaggeration, but Professor Müller gave it as his opinion that the labyrinth described did actually exist, and that the upper part, though no doubt highly embellished in the description, was not the mere offspring of fancy. He thought it quite probable that there was a square basement of regular masonry supporting five pyramids as recounted by Varro, but that the latter described the upper part from hearsay. He drew attention to the fact that a tomb somewhat of this nature is still in existence on the Appian Way at Albano, the pyramids being represented in this case by cones. It is commonly called the Tomb of the Horatii and Curiatii.

In the early part of last century a British traveller, G. Dennis, made a study of the antiquities of Etruria and gave particular attention to the remarkable rock-cut labyrinths of which that province furnishes several examples.

He pointed out that the possession of a labyrinth was the distinguishing feature of Porsena's tomb which alone caused Pliny to mention it. The expression "Sub Clusio" used by Pliny, he says, led subsequent writers to infer that the subterranean passages beneath Chiusi were intended, but such an arrangement would be at variance with the general sepulchral practice of the Etruscans, and the tomb of Porsena must be looked for outside the city walls. Dennis then goes on to describe the great cemetery that had recently been discovered in the hill called Poggio Gajella, about three miles to the northeast of Chiusi. His sketch of the principal "storey" of this labyrinthine excavation is shown in Fig. 14.

Here again we may note that the design of the passages, although perhaps puzzling to a stranger, especially with imperfect illumination, in no respect approaches the traditional "labyrinth" pattern. That the conventional form was not unknown to the Etruscans, however,

39

is shown by the occurrence of a design of this type on a vase found at Tragliatella which we shall mention later.

It is, of course, possible that the tomb of Porsena was erected on the hill above this labyrinth, but we have not much evidence on the point. If the tomb possessed a labyrinth, no doubt the latter would have been something of this type. Dennis also mentions various other labyrinths of this nature in Etruria—for example, one near Volterra, "a long passage cut in the rock, six feet wide but only three high, so that you must travel on all-fours. From time to time the passage widens into chambers, yet not high enough to permit you to stand upright, or it meets the passages of similar character opening in various directions and extending into the heart of the hill, how far no one can say. In short, this is a perfect labyrinth in which, without a clue, one might very soon be lost."

He also mentions one at San Pietro, Toscanella, "in the cliffs below the Madonna dell' Olivo, about half a mile from the town. Here a long, sewer-like passage leads into a spacious chamber of irregular form, with two massive columns supporting its ceiling and a rude pilaster on the wall behind. But the peculiarity of the tomb lies in a *cuniculus* or passage cut in the rock, just large enough for a man to creep through on all-fours, which, entering the wall on one side after a long gyration and sundry branchings, now blocked with earth, opens in the opposite wall of the tomb."

These Etruscan labyrinths were all of a sepulchral character, and one is naturally reminded of the catacombs of Rome, Paris, and Naples, to which, however, the term "labyrinth" is not customarily applied. Strabo uses the word in reference to a catacomb near Nauplia, which he calls the Labyrinth of the Cyclops. In Pliny's time the word would appear to have been used to denote a winding path following a more or less formal design of intricate

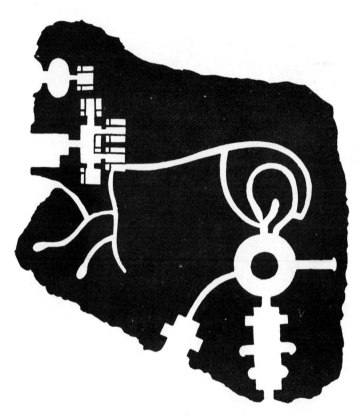

Fig. 14.   Poggio Cajella.   Labyrinthine Cemetery.   (Dennis)

Fig. 12.   Bronze Double Axe from Tomb of the Double Axes.
(From *Archæologia*, by kind permission of the Society of Antiquaries and Sir Arthur Evans)
(see page 33)

Figs. 15, 16, 17, 18.   Early Egyptian Seals and Plaques.   (British Museum)

pattern, but not necessarily connected with sepulchral purposes.

When speaking of the Labyrinth of Crete he says, "We must not compare this to what we see traced upon our *mosaic pavements* or to the *mazes formed in the fields* for the entertainment of children, and thus suppose it to be a narrow path along which we may walk for many miles together, but we must picture to ourselves an edifice with many doors and galleries which mislead the visitor. . . ." This passage shows that the term "labyrinth" had come to have a fairly broad significance. It had long been used in a metaphorical sense, even as we find Plato, over four centuries earlier, employing it to describe an elaborate argument. We also find it applied by extension to other objects, such as traps for fish, to judge by a certain passage in the works of Theocritus.

The only buildings to which the ancient writers applied the term, however, were those to which we have already referred.

Of the two phrases which we have italicised in the above quotation from Pliny, the second is of interest in connection with a matter we shall deal with later on, whilst the former brings us to the subject of our next chapter.

CHAPTER VIII

THERE has been considerable speculation as to how the typical labyrinth form first came into existence. It became stereotyped long before the Christian era and retained its character for many centuries.

The coins of Knossos furnish us with abundant examples of it, and, from the fact that in certain of the earlier specimens the corresponding figure is a simple repeated meander, it has been supposed that the typical labyrinth design arose by elaboration of the meander. The resemblance between this form and the very widespread and primitive sign known as the *fylfot* or *svastika* has also attracted some attention. It is a somewhat long step, however, from a loose combination of meanders like that shown in, say, Fig. 20, to the compact conventional labyrinth of Fig. 30. The adoption of the former design may possibly have been inspired by the fresco on one of the walls of the Minoan palace, to which we have made reference in Chapter VI (Fig. 8), portions of which may have been visible among the ruins for several generations. There does not appear to be any evidence that the complex meander pattern of the fresco was an allusion on the part of the Minoans to an actual constructional labyrinth; it may quite well have been a purely ornamental conception, without any symbolical significance. Meander designs were used by the Minoans at a

42

much earlier date than this, one example, though of simpler character, having been found in the older palace, and others, either snake-like or of a squarish nature, on ivory seals unearthed at other Minoan sites (Zakro and Hagia Triada). Similar designs exist on certain Egyptian "button-seals" of an approximately contemporary period—from the VIth Dynasty onwards—and Sir Arthur Evans has expressed the opinion that these will possibly prove to constitute the source of the Labyrinth in Art. Figs. 15, 16, 17, 18 show specimens of early Egyptian seals and plaques of this character in the British Museum. Professor Flinders Petrie very kindly drew the writer's attention to a steatite plaque in his collection at University College, London, which is somewhat similar to one of those mentioned above, but of rather more elaborate design (Fig. 19). The labyrinthine pattern on this is surmounted by a representation, in the peculiar "linear" fashion often adopted by early Egyptian artists, of two seated human figures facing one another, the

Fig. 19.—Early Egyptian Plaque or Amulet. (Prof. Petrie's Collection, University College, London.)

knees being drawn up. Professor Petrie acquired the plaque at Memphis. He considers that it dates from a period round about 3000 B.C., and points out that if the broken lines be completed there would appear to be five false turns to be avoided before reaching the centre.

In discussing the designs on these seals and plaques, Sir A. Evans alludes to a possible connection with two of the hieroglyphs of the period, which are of the nature of simple square meanders of a kind extensively employed in ancient ornament. One of them (*mer*) is the sign used for indicating irrigated land. The other (*aha*)

43

is a simplified form of a more elaborate sign representing the plan of a palace court, a figure to which one of the Minoan signs bears a close resemblance.

The Knossian coins shown in Figs. 20 to 31 are from the British Museum collection and are reproduced by the courtesy of the Keeper of the Coins and Medals Department, who supplied the writer with plaster casts for the purpose. They date, of course, from times greatly posterior to those of the Minoan civilisation, from times when the culture of Greece had long replaced that of the Mycenaeans, or whatever similar race it was that succeeded the Minoans (see Appendix IV, i.).

Figs. 20, 21, and 22 show silver coins dating from about 500 to 430 B.C. They portray on one side the Minotaur and on the other a symmetrical meander pattern which, it needs very little imagination to see, has reference to the labyrinth in which the monster was alleged to dwell.

Fig. 23 shows a silver coin of a rather later date, representing on its obverse a female head which is thought to be that of Demeter or Persephone, and on the reverse a meander-labyrinth containing a star at its centre.

Fig. 24 shows a similar obverse, but on the reverse we see a bull's head surrounded by a simple meander frame.

Fig. 25, the obverse of which is likewise adorned with a female head, gives on the reverse the design of a square labyrinth of the conventional type that thereafter predominates.

Fig. 26 shows a bronze coin having on one side the head of Apollo and on the other a labyrinth with a star.

The four coins last described date from a period between 430 and 350 B.C. The next (Fig. 27) is rather later in date and shows on its obverse the head of Hera and on the reverse a square labyrinth together with an arrow-head and thunderbolts and the Greek characters ΚΝΩΣΙΩΝ.

The bronze coin of about 220 B.C., shown in Fig. 28,

44

Figs. 20 to 25. Coins of Knossos. (British Museum)

Fig. 20.

Fig. 21.

Fig. 22.

Fig. 23.

Fig. 24.

Fig. 25.

Fig. 29.

Fig. 30.

Fig 31.

Fig. 26

Fig. 27.

Fig. 28.

bears on its obverse the figure of Europa seated on a bull, with two dolphins below, and on the reverse a square labyrinth, the Knossian superscription being again evident.

The remaining three figures represent silver coins of the two succeeding centuries, but not later than 67 B.C.

Fig. 29 exhibits on one side the head of Pallas, and on the reverse a little square labyrinth placed beside an owl standing upon a prostrate amphora.

In Fig. 30 the obverse is occupied by the head of Apollo, the reverse by a labyrinth of circular shape, but conforming to the conventional plan.

The head on the coin shown in Fig. 31 may be intended for that of Minos or Zeus. On the reverse is a square labyrinth.

Labyrinthine designs are also found on certain Lydian, Phrygian, and Ionian coins.

It will be noticed that when once the labyrinth pattern has been definitely conventionalised it remains very constant in principle, whether its general conformation be rectangular or circular. Starting from the exterior, the "path" runs inwards a short distance, turns so as to run parallel with the outer wall until nearly a full circuit has been completed, then doubles back on itself and runs round in the opposite direction, doubles upon itself again, and so on until it finally comes to a stop in a blind end, having traversed all of the space within the outer walls without covering any part twice and without forming any branches or loops.

Obviously there is no "puzzle" about this kind of labyrinth; one has simply to follow the one path, either to penetrate to the inner goal or to escape thence to the exterior.

A labyrinth of precisely this type was discovered traced on the surface of a crimson-painted pillar in the peristyle of the building known as the House of Lucretius, in the excavated portion of Pompeii (Fig. 32). It

45

was evidently scratched with a nail or stylus by some idler of 2000 years ago (Pompeii was overwhelmed by Vesuvius in A.D. 79) and is accompanied by the words "LABYRINTHUS. HIC HABITAT MINOTAURUS," possibly in waggish reference to the owner or occupier of the premises.

Another house has, in consequence of its mosaic and pictorial references to the Cretan Labyrinth, received the name of the Casa del Labirinto or House of the Labyrinth. One mosaic discovered therein depicts Theseus

FIG. 32.—*Graffito* at Pompeii. (Museo Borbonico.)

and the Minotaur struggling on the ground, watched by a group of affrighted maidens.

The Romans excelled in the art of designing and executing mosaic pavements, abundant remains of which have been preserved. These were of various kinds. There was the *pavimentum sectile*, composed of pieces of marble of various sizes, shapes, and colours arranged in uniform sets, so as to form when put together an ornamental pattern; the *pavimentum tessellatum*, in which the pieces of marble, though variously coloured, were all of the same size and shape, generally small squares; the *pavimentum vermiculatum*, composed of very small pieces of coloured

46

marble of irregular shape so arranged as to portray objects in their natural shapes and colours; and finally the *pavimentum scalpturatum,* in which the design was engraved or inlaid. *Opus alexandrinum* is a variant of *sectile.*

Several Roman pavements embodying labyrinthine devices, and in some cases commemorating the victory of Theseus over the Minotaur, or other exploits of

FIG. 33.—Mosaic at Salzburg. (Kreuzer.)

the hero, have come to light from time to time, not only on the continent of Europe but also in England; they are usually executed in *opus alexandrinum.*

Fig. 33 shows in outline a beautiful specimen, 18 ft. long and 15 ft. broad, discovered at Salzburg, in Austria. It bears the device of a labyrinth, with, at the centre, a representation of Theseus about to give the fatal blow to the Minotaur.

On the left side we see Theseus and Ariadne joining hands over the altar. In the upper panel Theseus appears

47

to be putting Ariadne ashore, and to the right we see the disconsolate maiden deserted by her lover, presumably on the Isle of Naxos.

A labyrinth of the type shown also occurs on a Roman mosaic which was unearthed in the churchyard at Caerleon-on-Usk. It was in a poor state of preservation, but sufficient remains to show that the labyrinth, of a design similar to that of the Salzburg specimen, is surrounded by scrolls proceeding from two vases (Fig. 34).

A very fine specimen of this type of labyrinth was discovered in 1904 beneath a ploughed field at Harpham, in the East Riding of Yorkshire. Another, of which details are not to hand, is said to have been found in Northamptonshire.

In 1790 a pavement, about eighteen feet by twelve, was unearthed at Aix, near Marseilles. It portrayed the combat between Theseus and the Minotaur, within a framed square, the remainder of the mosaic consisting of a complicated interlaced meander representing the labyrinth.

In Fig. 35 is reproduced from A. de Caumont's "Abécédaire d'Archéologie" a rough sketch of the Roman baths at Verdes (Loir-et-Cher), showing a pavement with a labyrinth mosaic.

A pavement found in 1830 at Cormerod, in the Canton of Friburg, Switzerland, is shown in Fig. 36. A few years afterwards another was brought to light in the neighbouring Canton of Vaud, from beneath the ruins of the ancient town of Orbe.

A splendid mosaic labyrinth of Roman times was found some forty or fifty years ago on a family tomb in the ancient necropolis of Susa, Tunis (*Hadrumetum*). It was afterwards destroyed by looters, but a careful drawing of it was fortunately made on its first discovery (Fig. 37). The whole mosaic measured about seventeen feet by ten, and contained a very finely executed labyrinth of four paths, like the Harpham and Caerleon examples

48

Fig. 34.   Mosaic at Caerleon, Mon.   (O Morgan, in Proc. Mon.
and Caerleon Ant. Ass'n, 1866)

Fig. 36.   Mosaic at Cormerod, Switzerland.
(Mitt. Ant. Ges. Zurich, XVI.)

mentioned above, the central space being occupied by
the Minotaur, who is shown in an attitude of defeat.

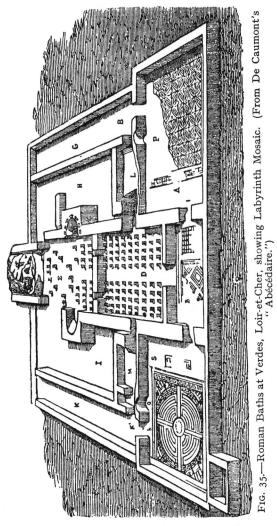

FIG. 35.—Roman Baths at Verdes, Loir-et-Cher, showing Labyrinth Mosaic. (From De Caumont's "Abécédaire.")

Sailing towards the labyrinth was a boat containing
figures which presumably represented Theseus and his

49

companions. The design was accompanied by the words "HIC INCLUSUS VITAM PERDIT."

Another well-preserved mosaic of this character was

FIG. 37.—Mosaic at Susa, Tunis. (C. R. Acad. Inscriptions, Paris.)

discovered in 1884 at Brindisi, and placed in the municipal museum of that town. It measures 17 ft. by 10 ft. 6 in., and shows within a square labyrinth Theseus in the act of clubbing the Minotaur, who has fallen on his knees. Around the labyrinth are various perches with birds thereon, perhaps in allusion to the automatic birds reputed to have been made by Daedalus (*cf.* Fig. 36).

We shall examine other mosaic and pavement labyrinths when we come to consider the question of the use of this symbol by the Church.

Apart from the designs on Knossian coins, Greek art does not appear to have left us any definite representations of the labyrinths, although with the Romans, who acquired the idea at a later date, it was a favourite *motif*.

We cannot, however, ignore the suggestion that has been made that certain structures discovered in the ruins of Tiryns and Epidaurus, two cities in that part of ancient Greece known as the Argolid, are architectural labyrinths, used for ritual purposes. The foundations of the *tholos*, or rotunda, of the sanctuary of Aesculapius at Epidaurus, which was excavated by P. Kabbadias, Director of the Greek Archaeological Society, in the 'eighties, do certainly suggest something of the kind. They consist of concentric circular walls, the three innermost being connected by a radial wall, separated by narrow spaces which intercommunicate by an opening or doorway in each wall, forming in plan a figure somewhat in the style of the "Pigs in Clover" toy mentioned in a later chapter. When the peculiar nature of the upper part of the building is considered, however, it seems very reasonable to suppose that these walls, with their passages, were designed only with a view to the requirements of the superstructure which they had to support.

As for the slightly similar concentric foundations unearthed by German excavators at Tiryns in 1912, the analogy is too imperfect to afford reliable grounds for the statement in question.

Greek ceramic art, on the other hand, furnishes us with very many allusions to the Theseus-Minotaur myth, and also with a profusion of frets and meanders, which are thought in some cases to be symbolical of the labyrinth.

51

Consider, for instance, the "*kylix*" or bowl in the British Museum which is shown in Fig. 38. (A similar bowl is preserved in Harrow School Museum.) On it are represented most of the exploits of the hero up to his Knossian adventure. All who are familiar with the legend will recognise at a glance Periphetes the Club-bearer, Sinis the Pine-bender, the Wild Sow of Krommyon, Kerkyon the Wrestler, Procrustes of the Standard Bed, and other gentlefolk that Theseus successively encountered and appropriately dealt with on his initial journey to Athens. In the centre of the bowl is shown the adventure of the Labyrinth, the hero being seen in the act of despatching the monster at the very door of his lair. The meander on the door-post has been thought to symbolise the Labyrinth, but there is more reason to suppose that it is purely decorative.

The Minotaur exploit is also shown on the smaller bowl shown in Fig. 39.

In the previous chapter we have already referred to an Etruscan vase found at Tragliatella. This was very roughly decorated with incised figures, representing amongst other things a circular labyrinth of the traditional type and some horsemen who are thought to be engaged either in the attack on Troy or in the game known as the *Lusus Trojae* or Game of Troy. That there can be no doubt about the artist's identification of the labyrinth in some way with the celebrated city in question is clear from the word *Truia* scratched within it (Fig. 133).

Representations of the labyrinth were sometimes engraved on ancient gems, a fine specimen of which is figured in P. A. Maffei's "Gemme Antiche" (Fig. 40), published in 1707. The Minotaur in this case is shown as a centaur. A similar representation appears on a sixteenth-century bronze plaquette of Italian workmanship exhibited in the Plaquette Room at the British Museum (Fig. 41. See plate, p. 60).

Before leaving the subject of the Labyrinth in ancient

Fig. 38.

Fig. 39.

Figs. 38, 39. Greek Kylices shewing Exploits of Theseus. (British Museum)

art we must take notice of a reference in an ancient manuscript which tends to show that the symbol figured on the robes of Roman Emperors. This manuscript was discovered by A. F. Ozanam in the Laurentian Library at Florence. It is entitled "Graphia Aurea Urbis Romae" and contains, under the heading "De diarodino imperatoris," the following passage:

Habeat et in diarodino laberinthum fabrefactum ex auro et margaritis, in quo sit Minotaurus, digitum ad os tenens ex

Fig. 40.—Labyrinth engraved on an ancient gem. (Maffei.)

smaragdo factus, quia sicut non valet quis laberinthum scrutare, ita non debet consilium dominatoris propalare.

"Let there be represented on it (the Emperor's robe) a labyrinth of gold and pearls, in which is the Minotaur, made of emerald, holding his finger to his mouth, thus signifying that, just as none may know the secret of the labyrinth, so none may reveal the monarch's counsels."

It has been pointed out by Mr. A. B. Cook that in the Fitzwilliam Museum at Cambridge is a painting by Bartolommeo Veneto (1502–1530) representing an unknown man who wears on his breast a labyrinth resembling that described above.

53

CHAPTER IX

CHURCH LABYRINTHS

The consideration of labyrinths worked in Roman mosaic pavements leads us on to a very interesting development of the subject which deserves a chapter to itself, namely, the Labyrinth in the Church.

Probably the oldest known example of this nature is that in the ancient basilica of *Reparatus* at Orléansville (Algeria), an edifice which is believed to date from the fourth century A.D. In the pavement near the north-west entrance of the church is the design shown in outline in Fig. 42. It measures about 8 ft. in diameter and shows great resemblance to the Roman pavement found at Harpham and the tomb-mosaic at Susa. At the centre is a *jeu-de-lettres* on the words SANCTA ECLESIA, which may be read in any direction, except diagonally, commencing at the centre. But for the employment of these words the labyrinth in question might well have been conceived to be a Roman relic utilised by the builders of the church to ornament their pavement. Such pavement-labyrinths, however, with or without central figures or other embellishments, and of various dimensions and composition, are found in many of the old churches of France and Italy.

They seem to have been constructed chiefly during the twelfth century, and although several of them have been destroyed many fine examples still remain. Some

54

FIG. 42.—Labyrinth in Church of Reparatus, Orléansville, Algeria.
(Prevost.)

FIG. 43.—Labyrinth in Lucca Cathedral. (Durand.)

are formed on the walls instead of the pavements, and in such cases are of smaller dimensions.

On the whole, too, those in the Italian churches are much smaller than the French specimens. On the wall of Lucca Cathedral (Fig. 43) is one of a diameter of only 1 ft. $7\frac{1}{2}$ in. It formerly enclosed at the centre a representation of Theseus and the Minotaur, but owing to the friction of many generations of tracing fingers this has

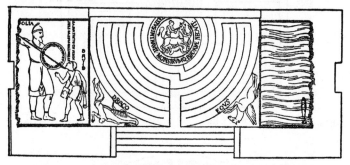

Fig. 44.—Labyrinth in S. Michele, Pavia. (Ciampini.)

become effaced. Opposite the "entrance" is the inscription:

HIC QUEM CRETICUS EDIT
DAEDALUS EST LABERINTHUS,
DE QUO NULLUS VADERE
QUIVIT QUI FUIT INTUS,
NI THESEUS GRATIS ADRIANE
STAMINE JUTUS⟨

A similar small labyrinth, with a central Theseus-Minotaur design, is to be found on the wall of the church of San Michele Maggiore at Pavia (Fig. 44). It is thought to be of tenth-century construction. This is one of the few cases where the Minotaur is represented with a human head and a beast's body—as a sort of Centaur, in fact. It is accompanied by the words "TESEUS INTRAVIT MONSTRUMQUE BIFORME NECAVIT."

56

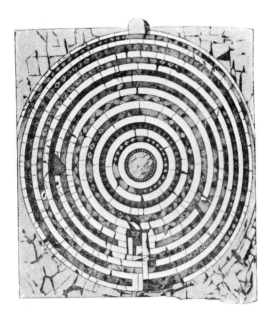

Fig. 45.   Labyrinth in S. Maria-di-Trastavera, Rome.   (Durand)

Fig. 46.   Labyrinth in S. Vitale, Ravenna.   (Durand)

Of about the same period was the example in the church of San Savino at Piacenza. It is described by P. M. Campi in his "Ecclesiastical History of Piacenza" (1651), under the year A.D. 903. The signs of the Zodiac were placed in juxtaposition to it. The accompanying legend in this case consisted of four hexameters, to the effect that the labyrinth represented the world we live in, broad at the entrance, but narrow at the exit, so that he who is ensnared by the joys of this world, and weighed down by his vices, can regain the doctrine of life only with difficulty.

HVNC MVNDVM TIPICE LABERINTHVS DENOTAT ISTE :
INTRANTI LARGUS, REDEUNTI SET NIMIS ARTVS
SIC MVNDO CAPTVS, VICIORVM MOLLE GRAVATVS
VIX VALET AD VITE DOCTRINAM QVISQVE REDIRE.

In the Cathedral of Cremona, which, like Pavia and Piacenza, is on the banks of the River Po, is a mutilated mosaic of early date—possibly eighth or ninth century—showing part of an interlaced pattern which was evidently intended to refer to the Cretan Labyrinth, as it was placed close to two figures in fighting attitudes and armed with swords and shields, the right-hand figure having the head of a beast and the label "CENTAVRVS." (There was apparently little distinction between a Minotaur and a Centaur in the minds of some mediaeval artists.)

A rather larger specimen, 5 ft. in diameter, may be seen in the church of Sta. Maria-in-Aquiro, Rome. It is composed of bands of porphyry and yellow and green marble, surrounding a central plate of porphyry, and is similar in design to that at Lucca. Another church in the same city, Sta. Maria-di-Trastavera, has a labyrinth composed of variously coloured marbles worked in the floor.

It is 11 ft. across and was probably constructed about
1190 A.D. (Fig. 45). It is now somewhat mutilated, but
was originally a most beautiful example. The fact that
the inner paths consist of a series of concentric rings
rather suggests that it has at some time been repaired
without regard to the original design; unless we accept
the hypothesis of M. Durand that they bore a symbolic

Fig. 47.—Labyrinth in Chartres Cathedral. (Gailhabaud.)

reference to the various degrees of beatitude by which
the soul approaches heaven, as figured by Dante. Fig. 46
shows another old Italian specimen. It is nearly 11½ ft.
in diameter and is to be found in the church of San Vitale,
Ravenna.

Designs of this nature were widely employed by the
mediaeval church builders in France, and, although many
of them were destroyed at the Revolution and at other
times, several fine examples still exist. They seem to have

58

been mostly built at a rather later date than those already described. The largest now remaining is that in Chartres Cathedral (Fig. 47). It is formed of blue and white stones and is about 40 ft. in diameter. The French poet Bouthrays, in his "Histoire de Chartres" (1624), describes it in a set of Latin verses. A fine sketch of it appears in the "Album" of the thirteenth-century architect, Villard de

FIG. 48.—Labyrinth in Amiens Cathedral. (Gailhabaud.)

Honnecourt. In a ninth-century French manuscript, formerly belonging to the Abbey of St.-Germain-des-Prés, there is a sort of frontispiece consisting of a labyrinth of similar type, with a funny little horned Minotaur at the centre, seated, hands on knees, on a kind of throne.

The Chartres labyrinth formerly went by the name of "La Lieue," an expression which would ordinarily be rendered as "the league." The French league, however, was about 2282 yards, a much greater length than the total extent of the path in any of the existing pavement-labyrinths, that at Chartres, for example, having a length of only about 150 yards. Possibly the term had some etymological connection with the old Gaulish measure *leuca, leuga* or *leuva*, which was 1500 paces.

In other cases the labyrinth was known as a "*Chemin de Jérusalem*" "*daedale*," or "*meandre*," terms which need

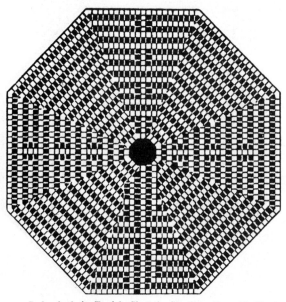

FIG. 49.—Labyrinth in Parish Church, St. Quentin. (Gailhabaud).

no explanation. The centre was called "*ciel*" or "*Jérusalem*." The labyrinth formerly in the nave of Amiens Cathedral was larger than that at Chartres, being 42 ft. in diameter (Fig. 48). It was constructed in 1288 and was destroyed in 1825. In plan it was similar to that at the entrance to the parish church of St. Quentin (Fig. 49). The latter, however, is only 34½ ft. in diameter.

Rheims Cathedral formerly possessed a fine design of this class (Fig. 50). It was laid down in 1240 and was

Fig. 41.
Bronze Plaquette, Italian, XVIth Century. (British Museum)

Fig. 50. Labyrinth in Rheims Cathedral. (Gailhabaud)

Fig. 51. Amiens.
Central Plate of Labyrinth. (Gailhabaud)

Fig. 52. Labyrinth in Bayeux Cathedral. (Amé)

composed of blue stones or marbles. It was destroyed in
1779 by order of a certain Canon Jacquemart, who ob-
jected to the noise made by children and others in tracing
its course during the progress of divine service.

The labyrinths of Rheims, Chartres, and Amiens
possessed in common a feature which has given rise
to much discussion, namely, a figure or figures at the
centre representing, it is believed, the architects of the
edifices.

That of Amiens is preserved in Amiens Museum and
consists of an octagonal grey marble slab (Fig. 51) with
a central cross, between the limbs of which are arranged
figures representing Bishop Evrard and the three architects, Robert de Luzarches, Thomas de Cormont and his
son Regnault, together with four angels. A long inscription accompanied it, relating to the foundation of the
Cathedral.

There is a very fine labyrinth in the chapter-house of
Bayeux Cathedral (Fig. 52). It measures 12 ft. across
and is composed of circles of tiles ornamented with
shields, griffins and fleur-de-lis, separated by bands of
small, plain, black tiles.

Sens Cathedral formerly possessed a circular labyrinth
(Fig. 53), 30 ft. in diameter and formed of incised lines
filled in with lead, but it was destroyed in 1769. A similar
specimen in Auxerre Cathedral was demolished about
1690.

In *The Builder* for May 12, 1916, appeared a diagram
accompanied by a note from a firm of publishers who
stated that they had received the sketch from one of their
travellers who was then serving on the Arras front. "He
informs us," they state, "that it is not a puzzle, but a
plan of the labyrinth under the cathedral. He found the
prints in a ruin in the vicinity, a house which appears to
have been occupied by a librarian from what he saw
among the débris." The sketch in question is of an
octagonal pattern resembling that of the St. Quentin

61

labyrinth, and represents the pavement-labyrinth that formerly existed in the now ruined cathedral, not, of course, a system of subterranean passages, as the correspondent evidently inferred. It was about 34½ ft. in diameter and was composed of small blue and yellow squares. The destruction of this labyrinth cannot be debited to the account of the aggressors in the Great War, as it was carried out during the French Revolution.

FIG. 53.—Labyrinth in Sens Cathedral.   (Gailhabaud.)

A labyrinth of rather striking design (Fig. 54) was formerly in the pavement of the old Abbey of St. Bertin, an edifice which has long been a picturesque ruin, in the lower part of the town of St. Omer. A description of it was first published nearly a century ago by Emmanuel Wallet (or Vallet). Our figure, which accords with his notes, differs slightly from that which has usually accompanied the references of subsequent writers—many of whom, by the way, erroneously speak of it as being in the cathedral, which is in the upper part of the town, and at some distance from St. Bertin. Most illustrations of the labyrinth in question show the path as crossing itself at one point, an arrangement which is most unlikely to have been adopted. Wallet based his description on a manuscript which, judging by the watermark in the paper, he attributed to a former English student at the college in the vicinity.

Fig. 54.—Labyrinth in Abbey of St. Bertin, St. Omer. (Wallet.)

This labyrinth was apparently destroyed at about the same time as that at Rheims, and for a similar reason.

In the cathedral there is no pavement-labyrinth, although it may possibly have possessed one in former times, but beneath the organ, at the west end of the nave, is a curiously engraved slab which is worth mentioning

63

in this connection, for it represents a sort of "chemin de Jérusalem," though not indeed of the usual type. It shows, around a large circle, mountains, rivers, towns, roads, and animals, together with the word ihervsalem, whilst the interior of the circle is divided into three horizontal compartments, in each of which are placed various objects indistinguishable through wear. The slab was very

Fig. 55.—Labyrinth in Poitiers Cathedral. (Auber.)

much worn when described by Wallet and has possibly been replaced by now.

A queer type of labyrinth was formerly represented in the Cathedral of Poitiers. It perished long ago, but for some time subsequently there remained on the wall of the north aisle a sketch of it (Fig. 55), which, however, gave no clue to the dimensions of the original. It will be seen that the construction is such that he who traces the path eventually emerges—like the poet of the "Rubaiyat" —by that same door at which he entered; he will have

64

encountered no "stops," but he may have "looped the loop" an indefinite number of times.

In the old abbey of Toussaints, Châlons-sur-Marne, which was destroyed in 1544, there was a series of tiles each bearing a small labyrinth of the conventional Cretan type (Fig. 56. See plate, p. 74). Pavement-tiles with labyrinths were also found in the Abbaye de Pont l'Abbé (Finistère).

A pavement labyrinth has been described as existing in the floor of the guard chamber of the Abbey of St. Stephen at Caen. Dawson Turner, in his "Tour in Normandy," thus refers to it: "The floor is laid with tiles, each near five inches square, baked almost to vitrification. Eight rows of these tiles, running east to west, are charged with different coats of arms, said to be those of the families who attended Duke William in his invasion of England. The intervals between these rows are filled up with a kind of tessellated pavement, the middle whereof represents a maze or labyrinth, about ten feet in diameter, and so artfully contrived that, were we to suppose a man following all the intricate meanders of the volutes, he could not travel less than a mile before he got from one end to the other. The remainder of the floor is inlaid with small squares of different colours, placed alternately and formed into draught or chess boards, for the amusement of the soldiers while on guard." The pavement was destroyed in 1802.

It has frequently been stated that a pavement labyrinth existed in a church at Aix near Marseilles, but probably this is due to confusion with the Roman pavement already referred to.

The only examples recorded as having existed in Germany were situated in two churches at Cologne, but these have long since disappeared.

In view of the widespread occurrence of these devices in mediaeval churches it would be surprising if the idea were not sometimes utilised by modern architects attempting to reproduce the spirit of the old buildings, and in fact this was done in the case of the prize plans submitted[1] by the English architects Clutton and Burges for the Church of Notre-Dame de la Treille at Lille. Burges designed for the nave a "Chemin de Jérusalem" of a wonderful pattern, the topography of "Jerusalem" being based upon the account in the "Ecclesiastical History" of the Venerable Bede (V. ch. 16). A good modern

Fig. 57.—Labyrinth in Ely Cathedral. (W. H. M.)

example, 20 ft. square, may be seen in the pavement of Ely Cathedral, near the west door (Fig. 57). It was constructed by Sir Gilbert Scott during his restorations in 1870. Some other modern specimens will be mentioned presently.

As to the function and meaning of the old church labyrinths, various opinions have been held. Some authorities have thought that they were merely introduced as a

[1] These plans, although awarded the prize, were not adopted, the designs actually carried out being some by a native architect who obtained tenth place in the competition.

66

symbol of the perplexities and intricacies which beset the Christian's path. Others considered them to typify the entangling nature of sin or of any deviation from the rectilinear path of Christian duty. It has often been asserted, though on what evidence is not clear, that the larger examples were used for the performance of miniature pilgrimages in substitution for the long and tedious journeys formerly laid upon penitents. Some colour is lent to this supposition by the name "Chemin de Jérusalem." In the days of the first crusades it was a common practice for the confessor to send the peccant members of his flock either to fight against the infidel, or, after the victory of Geoffrey of Bouillon, to visit the Holy Sepulchre. As enthusiasm for the crusades declined, shorter pilgrimages were substituted, usually to the shrine of some saint, such as Our Lady of Loretto, or St. Thomas of Canterbury, and it is quite possible that, at a time when the soul had passed out of the crusades and the Church's authority was on the ebb, a journey on the knees around the labyrinth's sinuosities was prescribed as an alternative to these pilgrimages. Perhaps this type of penance was from the first imposed on those who, through weakness or any other reason, were unable to undertake long travels.

In the case of the wall labyrinths, of course, the journey would be less arduous still, being performed by the index finger.

Whether such practices ever obtained or not, most writers who have had occasion to mention church labyrinths during the past century have adopted, more or less without question, the view that not only were the labyrinths used in this way, but that they were in fact designed for the purpose.

This view seems to rest chiefly on a statement by J. B. F. Géruzez in his "Description of the City of Rheims" (1817), to the effect that the labyrinth which formerly lay in the cathedral was in origin an object of devotion, being the emblem of the interior of the Temple of Jerusalem, but Géruzez quotes no authority for his assertion. Another explanation, based upon the occurrence of the figures of the architects or founders in certain of the designs, is that the labyrinth was a sort of masonic seal, signifying that the pious aim of the builder had been to raise to the glory of God a structure to vie with the splendours of the traditional Labyrinth. It is also said that in some cases the "Chemins" were used for processional purposes.

Some writers have held that the labyrinth was inserted in the church as typifying the Christian's life or the devious course of those who yield to temptation. Some have thought that it represented the path from the house of Pilate to Calvary, pointing out that Chateaubriand, in his "Itinéraire de Paris à Jérusalem," mentioned two hours as the period which he took to repeat Christ's journey, and that the same time would be taken in traversing the average pavement labyrinth on the knees.

The use of the labyrinth as a simile for the Christian's life is shown in a stone inscription in the Museum at Lyons:

HOC SPECVLO · SPECVLARE LEGENS · QVOD
SIS MORITVRVS:
QVOD CINIS IMMOLVTVM QVOD VERMIBVS
ESCA FVTVRVS:
SED TAMEN VT SEMPER VIVAS · MALE
VIVERE VITA:
XPM QVESO ROGA · SIT VT IN XPO MEA
VITA:
ME CAPVT APRIL' · EX HOC RAPVIT LABER-
INTO:
PREBITVM · DOCEO VERSV MĀ FVNERA
QÑTO:
    STEPHANVS · FECIT OC.

Whether this inscription was ever attached to a labyrinthine design is not known.

68

It is strange if, amongst all the great mass of mediaeval ecclesiastical literature, there is actually no indication of the use or significance of these monuments in the service of the Church; but no light appears to be forthcoming from this source, and certainly the writings of the chief authorities of these times give no support to any of the theories mentioned above.

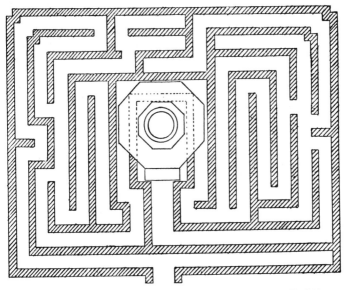

FIG. 58.—Labyrinth in Church at Bourn, Cambs. (W. H. M.)

It is noteworthy that in none of the known examples do any distinctively Christian emblems occur, and that, amongst all the myriad inscriptions, paintings, and carvings of the early Christians, in the catacombs of Rome and elsewhere, the labyrinth never once figures.

So far as these islands are concerned the practice of placing labyrinths in churches does not seem to have become common.

In the "Architectural Dictionary" (1867) mention is

69

made of one formerly existing in Canterbury Cathedral, but no particulars are given.

On the floor below the tower of the church at Bourn, Cambridgeshire, is a maze (Fig. 58) worked in black and red tiles, the centre being occupied by the font, the step of which forms the terminus of the path. From the fact that an intermediate portion of the path is concealed beneath the base of the font it is plain that the position of the latter is an after-thought, and from the design of the maze, no less than from the character of the tiles of which it is composed, the work would appear to be of comparatively modern date. The modern specimen at Ely has already been mentioned.

There is also a labyrinth, in this case engraved on the floor of the church porch, at Alkborough, Lincolnshire, but this is a modern replica of the turf maze in the locality—a point which brings us to the subject of our next chapter.

CHAPTER X

TURF LABYRINTHS

WE have just remarked that the custom of placing labyrinth designs in churches does not appear to have become general on this side of the English Channel. We have in England, however, a class of survivals peculiar to this country which may be regarded as the equivalent of the former. These are the *turf mazes* which are to be found in various counties, usually under some local name, such as "Mizmaze," "Julian's Bower," "Troy Town," or "Shepherd's Race."

One of the best-preserved examples is that at Alkborough, or Aukborough, a pretty village on the east side of the Trent falls, where the Ouse and Trent join to form the Humber. Crowning the hill is a square earthwork called the Countess Close, supposed to be the remains of a Roman Camp, and possibly the site of the ancient Aquis. On the side of the hill is a basin-shaped depression, in the turf of which is cut, to a depth of about 6 in., a labyrinth known as "Julian's Bower," or "Gilling Bore," about 40 ft. in diameter. Our illustration (Fig. 59) is reproduced from a drawing kindly supplied by the Rev. G. Yorke, Vicar of Alkborough. The configuration of the maze is exactly the same as in a figure published about a century ago in a little book called "Terra Incognita of Lincolnshire," by Miss S. Hatfield.

In recent years it has been several times cleared out

71

and trimmed up at the expense of Mr. J. Goulton Constable, J.P., F.S.A., of Walcot Hall, who is lord of the manor. Mr. Constable also caused the design of the maze to be cut in the stone floor of the church porch, the

FIG. 59.—" Julian's Bower," Alkborough, Lincs. (From a litho. supplied by Rev. G. Yorke.)

grooves being filled with cement, when the church was restored in 1887.

In Saxon and Norman times, from about A.D. 1080 to 1220, there was a small monastic grange in the neighbourhood, an offshoot of a Benedictine Monastery at Spalding. Its site is now occupied by a farm-house belonging to Magdalene College, Cambridge. The proximity of the maze to an ancient ecclesiastical site is not peculiar to this particular specimen, as we find a similar juxtaposition in the case of many of the other earth-mazes.

A correspondent, "J. F.," writing to *Notes and Queries* about the Alkborough Julian's Bower in 1866, says that he has lively impressions of the oft-repeated pleasure derived from the feat of "running it in and out," in company with others, sixty years previously, and of seeing the villagers playing May-eve games about it, "under an indefinite persuasion of something unseen and unknown co-operating with them." If this last-quoted phrase is anything more than a whim of retrospective old age it affords an interesting fragment of material for the student of "folk-memory." There is a description of this maze, under the name of Gillian's Bore, in the Diary, written between 1671 and 1704, of Abraham de la Pryme, "the Yorkshire Antiquary." He mentions at the same time one situated at Appleby, about six miles away, towards Brigg. This, he says, is called "Troy's Walls." He describes them both as Roman games and says "they are nothing but great labarinths cut upon the ground with a hill cast up round them for the spectators to sit round about on to behold the sport." The Appleby maze was placed close to the Roman road that runs through there, and has long since perished. No trace of it remained when Allen's "History of Lincolnshire" was published in 1834.

There is a turf labyrinth of a design similar to that at Alkborough in a secluded romantic spot on land forming part of the estate of the Hulse family, to the rear of their beautiful country seat, Breamore House, Hants. It is known as the Mizmaze, and consists of a grassy path 3 ft. in width, the overall diameter being 87 ft. The "goal" in the centre is 18 ft. in diameter, and forms a low mound. Every curved portion of the path is slightly inclined towards the centre of the maze, as if to afford a firmer footing to runners. When the writer visited it in July 1920 the grooves were rather overgrown, but the maze receives periodical attention from its owners, and is in no present danger of becoming obliterated. It lies in that sparsely populated corner of Hampshire which protrudes into Wiltshire, between Salisbury and Cranborne Chase, and is somewhat difficult to discover without directions, as it is on a hilltop, and is surrounded by a thick copse, with many other wooded hilltops in the neighbourhood. In the few references that have been made to it by writers, it has been variously described as being situated at Breamore, at Rockbourne, Hants, and at Wickdown Hill, Wilts. It is remote from the villages, but is best approached from Breamore (pronounced *Bremmer* or *Brimmer*), which is on the main road from Fordingbridge to Salisbury. From this village to Breamore House is a pleasant twenty-minutes' walk, and thence through the beautifully wooded and gently rolling grounds of the estate to the Mizmaze, a delightful half-hour's stroll. It is advisable to seek precise directions before setting out, because the path through the woods disappears after a while in a meadow, and the copse in which the maze is embedded appears at first impenetrable, having a narrow opening on one side only, on the side remote from the direction of approach. A local tradition says that a man could run from the maze to Gallows Hill, more than half a mile distant, and back again, while another ran round the maze.

A charming little sketch of this maze, by Heywood Sumner, accompanies a reference in Williams-Freeman's "Field Archaeology in Hants."

Near Wing, in Rutland, a few miles to the north-east of Uppingham, there is preserved a maze of very similar design (Fig. 60). It is maintained in good condition and is still the object of periodical visits by the village folk on certain holidays. Just to the south of it is a flat-topped bowl-shaped tumulus, over 70 ft. in diameter and

74

Fig. 56.
Labyrinths on Tiles, Toussaints Abbey, Chalons-sur-Marne.   (Amé)
(see page 65)

Fig. 60.   Turf-Labyrinth at Wing, Rutland.
(Photo, W. J. Stocks.   By permission of Rev. E. A. Irons)

4 ft. high. It may be that the frequent association of turf mazes with ancient earthworks of various kinds is something more than accidental, but we do not seem to have sufficient evidence to establish a necessary connection between the two things.

Lyddington, another Rutland village, has also been mentioned as possessing a turf maze. A writer in the *Rutland Magazine* in 1907, for instance, says, in speaking of Priestly Hill, which overlooks the village on the east, "at one time there was a turf maze on its slope, where, as our old people tell us, their grandparents, when children, used to play." The writer in question, however, does not make it clear whether he is really quoting an oral tradition of the locality or is basing his statement on the brief mention of Lyddington as a reputed maze-site which appears in Trollope's 1858 memoir. It is at any rate very difficult to trace any reliable evidence of such a maze, and it seems not unlikely that Trollope's reference, which is quite devoid of detail, may have had its origin in a misinterpretation of the elaborate series of ancient trenches situated in a field to the north-east of the church. These trenches have been identified as the "fish-stews" belonging to the old manor-house of the Bishops of Lincoln.

The similarity between the designs of the turf mazes mentioned above and those of some of the French pavement labyrinths, that in Chartres Cathedral for example, cannot fail to be noticed.

At Boughton Green, in Northamptonshire, about half a mile from the village of Boughton and near the ruined church of St. John the Baptist, was, until recently, a turf maze of like design but having the innermost convolutions of purely spiral form (Fig. 61). It was 37 ft. in diameter and was called the "Shepherd Ring" or "Shepherd's Race." The "treading" of it was formerly a great feature of the three days' fair in June, an event dating from a charter by Edward III. in 1353.

75

In a "Guide-book to Northampton" by G. N. Wetton, published in 1849, the maze is spoken of as being in a neglected condition. In a later book, however, a novel named "The Washingtons," written by the Rev. J. N. Simpkinson in 1860, occurs the following passage: " He had just been treading the 'Shepherd's Labyrinth,' a complicated spiral maze traced there upon the turf; and

FIG. 61.—" Shepherd's Race," Boughton Green, Northants. (After Trollope.)

was boasting of his skill, how dexterously and truly he could pursue its windings without a single false step, and how with a little more practice he would wager to go through it blindfold."

Another novel, "The Last of the Climbing Boys," by George Elson, contains a reference to it, in which it is spoken of as being "An attraction which was the origin of the fair"—a statement which it would be interesting to verify if possible.

Unfortunately, this famous relic was destroyed by
76

some of our soldiers in training during the Great War; trenches were driven right across it, and practically all traces of it are now obliterated.

There was formerly a specimen of somewhat similar design on Ripon Common, Yorkshire, but this was ploughed up in 1827. One of identical pattern at Asenby, in the same county, was preserved until recent times. According to Mr. A. H. Allcroft ("Earthwork of England," 1908), it was sunk in a hollow at the top of a hillock called "The Fairies' Hill," and is in a ruinous condition, being quite unknown to most of the villagers, although persons still living (in 1908) relate that they have often trodden it on a summer's evening and knelt at the centre "to hear the fairies singing."

The counties of Yorkshire and Lincolnshire seem to have been particularly rich in records of these devices, for in addition to those already mentioned we read of one on the wold overlooking Louth, one at Horncastle, a dozen miles to the south-west of Louth, one in Holderness, between Marfleet and Paul, about four miles from Hull, and another at Egton, near Whitby, where the late Canon Greenwell in 1872 saw traces of it near the main road to the north of the village. "July Park," or "St. Julian's," near Goathland, is also said to have possessed a specimen, a fact which probably accounts for the name of the place. The Horncastle maze is referred to by Dr. Stukeley, a noted eighteenth-century antiquary, as a "Julian's Bower" which is "much talked of." He also mentions the Alkborough specimen and others, coming to the conclusion that they were ancient British relics, having been constructed as places of exercise, or *cursus*, for the soldiery of those times. He observes, somewhat contemptuously, that "lovers of antiquity, especially of the inferior classes, always speak of 'em with great pleasure, as if there was something extraordinary in the thing, though they cannot tell what."

The Louth "Gelyan Bower" is mentioned in a record

77

of 1544, "To nych mason for making at gelyan bower a new crose, iijs." In an old hostelry in Mercer Row, Louth, stood for some centuries a boulder of dolerite called the "Blue Stone," which is stated to have formerly occupied the centre of the maze. Trees planted at the maze served as a landmark to ships out at sea.

The Horncastle example occupied a site to the south-west of the town still known as the Julian Bower Close. It has long been effaced by the agriculturist, and numerous coins, fibulæ, and other Roman remains which have been turned up on the spot have lent colour to the theory, still maintained in the current county directory, that the maze was a Roman work. The question whether this, or any other turf maze in this country, is a relic of Roman times we will discuss presently.

The maze near Hull was dodecagonal in outline, 40 ft. across, and formed of grass paths 14 in. wide. Its plan was much like that of the Alkborough maze, but the paths were straight instead of curved. It was called "The Walls of Troy." A coloured illustration of it was given in Ackermann's "Repository of Arts" in 1815.

Although, as we have seen, Lincolnshire furnishes us with records of more of these labyrinths than any other county, there is no conclusive evidence that they were in fact more numerous there than elsewhere. The reason for our comparative wealth of information concerning their existence in that part of the country may be due to the fact that Dr. Edward Trollope, who first made a serious study of these antiquities, and whose paper in the *Archaeological Journal* for 1858 has been a fount of inspiration to subsequent writers on the subject, was Archdeacon of Stow, afterwards Bishop of Nottingham.

Turf labyrinths were formerly of general occurrence throughout the country, for, in addition to those we have already described, we find remains of them in counties so widely separated as Kent and Cumberland. They are also recorded as having existed in Wales and Scotland.

78

CHAPTER XI

A MILE or two outside Winchester and rising up above the village of Chilcombe is the rounded shoulder of St. Catherine's Hill, on the summit of which lies a curious squarish "Mizmaze," the execution of which is often ascribed by guide-books to a Winchester boy who, detained at school during the vacation, beguiled his time by the fashioning of this earthwork and by the composition of the Wintonian "Dulce Domum." The interest of this maze lies not so much in the fanciful ascription of its origin as in the fact that it has apparently been cut, or re-cut, by somebody who did not understand the meaning of the plan given him to work upon. For, as will be seen from our illustration (Fig. 62), the actual labyrinth is made, not by the turfed path, but by the narrow channel by which it is delimited. In the few drawings of this maze which the writer has been able to find the lines are all straight, instead of being slightly curved as in our figure, which was sketched on the spot, and it seemed possible that they might represent an earlier condition of it, but in each instance the labyrinth is formed by the groove, which is hardly likely to have been the case in the original design. The maze was re-cut by the Warden of Winchester, who was guided by a plan in the possession of a lady residing in the neighbourhood, about the middle of last century, when it had become almost effaced. Possibly

79

the misinterpretation of the plan occurred on this occasion. The maze is backed by a clump of pines, planted by Lord Botetourt in 1770.

There used to be, until a generation ago, a turf maze at Leigh, in the north-west of Dorset. A writer in *Notes and Queries* in 1868 describes it as being slightly hollow, circular, thirty-three paces in diameter, and

Fig. 62.—" Mizmaze," St. Catherine's Hill, Winchester. (W. H. M.)

enclosed by a bank three feet high. He adds: "I am sorry to say the turf has grown over the little trenches and that it is now impossible to trace the pattern of the maze." Sir Frederick Treves, in his "Highways and Byways in Dorset," 1906, speaks of this maze as having consisted of "low banks and trenches arranged in an intricate figure, which the youths of the village, accompanied no doubt by the maidens, were wont to thread at certain seasons of the year." He states that it is on high ground

in an open field and that of the winding passages no trace
now survives. Only the low bank and ditch surrounding
the maze remain visible.

At Pimperne, not far from Blandford, there was formerly a maze of a unique design (Fig.63). John Aubrey,

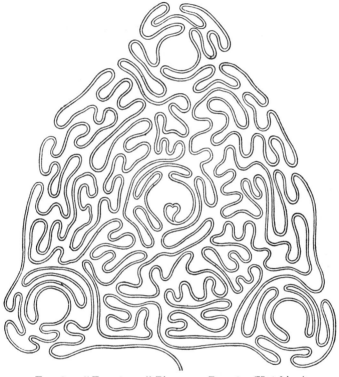

FIG. 63.—" Troy-town," Pimperne, Dorset. (Hutchins.)

writing in 1686, says it was "much used by the young
people on Holydaies and by ye School-boies." The path
was bounded by ridges about a foot in height. The maze
was destroyed by the plough in 1730. The memory of
another turf maze in the same country is preserved in
the name of Troy-town, applied to a locality about three

miles north-east of Dorchester. One is also said to have existed near Bere Regis. Aubrey goes on to refer to another at West Ashton, near Trowbridge, Wiltshire, and one "on the Cotteswold Downes, where Mr. Dover's Games were celebrated." He mentions them also in his "Natural History and Antiquities of Surrey," and concludes his reference by quoting what he calls a "Poetical Description" of them, by Thomas Randolph, a poet and dramatist of the seventeenth century, the so-called description being nothing more than an indictment of the lazy shepherd swain, who prefers to spend his leisure in sleeping under a bush when, according to the poet, he ought

> ". . . to tune his Reed and chant his layes
> Or nimbly run the windings of the Maze."

This is from Thomas Randolph's (or Randall's) "Eglogue on the Palilia and Noble Assemblies revived on Cotswold Hills by Mr. Robert Dover," one of a collection of eulogies—the *Annalia Dubrensia*—by various poets of the day of the then famous annual sports organised by Captain Dover on the hills near Chipping Campden. Mazes, or "laborinths," are referred to in the contributions of several of the other poets concerned, of whom we may mention Francis Izod, Nicholas Wallington, William Bellas and William Denny. A figure in the crude frontispiece conveys a similar allusion.

In Essex we have an example of rather larger dimensions than the majority, namely, that on the east side of the common at Saffron Walden (Fig. 64). A tall bank hides it from the Thaxted road, which runs within a few yards of it. The four bastions (or "bellows") and the centre are slightly raised. The overall dimensions are approximately 91 ft., excluding the bastions, and 138 ft. from corner to corner.

This maze is referred to in the Corporation account books for the year 1699, when it was apparently re-cut.

82

On several subsequent occasions it became neglected and almost obliterated, but fortunately there has always been some person sufficiently interested to cause its renovation. According to a local record, re-cuttings have taken place in 1828, 1841, 1859, 1887, and 1911. On

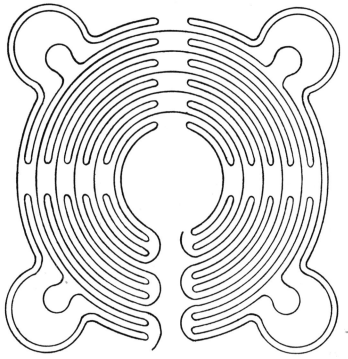

Fig. 64.—Turf Labyrinth, Saffron Walden, Essex. (W. H. M.)

the last occasion it was underlaid with bricks, to facilitate future renovations.

As in the case of the Winchester example, the "path" consists of the narrow and shallow groove instead of the raised turf, and this gives some weight to the tradition that it is only a copy of a much larger maze which formerly existed further to the east.

83

In a manuscript book of the latter part of the eighteenth century the maze is spoken of as a favourite resort for the young bloods of the town, a complicated system of rules and wagers (in gallons of beer) being laid down in connection with walking the maze.

It is stated that a large ash tree at one time occupied the centre, but that it perished by fire in the Guy Fawkes celebrations of November 5, 1823.

A few years ago some boys, playing on the central mound, discovered a Roman coin. This does not, of course, prove that the work is of Roman origin.

In the 1789 edition of Camden's "Britannia" a drawing of the maze exhibits merely a series of concentric circles with extensions on the outermost pair forming the "bastions." This illustration could hardly have been prepared on the spot.

About twenty miles to the north-west of Saffron Walden and a few miles to the west of Cambridge lies the little village of Comberton (Cambs). The playground of the village school occupies one corner at the cross-roads, and in the south-west angle of this, enclosed by iron railings, lies a turf maze of a pattern similar to that at Alkborough. Owing to the use which the school children make of it the paths are nearly denuded of grass, but the ridges are well defined, as shown by the photograph (Fig. 65), which was taken in March 1921. The present maze is a faithful copy of that which was formerly situated a few yards away, and which, when the school was built, occupied an inconvenient position just outside the scholars' entrance. The old maze was known as the "Mazles." It used to be the custom in the village to have a feast once every three years, and at such times the maze was re-cut.

Comberton, by the way, is almost the next village to Bourn, where, as we have seen, a peculiar pavement maze occupies the floor of the church tower.

In the neighbouring county of Huntingdon we find

84

[*Photo : W.H.M.*

Fig. 65.   " The Mazles," Comberton, Cambs.

[*Photo : W.H.M.*

Fig. 67.   Turf-Labyrinth, Hilton, Hunts.

a splendidly preserved maze, of curious plan, in a corner
of the green in the rambling and out-of-the-way but
charming village of Hilton (Fig. 66).

These turf labyrinths are in most cases liable to
escape the notice of all but the intentional seeker, owing

Fig. 66.—Turf Labyrinth, Hilton, Hunts. (W. H. M.)

to their flat and grassy nature, and the difficulty is accen-
tuated in the case of Hilton by reason of the fact that the
maze is at some little distance from the road, and is,
moreover, sunk to a depth of several inches below the
general level of the surrounding turf. It may easily be
located, however, if one remembers that the centre is
marked by a square stone obelisk surmounted by a ball.

This obelisk has indications of a sun-dial on the north face, with the words "A.B. hoc." On its south face it bears a coat of arms, engraved within a circle, and the inscription: "Sic transit gloria mundi. Gulielmus Sparrow, Gen., natus ano. 1641. Aetatis sui 88 quando obiit, hos gyros formavit anno 1660." On the east face is engraved, "William Sparrow departed this life the 25th August, Anno Domini 1729, aged 88 years." The west face bears only the words "Dep. hoc." Our photograph (Fig. 67) shows the obelisk and as much of the maze as could conveniently be included with the camera used. It will be noticed that the trenches between the paths are fairly wide and deeply cut.

The good state of preservation is no doubt greatly due to the fact, remarked by a writer of half a century ago, that the paths are made up with pebbles. No sign of the latter is now evident amongst the thick turf. The plan of the maze shows some interesting variations on the older and more conventional designs of Alkborough, Comberton, etc., the most remarkable point being that the path from the exterior to the centre is almost direct, the labyrinth proper being composed of paths which commence and terminate at the central plot. The Hilton maze appears to be unique in this respect.

Whatever may have been the original purpose of turf labyrinths in this country as a whole, it is fairly clear that the Hilton example at any rate was not made for ecclesiastical purposes if, as stated on the obelisk, it was constructed in 1660. On the other hand, the reflection that at that date Puritan influences were on the decline and the restoration of the Monarchy was imminent leads one to conclude that this somewhat exuberant design of a youth of nineteen was intended for purposes of rustic enjoyment.

Fig. 68 shows a labyrinth formerly incised in the turf of the marshes of Rockcliffe in Cumberland, near the shores of the Solway Firth. It covered a space of

86

26 ft. by 24 ft. and had a 9-in. path bounded by an 8-in. groove. It went by the name of "The Walls of Troy." The two villages of Burgh and Rockcliffe are distant from one another about two miles and a half, and the river Eden bisects the intervening marshes and occasionally floods them. A certain point on the marsh is known as "Willie of the Boats," from the fact that prior to 1816, when the main road from Carlisle to Glasgow passed this way, a man of that name lived here and

Fig. 68.—"Walls of Troy," Rockcliffe Marsh, Cumberland. (After Ferguson.)

acted as guide through the marshes and over the river fords. A maze existed close to this spot and is said to have been cut in 1815 by a man named Christopher Graham. Whether Graham designed the maze himself or whether he copied an already existing specimen cannot now be determined, but it is stated that a smaller and probably older maze existed side by side with his. Both have now entirely disappeared. The maze figured, however, was about a mile from this spot and was still in existence in 1883, though much overgrown. The local tradition declared it to have been cut by Robert Edgar, a sailor, who was subsequently drowned at sea. All three

87

of the mazes mentioned were apparently of similar design. A friend of the writer was unable to find any traces of a maze in the locality in 1920.

On the summit of a hill by St. Anne's Well, Sneinton, Nottingham, there formerly existed a maze called "Robin Hood's Race," or "Shepherd's Race." It was of a design somewhat similar to that at Saffron Walden, but having each of the four bastions ornamented with an incised figure of the type known in heraldry as a "Cross, crosslet, fitchy." The path was stated to be 535 yards in total length. When the lordship of Sneinton was enclosed, in February 1797, the maze was ploughed up. An enterprising printer of Nottingham, J. Wigsby by name, preserved for us the plan by publishing in the following month an illustrated pamphlet in commemoration of the maze, "Sixpence plain, eightpence coloured."

Another turf maze used to exist in the same neighbourhood, namely, at Clifton, about four miles or so from Sneinton, on the opposite side of Nottingham. This was of a square design similar to that of the garden maze shown in Fig. 75.

At Somerton, near Banbury, Oxfordshire, there has been well preserved a very good "Troy-town" (Fig. 69), of a plan which recalls that on the tiles of Toussaints Abbey. It is situated in the garden of a farm-house, named after it "Troy," and is surrounded by beautiful trees and shrubs. Our drawing is made from a sketch kindly supplied by the brother of the present occupier, Mr. J. F. Godwin. Its dimensions are 57 ft. by 50 ft., and the turf path, one foot in width, has a total length of 400 yards.

Near Piddington, on the border of the same county, rises to a height of nearly 400 ft. above the village the eminence known as Muswell Hill. Close to the summit of the hill is an earthwork having the form of a square turfed level surrounded by a low bank and bearing the traditional name of "The Wilderness." It is often spoken of locally as a Roman camp, but there is nothing in its structure to suggest such an origin: no satisfactory explanation of its origin or purpose has, in fact, been hitherto forthcoming. Now the word "wilderness," as we shall see in a subsequent chapter, was employed during a certain period to denote a maze of the horticultural type, and it

Fig. 69.—"Troy-town," Somerton, Oxon. (From sketch by O. W. Godwin.)

is not improbable that it was used in connection with mazes in general. May we not, therefore, allow it to be within the realms of legitimate surmise that this mysterious work constitutes the remains of a square turf maze, perhaps of a design similar to that of the Clifton maze mentioned above? The situation, the enclosing bank, and the regular outline of the latter accord well with this supposition, though the dimensions—250 ft. square—are rather excessive unless we allow for a considerable margin between the bank and the maze itself.

Another Oxfordshire locality, Tadmarton Heath, is mentioned as a turf-maze site in a manuscript by the Rev. T. Leman, quoted in a county history published in 1861, but if such a work ever existed there all traces of it have now disappeared; the same is true with regard to another reputed maze site to which reference is made in the manuscript, namely, the Herefordshire Beacon, in the Malvern Hills. In both cases the situations are such as might well have been selected for the purpose, judging by analogy with other known turf-maze sites. Sixty years is none too long a period to allow of the complete obliteration of the turf figures, if such existed, in the absence of care and attention, so that it is not surprising if we now find ourselves unable to trace them, especially if they possessed no circumscribing bank or ditch.

In Surrey a "Troy-town" was formerly well known in the neighbourhood of Guildford. It was cut in the turf on Hillbury, between Guildford and Farnham. It may be that the earth-rings of which traces are yet visible on St. Martha's Hill, on the other side of Guildford, constitute the remains of a similar work. It is said that the youths and maidens of the town used to congregate here on Good Friday and indulge in boisterous celebrations, the origin of which is not known. Another Surrey spot formerly· alluded to as having a turf maze is Putney Heath. Unfortunately, however, we cannot at present point to any authentic traces of a single specimen in the whole of the county.

At Chilham, near Godmersham, in Kent, is an earthwork on the downs known as Julaber's Barrow or Juliberry's Grave. It bears no traces of mazy paths, but the name carries strong suggestion of "Julian's Bower," and there is perhaps as much force in this suggestion as in the opposing view that the mound is the grave of Quintus Laberius Durus, one of Julius Caesar's tribunes (hence

Julii Laberius), who was killed by the Britons. The latter theory was, however, maintained by a writer to *The Times* as recently as April 5, 1920. The fact that as late as 1893, according to a letter to *Notes and Queries* of that year, traces of a "bower" or "Troy-town" were still observable in the neighbourhood of Walmer, shows that the Chilham work, if a turf maze, would not have been unique in the county. It is also said that one formerly existed near Westerham; the name "Troy-town," moreover, survives in other parts of the county (see p. 211). Additional support for the theory of a turf maze site at Chilham is found in the occurrence of the name Bowerland, applied to a district to the north of the village. We find, too, a hamlet of Bower, only a few miles to the south-west.

In Bedfordshire, not far from Dunstable, there is a circular earthwork on the downs called "Maiden Bower." Stukeley refers to it in his discussion on Julian's Bowers as being in his opinion the site of a former turf maze, and there is some force in this contention. He mentions in the same reference a similar work at Ashwell.

Dr. Trollope stated that specimens had been reported also from the county of Devonshire and in Scotland, but actual details are not at the moment available.

There is no doubt that the custom of cutting these devices in the turf was formerly very widespread throughout the land, although comparatively few examples now exist. Even during the past generation, as we have seen, some are known to have disappeared. Let us therefore hope that all possible care will be taken to preserve those that remain to us.

CHAPTER XII

In 1858—the year in which Archdeacon Trollope published the results of his researches—Capt. W. H. Mounsey drew attention to the description in a Welsh history book ("Drych y Prif Oesoedd," published in 1740) of a curious custom formerly prevalent among the Welsh shepherds. This custom consisted of cutting in the turf a figure in the form of a labyrinth, which they called Caerdroia, *i.e.* the walls, or citadel, of Troy. He also remarked that the herdsmen of Burgh and Rockcliffe "at the present day are in the habit of cutting this labyrinthine figure, which they also call 'the Walls of Troy.' " He drew the tentative conclusion that this name "would seem to be an after-thought of pure Cymric origin, suggested by the similarity between *Caerdroia*, the City of Troy, and *Caer y troiau*, the city of windings or turnings." A similar suggestion had already been made in the *Transactions of the Cymmrodorion Society* in 1822, the writer ("Idrison") holding that the turf figures, and also those on the Knossian coins, had reference to the courses of the sun as conceived by ancient worshippers of that orb.

Captain Mounsey was promptly answered by Dr. Trollope, who referred to the wide distribution of these devices throughout England and commented on their total absence from Brittany, where, if they were of ancient Cymric origin, one would have expected to find at least

92

some trace of them. He also stated that they first received the name of "Troy-towns" in Tudor days, when "subtleties" of all kinds were in vogue, the term being used simply to indicate, by analogy with the Troy of legend, the difficulties to be overcome before the centre could be reached. Dr. Trollope gave it as his considered opinion that they were originally cut for penitential purposes by ecclesiastics, and this opinion has since his time remained practically unchallenged. In his memoir on the subject he reproduces a sketch showing the St. Anne's Hill maze with two gowned and kneeling persons in the act of performing a penitential circuit. Both the sketch and Dr. Trollope's conclusion are based on inference, however; there does not appear to be any direct evidence in the matter.

The theory of an ecclesiastical origin of the turf mazes is chiefly supported by analogy with the continental church-labyrinths which many of them so strongly resemble. Against the argument of their frequent proximity to an ecclesiastical site we may place that of their equally frequent proximity to known Roman remains and the fact that many of our old churches were founded on Roman sites.

The Welsh custom above referred to was also described by P. Roberts in his "Cambrian Popular Antiquities," published in 1815. He gives a plan of the figure as usually cut—a design resembling the circular labyrinths on Knossian coins, but flattened on the side where the entrance is situated—and expresses dissatisfaction with it because there are "no means of losing the way into the citadel, the supposed way continuing regularly through all its windings unbroken, which could scarcely have been the design of the inventor " (Fig. 70).

This figure, he says, is the plan of a labyrinth which is sometimes cut out in the turf by shepherd boys whilst they are tending their flocks on the mountains of Wales, and is sometimes drawn and presented as a puzzle by boys to exercise the ingenuity of their school-fellows, either in finding their way to the citadel at the centre or in drawing the plan. The tradition which accompanies the plan is that the city of Troy was defended by seven walls represented by the seven exterior lines and the entrance made as intricate as possible in order to frustrate an attacking force.

On the question whether turf mazes were, as Dr. Trollope affirmed, constructed by ecclesiastics for penitential purposes, there does not appear to be sufficient evidence to form a final decision. Even if it be true that they, and the pavement labyrinths, were actually used in the manner mentioned — a statement for which we do not seem to have definite proof—it by no means follows that they were designed with that object. We do know for certain that they were, from Tudor times onwards, used for recreational purposes. In his "Midsummer Night's Dream" (Act II., Sc. i.) Shakespeare makes Titania say, in her reply to Oberon (after the latter had twitted her with her love for Theseus):

FIG. 70.—" Caerdroia." (After P. Roberts.)

"... the quaint mazes in the wanton green,
For lack of tread are undistinguishable."

In "The Tempest" also (Act III., Sc. iii.) he makes the old counsellor Gonzalo say:

"By'r lakin, I can go no further, sir,
My old bones ache: here's a maze trod indeed
Through forth-rights and meanders: by your patience
I needs must rest me ";

94

and further on (Act V., Sc. i.) he puts a similar phrase into the mouth of Alonso:

"This is as strange a maze as e'er man trod:
And there is in this business more than nature
Was ever conduct of."

It is most likely that the turf mazes were in existence long before Shakespeare's time. The similarity of design between some of them and certain of the continental church labyrinths, which has already been alluded to, furnishes some grounds for supposing that they were contemporary with the latter in origin, in which case they would most probably have been constructed in the twelfth or thirteenth centuries. The fact that several of them were situated in the neighbourhood of some religious institution also lends support to the assertion that they were of monastic workmanship. There is no reason, however, to suppose that their construction and the handing on of the labyrinth tradition was confined to ecclesiastics.

According to M. Berthelot, who made a special study of the work of the ancient and mediaeval alchemists, a similar figure was employed by the latter. At any rate he found in an eleventh-century alchemistic manuscript, which he refers to as the Manuscript of St. Mark, Venice, a labyrinth drawing closely resembling the ecclesiastical type, accompanied by a commentary in Greek verse. He, however, expresses the opinion that both the labyrinth and the verses are an addition of the fourteenth or fifteenth century. The figure, he says, is referred to as "The Labyrinth of Solomon."

The name of Solomon was in use at least as late as 1844 in connection with labyrinthine figures. In that year M. Didron, a noted French archaeologist, whilst making a tour through Greece, visited the convent of St. Barlaam, a building perched high up on a huge crag and approached only by a rope. On the wall of the guest-

95

room he observed a red tracing of a labyrinth resembling that on the floor of Chartres Cathedral. M. Didron inquired as to the origin of it, and was informed that it was called the "Prison de Salomon" and that it had been copied on the wall long before by a monk who had found the design in a book. The monk was dead and the book lost. This "Solomon's Prison" was of the same character as the "Solomon's Labyrinth" described by M. Berthelot, but very probably these and similar terms were at one time as popular as "Chemin de Jérusalem," "Julian's Bower," and so on, in their application to all sorts of labyrinthine devices.

A simple "interrupted-circle" type of labyrinth was adopted as a heraldic device by Gonzalo Perez, a Spanish ecclesiastic who acted as Secretary to Charles V and Philip II, and published in 1566 a translation of Homer's "Odyssey." The labyrinth was shown in perspective, with the Minotaur, in fighting attitude, at the centre. It was surmounted by the motto *In silentio et spe*.

No doubt continental heraldry could furnish us with many similar references of the sort, although nothing of the kind seems to occur in English heraldry. In Fig. 71, for instance, is shown one used by Bois-dofin de Laval, Archbishop of Embrun. The motto in this case was *Fata viam invenient* ("The Fates will find a way"), a motto adopted in England by the Berkshire Vansittarts. Our illustration is copied from an early seventeenth-century book entitled "Devises Héroïques et Emblèmes," by Claude Paradin.

In the text it is stated that "par ce labyrinthe . . . se pourroit entendre que pour rencontrer la voye, & chemin de vie eternelle, la grace de Dieu nous adresse: nous mettant entre les mains le filet de ses saincts commandemens. A ce que le tenans & suivans tousiours nous venions a nous tirer hors des dangereux foruoyemens des destroits mōdains." In other words, the device may be taken as emblematical of the temptation-labyrinth of this

96

worldly life, which can only be safely traversed by means of the Ariadne thread of divine grace.

The design in this case is of a peculiar type, but it may be very easily derived from the simple split-ring or "Pigs in Clover" design (Fig. 144).

We have in the two cases just mentioned, as in the case of the pavement labyrinths, an association with the

FIG. 71.—Labyrinth Device of Archbishop of Embrun. (After C. Paradin.)

Church or with ecclesiastics. At the same time we know that, in England at any rate, the turf mazes were used for sportive purposes in the days of Elizabeth, and there is, so far, a lack of contemporary reference to their employment in a devotional or penitential capacity. "Treading" or "threading" the maze was a favourite game for several generations. Seeing that the path in the turf maze has as a rule no branches or dead-ends, the sport in question would appear to have been rather simple in character, unless we imagine the participants to have been blindfolded for the purpose or primed with a tankard or two of some jocund beverage.

Let us refer once more to that chapter of Pliny's "Natural History" in which he says that we must not compare the Egyptian and other labyrinths with "what we see traced on our mosaic pavements *or to the mazes formed in the fields for the entertainment of children.*" The italicised words clearly show that the construction of something akin to our turf mazes was practised by the Romans. It seems very reasonable to infer that, if the custom were so common as Pliny seems to imply, it would have been carried to the Roman colonies in these islands. An argument which has often been brought forward in this connection is that from very early times the game of Troy, the *lusus Trojae*, was played by Roman youths. Virgil describes it in the fifth book of his "Aeneid," and draws attention to the similarity between the mazy windings of this sport—which was performed on horseback—and the sinuous path of the Cretan labyrinth (see Chapter XVIII). The inference drawn from this is that our "Troy-towns" and the sports connected with them are in the direct line of descent from this classic game and are therefore a legacy of the Roman occupation of Britain.

Dr. Stukeley, whom we had occasion to mention with reference to the Horncastle maze, suggested that the term Julian's Bower was derived from the name of Iulus, the son of Aeneas, who is described as having taken part in the game. We see, then, that there is a good deal to be said for the claim of a Roman origin.

Assuming for the moment that such was the case, we are faced with some difficulty in accounting for the preservation throughout the intervening ages of a class of earthwork which, without attention, is liable to become effaced in a few decades.

Is it likely that the Britons, after the Roman recall,

98

would trouble to preserve the playgrounds of their late rulers' children? Is it at all probable that the successive waves of immigrants, Anglo-Saxons, Danes and Norsemen, would concern themselves with the maintenance of such alien frivolities?

Is there not a chance that perhaps some of these invaders brought the custom with them?

If we had to rely solely on our own historical records, we should find it extremely difficult to arrive at any conclusion in the matter. Researches of recent decades have, however, rendered it possible to approach the matter from a much wider angle, and, before we attempt any further to inquire into the origin of our own turf mazes, we shall find it necessary to go back very far indeed in the history of European civilisation, and to look at the question of labyrinth origins from another point of view.

Before doing so, however, we will review a development which, in the eyes of the archaeologist an insignificant side-line, is perhaps to many readers a matter of greater interest than anything we have yet dealt with, embracing as it does that type of labyrinth which is familiar to all in the famous Hampton Court specimen.

CHAPTER XIII

THE FLORAL LABYRINTH AND THE DWARF-SHRUB
MAZE

THE mention of the word "maze" most frequently calls to mind a block of tall shrubs penetrated by a puzzling branching path, which terminates in an arbour or goal of some sort. But just as we have seen that the horticultural maze is far from being the sole form of expression of the idea, so we must now recognise that even in horticulture the well-known hedge maze is not the only type of verdant labyrinth.

The dwarf box, although a favourite material for delimiting flower beds and edging paths, is merely a subordinate or "accompanying" instrument, so to speak, in the gardener's orchestra. Yet we do occasionally see it employed as a soloist, executing its modest little arabesques between the strepitant choruses of the chromatic parterres on the terrace of some stately country home. In such cases we see a relic of the "knots" which formed an important feature in the gardens of our forefathers.

These devices were composed of various herbs or low shrubs and great ingenuity was displayed in their fashioning, amongst other forms being several varieties of labyrinths. The praises of the dwarf box in this connection were sung by John Parkinson, herbalist to Queen Elizabeth and King James the First. In his "Paradisus" he mentions it thus: ". . . Boxe, which lastly I chiefly and

Fig. 72. Floral Labyrinth (De Vries).

Fig. 74. Floral Labyrinth (De Vries).

above all other herbs commend unto you, and being a small, low, or dwarfe kind, is called French or Dutch Boxe." This plant, he says, "serveth very well to set out any knot or border out any beds, for besides that it is ever greene, it being reasonable thicke set, will easily be cut and formed into any fashion one will, according to the nature thereof, which is to grow very slowly, and will not in a long time rise to be of any height, but shooting forth many small branches from the roote, will grow very thicke and yet not require so great tending, nor so much perish as any of the former . . .," and so on, in typical labyrinthine prose. The use of dwarf box in this way was not, of course, a novelty in Parkinson's time. In fact it was used by the Romans to border their paths and the flower-beds of that little garden in front of the porticoes which went by the name of the *xystus*.

In the sixteenth century, however, the planting of dwarf shrubs and herbs in long narrow beds twisted into various complicated figures seems to have become very fashionable.

Where maze patterns were introduced, a simple, unicursal form was sometimes followed, but in many instances very elaborate mazes were executed.

In a few of our libraries are to be found copies of a curious book of garden designs by Jan Vredeman De Vries, entitled "Hortorum Viridariorumque Formae," published at Antwerp in 1583. In it are represented many extraordinary and even fantastic plans for the lay-out of gardens, including no less than nine in the form of labyrinths. Some of the latter are designated by titles of a descriptive or of a quasi-classic character, "La Roue," "Ionica," "Corinthia," and so forth. We reproduce a few of these designs in Figs. 72, 73 and 74. Several other horticultural or architectural books of about the same period also mention labyrinths or figure them in their illustrations, but it is not clear, in many cases, whether these are intended to represent garden mazes or the

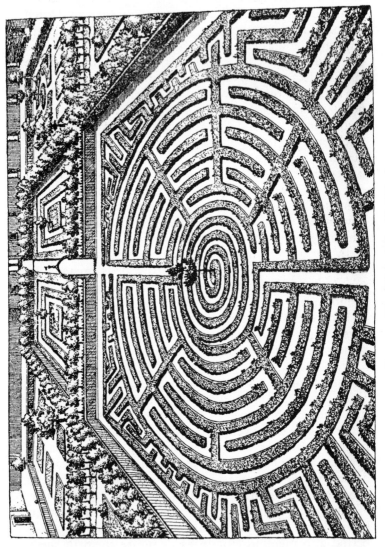

FIG. 73.—Floral Labyrinth. (De Vries.)

flower-bed labyrinths that we have just mentioned. In some instances, where the beds were occupied by shrubs, we have a sort of link between the garden labyrinth and the hedge maze proper. An illustration in a book of 1573 on the gardens of the Villa d'Este at Tivoli, dedicated to Catherine de Medici by the author, Stefano Duperac, shows four rectangular labyrinths, all of the same pattern. It is unlikely that in such circumstances they would all have been formed of tall hedges, and we may therefore judge them to have been of the flower-bed type or perhaps of dwarf box.

We find a reference to the herbal labyrinth in "La Maison Rustique," by Charles Estienne (Paris, 1573), under the heading of "Kitchen Garden Planning":

"Et sera bon dresser a ceste fin une planche de sauge . . . encore une de sariette, & hyssope, de cost, de basilic, aspic, baume, pouliot & une de camomille pour faire les siéges & labyrinthes, que l'on nomme Daedalus."

One of the best-known and most often quoted of the Tudor gardening books is that of Thomas Hyll, or Hill, whose work "A moste Briefe and Pleasaunt Treatyse Teachynge How to Dress, Sowe and Set a Garden" was published in 1563. It has a captivating charm, especially in the earlier, black-letter editions. In later editions the name of the author appears as "Didymus Mountaine" (Didymus = Thomas, Mountaine = Hill), and the book becomes "The Gardener's Labyrinth."

He published two figures of mazes, which we reproduce as Figs. 75 and 76. In the 1579 edition—"The Profitable Art of Gardening"—they are respectively placed at the heads of different chapters, the openings of which are worth quoting:

"Here by the way (Gentle Reader) I do place two proper Mazes, the one before this Chapter, and the other after, as proper adornments upon pleasure to a Garden, that who so listeth, having such roomth in their Garden, may place the one of them, which liketh them best, in

103

that voide place of the Garden that maye beste be spared
for the onelye purpose, to sporte in them at times, which

Fig. 75.—Herbal Labyrinth. (T. Hill, 1579.)

Fig. 76.—Herbal Labyrinth. (T. Hill, 1579.)

mazes being workmanly handled by the Gardner shal
much beautifie them in devising four sundry fruits to be

104

placed in each of the corners of the Maze and in the middle of it a proper Herber decked with Roses, or else some faire tree of Rosemary, or other fruits, at the discretion of the Gardener."

"And here, I also place the other Maze, which may be lyke ordered and used, as I spake before, and it may eyther be set with Isope and Time, or with winter Savery and Tyme; for these do wel endure all ye winter through greene. And there be some which set their mazes with Lavender, Cotton Spike, Majerome and such like. But let them be ordered in this point, as liketh best the Gardener, and so an end. For I doe not here set forth this, or the other Maze afore expressed, for any necessarie commoditie in a Garden, but rather appoint eyther of them (which liketh you best) as a beautifying unto your Garden: for that Mazes and Knots aptly made do much set forth a garden which neverthelesse I referre to your discretion for that not all persons be of like abilitie."

One would have expected to find some word concerning mazes in Lord Bacon's Essay on Gardening, but, strange to say, he makes no reference whatever to mazes or labyrinths. He abhorred topiary work. "I, for my part," he says, "do not like images cut out in juniper or other garden stuff—they be for children." Mazes he apparently considered unworthy even of mention.

Hill's square maze reappears, but with a tree at the centre, in another gardening book which achieved much popularity in the seventeenth century, namely, "A New Orchard and Garden," by William Lawson (1623), afterwards published (1638, 1648, etc.), bound up with "A Way to get Wealth," by Gervase Markham. This is a quaint little publication which embodies amongst other things a "Table of Hard Words." "Mazes well framed a man's height," says Lawson (ch. xvii.), may perhaps make your friend wander in gathering of berries, till he cannot recover himself without your help." In the division entitled "The Country Hous-Wife's Garden" we are told that "The number of Formes, Mazes and Knots is so great, and Men are so diversly delighted that I leave every House-wife to her selfe, expecially seeing to set downe many, had been but to fill much Paper; yet lest I deprive her of all delight and direction, let her view these few, choice, new Forms, and note these generally, that all Plots are square, and all are bordered about with Privit, Rasins, Fea-berries, Roses, Thorne, Rosemary, Bee-flowers, Isop, Sage or such like."

Let us hope that the Hous-Wife whose duty was to

FIGS. 77, 78.—Maze Designs in Seventeenth Century Manuscript.
(Harley MS.)

prepare and keep in order these "Choice new Forms" had plenty of time on her hands.

The two mazes included in a tiny book amongst the Harley Manuscripts (Figs. 77 and 78) were probably intended for flower-bed mazes. The book consists of a collection of 166 sketches of flower-beds, "knots," etc., and probably belonged to some seventeenth-century gardener.

These mazes, like most of the early forms, are of the "unicursal" type; that is, they have only one path, without loops or branches. It seems most likely that such mazes would be constructed either of flower-beds or of some low-growing shrubs, such as box. If constructed of high hedges the pattern would be invisible, except from

106

a superior eminence, and they would afford but a poor sort of entertainment to the visitor, who would have nothing to do but to follow the path until he came to a full stop, and then retrace his steps. Nevertheless there is no doubt that some of them were made in this way. On the other hand the flower-bed labyrinth was not necessarily unicursal, as we may see from the plans of De Vries.

The actual form of the unicursal type of labyrinth was,

Fig. 79.—Maze Design by Adam Islip, 1602.

in all the earlier designs, whether circular or square, in very close agreement with the classic model, but in later designs monotony was avoided by means of some ingenious modifications. One of the earliest of these is shown in Fig. 79, which is copied from a very rare book called "The Orchard and The Garden," gathered from French and Dutch sources and published by Adam Islip in 1602. Fig. 80 shows one of several specimens which are given in a Dutch book of about half a century later, "Nederlantze Hesperides," by J. Commelyn (1676). It is perhaps as likely, however, that these were intended as designs for a hedge maze, or "Doolhof," as the Dutch call it.

The box-edged paths of "Queen Mary's Bower" on the island of Inchmahome, by the Lake of Menteith, Stirlingshire, may mark the site of a former dwarf-box labyrinth. Tradition maintains that the maze was made for Mary Queen of Scots when she was staying there as

FIG. 80.—Maze Design by J. Commelyn, 1676.

a child. The original maze-pattern, if such existed, is lost by reason of the depredations of relic hunters, who for many years laid the bower under contribution and so denuded it that it had to be entirely replanted some fifty or sixty years ago. The box shrubs with which it was repaired, however, are said to have been taken from the gardens of Cardross, where they had been reared from cuttings derived from the original bower. They have now grown to a height of several feet, and the bower no doubt presents a very different appearance from that which it had in the days of the ill-starred Mary.

108

It consists of a winding box-bordered walk leading to a central thorn-bush, the whole affair being oval in outline, about thirty yards in circumference and surrounded by a paling. Close at hand, and enclosed within a square stone wall, is Queen Mary's garden, containing at the centre an old box tree which is affirmed to have been planted by the little princess herself.

Another Scottish relic which is said to mark the site of an old terrace maze is that near Stirling Castle, known since the fourteenth century as the "Round Tabill" or the "King's Knot."

There is a "Queen Mary's Bower," by the way, in the gardens at Hampton Court, but this is only a straight walk shaded by an avenue of pollarded elms, which forms a sort of verdant tunnel. It is situated at the summit of a bank rising above one side of the King's Privy Garden. An old tower planted with shrubs at Chatsworth bears the same name.

We shall have occasion to refer to "bowers" again later on, in another connection. The present mention of them forms a convenient transition from the subject of garden labyrinths to that of *hedge mazes*.

CHAPTER XIV

THE TOPIARY LABYRINTH, OR HEDGE MAZE

THE art of trimming hedges of evergreens is of great antiquity; probably it is almost as old as horticulture itself.

The Romans made much use of the services of the *topiarius*, or hedge-trimmer—he is referred to by Cicero and other writers—and it is quite possible that they had shrubs or bushes trained to enclose winding paths in the manner of a hedge maze.

In Pliny's "Natural History" (Book XVI, Ch. 33) the cypress is spoken of as being clipped and trimmed to form hedges or lengthened out in various designs for ornamental purposes. In Book XV he tells us that a shrub called *taxa* is also used in ornamental gardening, from which we might conclude that the yew (*taxus*) was intended. From the description in the context, however, it is more likely that Pliny was speaking of a plant something like our "butcher's broom" (*Ruscus aculeatus*). He also mentions the box and a species of laurel as being suitable for this kind of work.

A hint of something like a hedge maze is given in one of the epistles of the younger Pliny, where he describes the gardens of his *villa* in Tuscany. He speaks of having a *hippodromus*, a kind of circus consisting of many paths separated by box hedges and ornamented with topiary work.

We do not, however, find any actual description of

an indubitable hedge maze in the works of the classic writers. Amongst monastic manuscripts of the middle ages occur a few passages which have been thought to refer to something of the kind. For instance Henry, Abbot of Clairvaux, in speaking metaphorically of labyrinthine entanglements, says, "Non habent certos aditus, semitas ambulant circulares, et in quodam fraudium labyrintho monstra saevissima reconduntur" ("They have no definite approaches, but wander about in circular sidetracks, and most savage monsters are concealed in their labyrinth of deceptions"); but he may very well have been alluding simply to the traditional Cretan Labyrinth and not to actual constructions of his own period.

A perhaps more striking passage is that in a "History of the Counts of Guines, A.D. 800 to 1200," by Lambert of Ardres (*Lambertus Ardensis*), who lived in the twelfth and thirteenth centuries. Speaking of the building of a large residence at Ardres for Count Arnold, in the twelfth century, he says:

"Quam quidem Broburgensis artifex vel carpentarius, in hujus artis ingenio parum discrepans a Dedalo fabrefecit et carpentavit nomina Lodevicus et de ea fere inextricabilem fecit laberinthum et effigiavit, penus penori, cameram camerae, diversorium diversorio concludens . . ."; that is to say, a certain workman named Louis of Bourbourg, with a skill in woodwork very little different from that of Daedalus, was employed in building the house and made there a nearly inextricable labyrinth, containing recess within recess, room within room, turning within turning. Here again the description hardly answers to that of a hedge maze, but rather indicates an elaborate architectural structure and probably refers to nothing more than a large wooden house.

The common belief that our own King Henry II concealed his paramour "the fair Rosamond" within a maze at Woodstock may possibly, as sceptical historians aver, have no firmer foundations than that afforded by the imaginative efforts of mediaeval romancers, but from what we have just quoted it is evident that contrivances of the kind described in the legend may have been in existence not only in Henry's time but even in the previous century. In view of the great popularity of the story throughout succeeding generations we cannot altogether ignore it, but we will discuss it more conveniently in a later chapter.

The maze was introduced into the Low Countries, according to a book on Architecture in Belgium, some time during the thirteenth century, but this statement may be merely an inference from Lambert's History quoted above.

In France, as we have already seen, the pavement labyrinths were sometimes known as "dédales" or "maisons de Dédalus," in reference of course to the "house" built by Daedalus for the Minotaur, and in the fourteenth and fifteenth centuries we find the same titles applied to mazes formed of shrubs. Charles V, in the fourteenth century, is said to have laid out a *maison de Dédale* in the gardens of the Hôtel de St. Paul in Paris.

Of interest on this point is an Order of the Court of the Duchy of Anjou, dated September 18, 1477, in which the people of the Duchy were required to pay twelve *livres* to the keeper of King Réné's castle at Baugé "pour la nourriture des ouyseaux et nestoyer les espèces qu'il a en garde . . . et *reffaire le Dédalus* qui est és jardrins dudit lieu de Baugé."

We also read of a *dédalus* in the park of Louise de Savoie in 1513.

A sixteenth-century maze is depicted in a landscape by Tintoretto which is exhibited in the Queen's Private Chamber at Hampton Court Palace (No. 524 [787]). In the centre of the maze are seen four ladies seated at a table, their attendants standing by. In the background is the palace to which the maze and surrounding pleasure-grounds evidently appertain.

112

Hans Holbein, an early contemporary of Tintoretto, is also said to have painted a maze of this description.

Many mazes at that time were planned by the Italian architect Serlio, one of whose designs is shown in Fig. 81.

The late sixteenth century furnishes abundant evidence of the growing taste for the topiary labyrinth in the architectural works of Androuet du Cerceau, one of the great builders of the French Renaissance and architect to Catherine de Medici. We are bound to say, however,

FIG. 81.—Maze Design by J. Serlio (Sixteenth Century).

that the assertion of Horace Walpole, in his "Essay on Modern Gardening," to the effect that in Du Cerceau's works there is scarcely a ground plot without both a round and a square maze, is not borne out by reference to such editions as are generally available.

Du Cerceau's sketches of the mazes at Charleval and in the Palace garden of the Archbishop of Rouen at Gaillon—with modifications necessitated by the extreme roughness of the original blocks—are shown in Figs. 82, 83 and 84.

One of the best-known gardens of the Elizabethan

113

period was that made about 1560 for Lord Burleigh, or Burghley, at Theobalds in Hertfordshire. It was described by a contemporary as being "large and square, having all its walls covered with Sillery and a beautiful

Fig. 82.—Maze at Charleval. (After Du Cerceau.)

Figs. 83 and 84.—Mazes at Gaillon. (After Du Cerceau.)

jet d'eau in the centre." At the end was a small mount called the Mount of Venus, placed in the midst of a labyrinth, "upon the whole, one of the most beautiful spots in the world." The house and gardens, John Evelyn tells us in his Memoirs, under date April 15, 1643, were "demolish'd by the rebels."

114

A plan of this labyrinth is shown in Fig. 85. Theobalds was afterwards transferred by Burleigh's son, the Earl of Salisbury, to King James the First, in exchange for another noble seat in the same county, Hatfield House, still held by the present Marquis of Salisbury.

In the grounds to the rear of the latter mansion is to be seen at the present day one of the finest examples of

Fig. 85.—Maze at Theobalds, Herts. (After Trollope.)

a hedge maze, which, although of fairly modern construction, probably replaced an earlier specimen.

Our photograph, Fig. 86 (see Frontispiece), was taken, by kind permission, from the roof of Hatfield House. The hedge is of tall, thick yew throughout, and is perfectly formed, without any of those thin, straggly growths in the lower portion which, by tempting the unscrupulous maze-trotter to burst through them, soon necessitate renewal or unsightly patching.

The maze is 174 ft. in length and 108 ft. in width, and has two entrances (or exits), one at each end. The

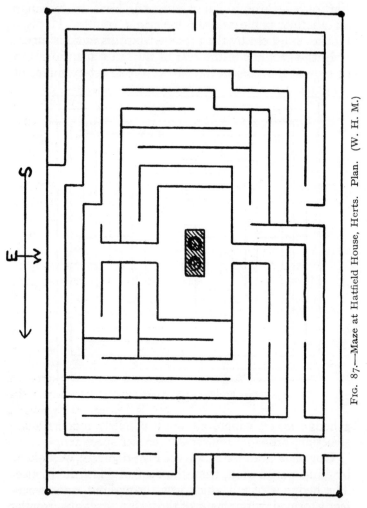

basin which formerly occupied the centre was replaced some years ago by a block of yew surmounted by topiary figures. Fig. 87 shows the maze in plan.

From the beautifully turfed level above the maze, or from the parterre terrace above that, one can overlook the hedges and enjoy, if so inclined, occasional glimpses of ensnared and perplexed visitors.

The type of hedge maze exemplified here, in which the paths are bounded by hedges of uniform thickness, is only one development. Another type arose in the late seventeenth century in which serpentinous footpaths penetrated blocks of shrubs or dense thickets. In some cases limes or hornbeams were "plashed," *i.e.*, their branches were so trained and intertwined as to form a continuous wall of verdure. In other cases the intervals between the paths were filled with loose aggregations of flowering shrubs and evergreens; such an arrangement as this was usually termed a "wilderness." (The term "plashing," by the way, should not be confused with "pleaching," which merely signified the process of ordinary trimming).

In practically all types of maze it became the fashion to relieve the monotony of the walks by placing statues, vases, seats, fountains, and other ornaments at various points. This kind of thing reached a climax of extravagance in the latter part of the seventeenth century, when J. Hardouin-Mansart constructed for Louis XIV the famous labyrinth in the smaller park at Versailles. This labyrinth is described in a book, now very rare, entitled "Labyrinte de Versailles," by C. Perrault, printed at the royal press, Paris, in 1677, and illustrated by Sebastien le Clerc. Our illustrations, Figs. 88, 89, 90 and 91, are selected from the book in question and show respectively the plan of the labyrinth and three of the thirty-nine groups of hydraulic statuary representing the fables of Aesop. At the entrance to the labyrinth were placed symbolical statues of Aesop and Cupid, the latter holding in one hand a ball of thread. Each of the speaking characters represented in the fable groups emitted a jet of water, representing speech, and each group was accompanied by an engraved plate displaying more or less appropriate verses by the poet de Benserade.

FIG. 89.—Labyrinth of Versailles. Fable Group: " The Hare and the Tortoise." (Perrault.)

We reproduce le Clerc's engravings of the groups illustrating respectively the fables of "The Hare and

Fig. 88.   Labyrinth of Versailles.   (Perrault)

the Tortoise," "The Fox and the Crow," and "The Snake and the Porcupine." The water for all these elaborate

FIG. 90.—Labyrinth of Versailles. Fable Group: "The Fox and the Crow." (Perrault.)

waterworks was conveyed from the Seine by a wonderful contrivance called the "Machine de Marli," constructed

FIG. 91.—Labyrinth of Versailles. Fable Group: " The Snake and the Porcupine." (Perrault.)

Fig. 93. Labyrinth at Choisy-le-Roi. (Blondel)

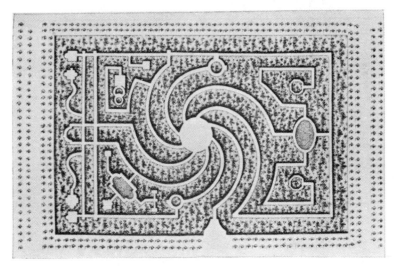

Fig. 94. Labyrinth at Chantilly. (Blondel)

Figs. 95 and 96.   Maze Designs by André Mollet, 1651.

by Swalm Renkin between 1675 and 1682. It is said to have cost the equivalent of £8,000,000 and contained fourteen water-wheels driving 253 pumps, some of which worked at a distance of three-quarters of a mile.

The labyrinth was destroyed in 1775 and its site is now occupied by the "Bosquet de la Reine."

The "Dial-garden" at Friar Park, Henley-on-Thames, is laid out on the plan of the Versailles labyrinth, but in place of the statuary groups are thirty-nine sun-dials, each having its motto or epigram. Adjoining it is a maze of original and ingenious design.

The Versailles example was only one of several well-known mazes which existed in or around Paris at that time. Evelyn, who spent some years in Paris, from 1643 onwards, remarks on the design and trimness of the box-hedge designs in the gardens of the Luxembourg and on the "labyrinth of cypresse" at the Tuileries, no doubt designed by Du Cerceau (Fig. 92). In another account of the Tuileries labyrinth, however, it is described as being made entirely of bent cherry trees. In was ultimately swept away by Le Nôtre to make room for enlarged parterres.

FIG. 92.—Labyrinth at the Tuileries. (After Du Cerceau.)

There is still a labyrinth in the Jardin des Plantes, formerly the Jardin du Roi, but it is of rather feeble design.

Another noted French maze was that constructed by M. Gabriel at Choisy-le-Roi (Fig. 93). One was designed for the gardens of Chantilly by Le Nôtre, but exists to-day only as an engraving on a stone in the park (Fig. 94). Madame de Sévigné, in a letter of June 1, 1689, mentions one at Les Rochers, her seat in Brittany, and we read of one at Sceaux on the occasion of a fête given to Louis XIV and Madame de Maintenon in 1685.

121

In most European countries the fashion had obtained
a hold either before or during the seventeenth century,

Figs. 97 and 98.—Mazes by G. A. Boeckler, 1664.

and we can usually be sure of finding a few drawings of
mazes in any horticultural book of that period.

Figs. 95 and 96 show two examples given in "Le

Jardin de Plaisir," by André Mollet, the royal gardener at Stockholm, in 1651. Figs. 97 to 106 show some very

FIGS. 99 and 100.—Mazes by G. A. Boeckler, 1664.

ingenious designs selected from a great number which accompany the drawings of castles and great houses in Germany and elsewhere, contained in the "Architectura curiosa nova" of G. A. Boeckler, 1664.

One of these (Fig. 105) is rather suggestive of the
Saffron Walden turf maze, whilst another (Fig. 101)

FIGS. 101 and 102.—Mazes by G. A. Boeckler, 1664.

is reminiscent of the Rheims pavement labyrinth. At
Enghien, in Belgium, the gardens of the château where
the Duke of Arenburg entertained Voltaire contained a

124

maze, as well as a "mechanical island" and various other
horticultural toys.

FIGS. 103 and 104.—Mazes by G. A. Boeckler, 1664.

In Spain, as elsewhere, the hedge maze attained great
popularity. In the magnificent gardens of the Alcazar at
Seville may still be seen the labyrinth laid out in the

sixteenth century for the Emperor Charles V, with tiled paths and fountains, and adjoining this is a hedge maze

FIGS. 105 and 106.—Mazes by G. A. Boeckler, 1664.

of roughly hexagonal outline enclosed within an irregular rectangle.

As regards Italy, we read that even the Pope himself,

Fig. 107. Maze at Gunterstein, Holland. (N. Visscher, 1719)

Fig. 108. Gunterstein. Plan of Gardens, showing Maze. (N. Visscher, 1719)

Fig. 109. Gardens at Loo, Holland, with Mazes. (W. Harris, 1699.)

Clement X, took pleasure in watching the endeavours of his domestics to extricate themselves from the maze of tall box hedges which adorned his garden at Altieri. Evelyn, in 1646, describing his visit to Vicenza, remarks of the gardens of Count Ulmarini, or Vilmarini, outside the town, "Here is likewise a most inextricable labyrinth."

Sir Philip Skippon, describing his own visit to Vicenza in 1663, refers to the gardens as those of Count Valmarana, and mentions "a labyrinth of myrtle hedges." Skippon also speaks of labyrinths in the gardens of the Duke of Bavaria at Munich.

The Dutch gardeners made a great feature of the *doolhof*, typical examples being those at the Duke of Portland's château at Sorgvliet, near the Hague, at Gunterstein (Figs. 107 and 108), and at the Palace of Loo, the Dutch home of William and Mary (Fig. 109). Our illustration of the last-named is taken from Dr. W. Harris's book "The King's Palace and Gardens at Loo" (1699). It will be seen that the maze to the left is described as a "wilderness," as is also the structure to the extreme right, but whereas the latter certainly presents little of a labyrinthine appearance, the former is evidently a hedge maze, although perhaps loosely drawn. Harris uses the terms "maze" and "wilderness" interchangeably. He says that the King's labyrinth was formed of clipped hedges with sandy walks between, while the Queen's was decorated with fountains and statues. William the Third exercised his taste for this kind of embellishment also in the grounds of his English palaces. His gardeners, George London and Henry Wise, have left us one which, although of no great complexity, has become world-famous, namely, the specimen which forms part of the "Wilderness" in the gardens of Hampton Court Palace.

CHAPTER XV

THE Hampton Court maze (Fig. 110) was constructed in 1690 and in all probability displaced an older maze, a relic of Wolsey's time. The maze is situated close to the Bushy Park entrance. Defoe speaks of it as a "labrynth," and tells us that the "Wilderness," of which it forms part, replaced the old orchard of the palace.

It is of no great complexity, but, as may be seen from Fig. 111, is of a neat and symmetrical pattern, with quite sufficient of the puzzle about it to sustain interest and to cause amusement but without a needless and tedious excess of intricacy. The area occupied by it is rather more than a quarter of an acre—not a great amount of space, but enough to accommodate about half a mile of total pathway. The longest side of the maze measures 222 ft.

Various diagrams of the maze have been published, some of them very incorrect and therefore misleading. Our sketch was made on the spot and represents at any rate the present (1922) disposition of the paths and hedges. The gate almost opposite the entrance should normally be closed. It is for the purpose of affording the gardener or attendant direct access to the "goal" and its approaches, or occasionally for facilitating the release of impatient visitors; if left open it spoils the fun. The goal is provided with two bench seats, each shaded by a leafy tree.

128

Fig. 110.   Maze at Hampton Court.

Fig. 113.   " The Little Maze."

The hedge was at first composed entirely of hornbeam, but, like most of its kind, it has required renewal at various points from time to time, and this has not always been carried out with the appropriate material. The result, as may be seen in our photograph, is a patchwork of privet, hornbeam, yew, holly, hawthorn and sycamore. It is nevertheless questionable whether the lack of uniformity in this respect causes any grief to the bulk of its visitors. The maze is as popular as ever, and in the financial year 1919–20 brought in a revenue of nearly

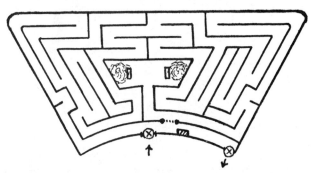

Fig. 111.—Maze at Hampton Court.   Plan.   (W. H. M.)

£775, which exceeded the estimate of the Office of Works by £325 !

Long may it remain! It may be a sad sight to the "highbrows" of horticulture, but to the unsophisticated many it is a never-failing source of innocent merriment. Those who incline to deplore the perpetuation of these "topiary toys" should spend an hour or two in the Hampton Court maze on a sunny holiday and witness the undiluted delight which it affords to scores and hundreds of children, not to mention a fair sprinkling of their elders.

The circular Troy-town or "Plan-de-Troy," formed of tall espaliers, which formerly co-existed with the present maze (see Fig. 112), has long been replaced by a sunken rockery, the path of which, however, is of a very meandering character and has earned from visitors the title of "The Little Maze" (Fig. 113). A topiary work of similar title, "The Siege of Troy," was one of William's pet horticultural adornments at Kensington Palace. It is

FIG. 112.—Hampton Court. The " Wilderness," with Maze and " Plan-de-Troy," in Eighteenth Century. (Engraving by J. Rocque, 1736.)

said to have been a verdant representation of military defence works, cut yew and variegated holly being "taught," as Walpole says, "to imitate the lines, angles, bastions, scarps and counter-scarps of regular fortifications."

The rather curious unicursal maze of three meanders shown in Fig. 114 is usually, *e.g.*, in the "Encyclopaedia

130

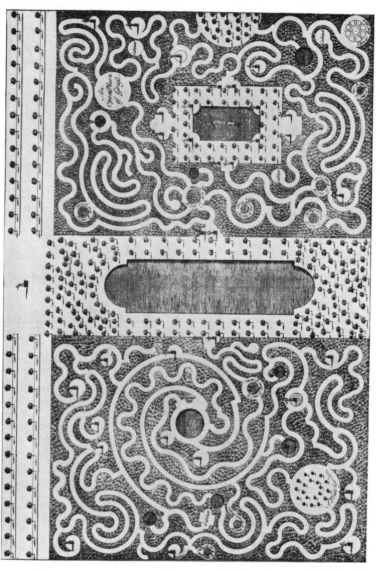

Fig. 116. Maze Design by Batty Langley (from *New Principles of Gardening*, 1728).

A Grove of ever greens

Cabinet.

Fig. 115.   Maze Design by Batty Langley. (from *New Principles of Gardening*, 1728

Britannica," attributed to London and Wise, and certainly it appears in a book which was issued by them in 1706 under the title of "The Solitary Gardiner" (subsequently published by Joseph Carpenter as "The Retir'd Gardner"), but this work is mainly a translation from an earlier French book, "Le Jardinier Solitaire," by Louis Liger of Auxerre, in which also the figure appears. Various other horticultural writers of the period make use of the same design.

"A Labyrinth," says the text, "is a Place cut into

Fig. 114.—Labyrinth Design by L. Liger (circ. 1700).

several Windings, set off with Horn-beam, to divide them from one another . . . The most valuable Labyrinths are always those that wind most, as that of Versailles, the contrivance of which has been wonderfully lik'd by all that have seen it" (*chacun à son goût!*). "The Palisades, of which Labyrinths ought to be compos'd, should be ten, twelve, or fifteen foot high; some there are that are no higher than one can lean on, but those are not the finest. The Walls of a Labyrinth ought to be kept roll'd, and the Horn-beams in them shear'd, in the shape of Half-moons."

As for the allurements of the much-winding labyrinths

of the Versailles type the reader will no doubt form his own opinion. Their popularity at that time is demonstrated by the great number of designs of this nature which we find in such books as, for example, those of Batty Langley, a few of whose plans we reproduce (Figs. 115 and 116).

An example of the "block" type of labyrinth was that at Trinity College, Oxford, of which a view is seen in an early eighteenth-century engraving (Fig. 117), from the "Oxonia depicta" of W. Williams. It was destroyed in 1813. Similar arrangements appear in several of the engravings of country seats, e.g., those of Belvoir Castle, Boughton, and Exton Park, in J. Kip's "Britannia Illustrata," 1724. In this work also appear mazes of the more familiar type, as, for example, in the engravings of Badminton and Wrest Park (Fig. 118).

The idea of Batty Langley and of the Versailles artist seems to have been not so much that of puzzling the visitor as of providing an entertaining and diversified promenade, but with many maze-architects the object was to provide as much bewilderment as the space available permitted. This is frankly avowed by Stephen Switzer in his somewhat tedious "Ichnographia Rustica," published in 1742. He gives the design shown in Fig. 119, and describes it as "a labyrinth of single hedges or banks, *after the ancient manner.*"

He speaks of the object of a labyrinth as being to provide "an intricate and difficult Labour to find out the Centre, and to be (as the Vulgar commonly like it for) so intricate, as to lose one's self therein, and to meet with as great a Number of Stops therein and Disappointments as possible; I thought the best way to accomplish it was to make a dubious Choice of which way to take at the very Entrance and Beginning it self, in order to find out the Centre, at which we are to end at B. into a little Arbour cradled over; for which Reason there is in the very first coming in, in the Centre, where the Grass-Plot

132

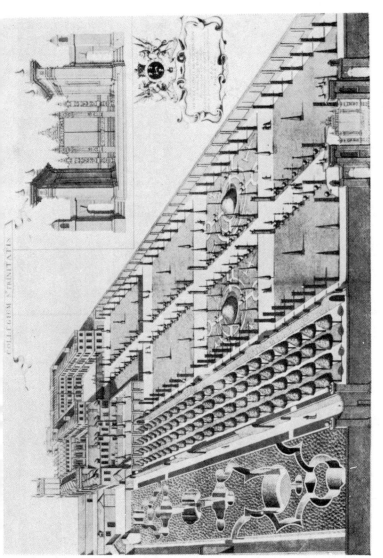

COLLEGIUM S.TRINITATIS

Fig. 117. Gardens of Trinity College, Oxford, with Labyrinth. (W. Williams, 1732).

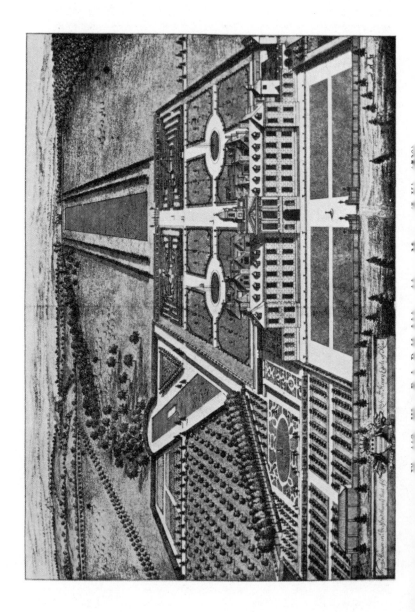

and Statue are design'd at A. six different Entrances whereof there is but one that leads to the centre and that is attended with some difficulties and a great many stops."

He might have added, ". . . like unto my own literary style."

A labyrinth of a most fantastic character is said to have occupied a large area in the palace garden of the Prince of Anhalt, in Germany. It was allegorical and was intended to typify the course of human life. It was

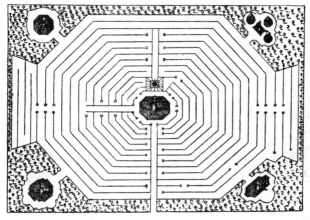

FIG. 119.—Maze Design by S. Switzer (1742).

composed not only of hedges, but of rocks and trees, streams and caverns, and tortuous deeply cut paths, which were for the most part covered in, with very scanty illumination. At every other turn the visitor was pulled up by some puzzling or terrifying allegory, or some didactic inscription after the manner of those which adorn the rocks at Tilly Whim, on the Dorset coast. By way of compensation he was refreshed here and there by the sight of a choice example of the sculptor's art, or a flowery dell, or some verdurous presentation of the architect's idea of Elysium. As in the case of Versailles, expense seems to have been no obstacle.

At H.M. Records Office is preserved in "Survey No. 72" a rather pathetic document headed "A Survey of the Manor of Wymbledon *alias* Wimbleton, with the Rights, Members and Appurtenances thereof, lying and being in the Countie of Surrey, late Parcell of the Possessions of Henrietta Maria, the Relict and late Queene of Charles Stuart, late King of England, made and taken . . . in the Moneth of November 1649." A transcript of the document was communicated to "Archaeologia" in 1792 by John Caley, F.A.S., the following portion being worth noting in connection with our present subject:

". . . On the South syde of the sayd turfed tarras there are planted one great maze, and one wilderness, which being severed with one gravelled Alley, in or near to the midle of the sayd turfed tarras, sets forth the maze to lie towards the east, and the wilderness towards the west; the maze consists of young trees, wood and sprayes of a good growth and height, cutt into severall meanders, circles, semicircles, wyndings and intricate turnings, the walks or intervalls whereof are all grass plotts; this maze, as it is now ordered, adds very much to the worth of the upper levell . . . which maze and wilderness over and besides the trees thereof, which are hereafter valewed amongst the other trees of the sayd upper garden and the materialls of the sayd two shadowe or summer houses, wee valew to bee worth £90. 0. 0."

Whether the maze referred to was afterwards destroyed is not clear, but possibly it was preserved and was identical with that mentioned by the writer of the "Encyclopaedia Britannica" article as having formerly existed at Wimbledon House, the seat of Earl Spencer, which was conjectured to have been laid out by Brown in the eighteenth century. ("Capability" Brown, we may note, was no lover of mazes, though his official residence at Hampton Court adjoined the maze.)

There are records of various other old mazes in the

134

immediate vicinity of London, apart from the "tea-garden" mazes of the last century. Pepys in 1666 speaks of "several labyrinths" in the gardens of Lord Brooke at Hackney, and Evelyn in 1700 mentions mazes at Marden, Surrey. Sutton Court also contained a fine example.

There was one in Tothill (or Tuttle) Fields, Westminster, in the seventeenth century, and perhaps earlier, for it is mentioned with familiarity in a play written by John Cooke in 1614, "Greene's Tu Quoque; or the Cittie Gallant; a Play of Much Humour," wherein one of the characters challenges another to a duel:

> *Staines.* I accept it ; the meeting place ?
> *Spendall.* Beyond the Maze in Tuttle.

The maze was renovated or remade in 1672, as shown by an entry in the Churchwardens' Accounts of St. Margaret, Westminster:

"*Item*, to Mr. William Brewer, for making a maze in Tuttlefields . . . . £2.0.0."

It was well known to John Aubrey, the antiquary and naturalist whose reference to turf mazes we have already quoted. In his "Remaines," 1686–7, he says:

"There is a maze at this day in Tuthill Fields, Westminster, & much frequented in summer-time in fair afternoons."

According to Mr. J. E. Smith's "Parochial Memorials of St. John the Baptist, Westminster," Tothill Fields were at one time known as "Tuttle-in-the-Maze."

In the large view of London and Westminster engraved by Wenceslaus Hollar (1607–1677) there is shown in the middle of Tothill Fields a clump of trees surrounding a sort of shelter, like a band-stand, but no sort of labyrinthine design is visible.

Another London maze mentioned by Aubrey, and one which has left its remembrance in the present-day nomenclature of the locality (Maze Pond), is that of Southwark.

135

"At Southwarke," says Aubrey, "was a Maze which is converted into Buildings bearing that name."

In another place he says, "On the south side of Tooley-street a little westward from Burnaby-street is a Street called the Maes or Maze, Eastward from the Borough (another name for Labyrinth). I believe we received these Mazes from our Danish Ancestors. . . ." This latter observation is one which seems to have been entirely over-looked by subsequent archaeologists and antiquaries, but its significance will be seen when we come to consider the subject of "stone labyrinths."

It is clear from the last phrase, that in this case Aubrey had in mind turf mazes rather than hedge mazes, and we are in doubt as to whether the Southwark maze was of the former or the latter species.

The Abbot of Battle had a residence there after the dissolution of the monasteries, and it has been stated that he had a maze in his garden, or, alternatively, that his garden paths were laid out in such an intricate manner as to suggest the name. But there are records of the name being applied to the locality before the dissolution of the monasteries, and it is quite possible that there was once a turf maze in the neighbourhood, perhaps before the abbot's time. According to a footnote in Strickland's "Lives of the Queens of England," the maze in South-wark once formed part of the garden of the Princess Mary Tudor, but the authority for this statement is not quoted.

Maze Hill, Greenwich, is said to derive its name from the former existence of a maze, traces of which are claimed to have been found near the entrance to Morden College, Blackheath. The name was formerly spelt Maize Hill and at one time Mease or Meaze Hill. We shall have a word to say about place-names towards the end of this book, but we may remark in passing that inferences as to the past existence of an object based solely upon a current homonymous place-name are obviously unsound.

136

CHAPTER XVI

THE TOPIARY LABYRINTH, OR HEDGE MAZE (*continued*)

Latter-day Developments

Towards the end of the eighteenth century the taste for mazes in private gardens had to some extent declined, but as an adjunct to places of public amusement the topiary labyrinth was still in great demand.

"Pleasure gardens" of the Ranelagh and Vauxhall type were then greatly in vogue, not only in the metropolis but in most of the fashionable health resorts, and, although it is only in comparatively few cases that we have definite records of their having possessed a maze, there is no doubt that very many were in existence, though probably most have since disappeared.

A favourite resort with dwellers in the north of London, up to about a century ago, was White Conduit House, in Islington, and here a maze formed one of the principal attractions.

In Harrow Road, N.W., No. 6 Chichester Place marks the site of a minor public garden called "The Maze," which flourished up to about the middle of last century.

Another northern pleasure garden which is recorded as possessing a maze was "New Georgia," in Turners Wood, near the Spaniards, Hampstead.

South of the Thames the celebrated Beulah Spa had

a maze, which, together with that at Hampton Court, is referred to by Dickens in his "Sketches by Boz."

Other well-known "tea-garden" mazes are those at the Crystal Palace and at the Rosherville Gardens, Gravesend.

A maze was erected at the request of the Prince Consort, in or about the year 1862, in the gardens of the Royal Horticultural Society at South Kensington. It was designed by Lieut. W. H. Nesfield, R.N., who relinquished a naval career to become a very successful gardener. Fig. 120 shows the plan of this maze as given in the R.H.S. official guide to the gardens in 1864. A statue of Galatea adorned the "goal."

This plan differs in some respects from Nesfield's original design, which was slightly simpler and provided for a central fountain and basin. The figure which illustrates the "Britannica" article—and which has been copied into a popular book on puzzles, accompanied by the remark that it is "a feeble thing"—unfortunately departs from the official plan in certain small but important details; it allows of an almost direct passage from a third external opening to the circular goal. The maze ultimately went to ruin and its site has long been built upon.

The maze in the beautiful little gardens at Saffron Walden which were presented to the public nearly a century ago by Mr. I. Fry, M.P., and are known as Bridge End Gardens, is still in excellent condition, although suffering in places from the illicit short-cuts made by impatient visitors. It is locally believed to be a replica of that at Hampton Court, but is of very different plan and is, in fact, much more elaborate. Our photographs, Figs. 121 and 122, were taken from the pulpit-like erection at one end of the central enclosure, looking roughly towards the south and the north respectively.

It will be noticed that a person standing on the erection is precluded from mapping out the maze therefrom,

138

by reason of the tall topiary upgrowths at various points, designed, no doubt, with this object. This maze is situated within a few hundred yards of the turf maze which we noticed in a previous chapter.

FIG. 120.—Maze by W. H. Nesfield, in R.H.S. Gardens, South Kensington, circ. 1862. (From R.H.S. Guide.)

Another modern hedge maze in the same county is that in the grounds of Mistley Place, Manningtree, the residence of E. M. Jackson, Esq., M.A., who has kindly furnished the writer with some details concerning it.

The maze was planted about fifty years ago, but unfortunately the choice of material was not of the most judicious, for, while the major portion is of beech, young oaks were planted in the outer circle and these have now grown up into large trees, overshadowing and ruining the neighbouring portions of the hedge, so that it is now difficult to trace the plan. Only the inner circles remain complete.

In the adjacent county of Suffolk there is another maze of about the same age but of very different pattern, at Somerleyton Hall, the seat of Lord Somerleyton (Fig. 123). The hedges in this case are of yew and are of great thickness, about six or seven feet in height. At the points marked "A" are situated two beautiful golden Irish yews. Clipped yews provide interesting variety at the points marked "B," and a little pagoda crowns the central knoll, approached by grassy ramps.

There is a hexagonal maze, of some complexity, in the splendid gardens of the Hon. J. Egerton Warburton at Arley Hall, Cheshire. It is formed of lime trees, planted about half a century ago.

We may also mention one, of circular and rather simple though distinctive design, at Belton House, the residence of Earl Brownlow, near Grantham, Lincolnshire.

In Gloucestershire there is one in the grounds of Sudeley Castle, the home of H. D. Brocklehurst, Esq., J.P., where, according to Kelly's county directory, "the old pleasaunce, with its paths and fountain, was discovered in 1850 and now forms part of the garden."

In Nottinghamshire there is one, planted by Colonel Thos. Coke in the 'fifties, at Debdale Hall, Mansfield Woodhouse (F. N. Ellis, Esq., J.P.).

Mr. W. W. Rouse Ball, in his "Mathematical Recreations and Essays," gives a drawing of an elaborate maze which he has erected in his own garden, presumably at Cambridge.

Possibly there are many others in the seclusion of

[*Photo: W.H.M.*

Fig 121.   Maze in Bridge End Gardens, Saffron Walden, looking South.

[*Photo: W.H.M.*

Fig. 122.   Maze in Bridge End Gardens, Saffron Walden, looking North.

large country gardens, but, as the owners of such contrivances are inclined to consider them as relics of a
bygone and discredited fashion, it is only by chance or
by individual enquiries that information concerning
them can be obtained, and it is of course impracticable

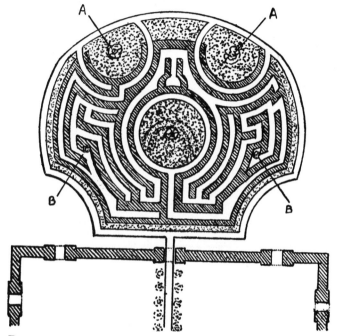

Fig. 123.—Maze at Somerleyton Hall, Suffolk. (W. H. M., from
sketch by G. F. G.)

to take an unofficial census on such a matter. It may be
taken as probable, however, that all the most notable
examples have been enumerated above.

In continental countries the occurrence of mazes is as
sporadic as at home. There are said to be some excellent
specimens in the neighbourhood of Barcelona, fragrant,
aromatic, and flowering shrubs being a characteristic
feature of their composition.

As regards Italy, Mr. Inigo Triggs, in his description of the Castellezo dei Arconati, near Milan ("The Art of Garden Design in Italy"), mentions two "labyrinths," one of which is an extensive work of closely cut hornbeam, partly laid out as a circular maze, whilst the other has a number of small enclosures and alcoves with fountains.

In France well-known mazes are those at the Priory of St. Michel, Toul, called *la Tour du Diable*, and at the Abbaye aux Dames, Caen, as well as the rather poor specimen at the Jardin des Plantes in Paris, to which we have already alluded.

A description of the popular Tivoli Gardens in Vienna, towards the close of the last century, refers to a labyrinth situated below a terrace from which spectators could observe the alarms and excursions of the enmeshed maze-trotters.

In the United States, where very few of the embellishments of bygone Europe have failed to achieve reproduction, there is a replica, with some slight modifications, of the Hampton Court maze. This is situated at Waltham, Massachusetts, on the property of Miss Cornelia Warren. It was planted in 1896, and is formed of thick hedges of arbor vitae, about a thousand shrubs being employed. The plan follows that of its original model, but the sharp rear angles of the Hampton Court design are replaced by rounded curves, and the hedges adjacent to the central space, which is also rounded, are correspondingly modified.

There is a pond at the centre and a rustic rostrum stands before the entrance. The shortest route to the centre is said to be about one-fifth of a mile in length and the total length of the paths about one-third of a mile.

A large hedge maze is also to be found at a place called Cedar Hill—and no doubt there are many others.

The decline in favour of the maze amongst gardeners of repute during the latter part of the eighteenth century is possibly to be accounted for in great part as the natural revulsion from the surfeit of elaborate designs produced in the preceding periods.

"In designing a garden," wrote Lord Kames (Henry Home), "everything trivial or whimsical ought to be avoided. Is a labyrinth therefore to be justified? It is a mere conceit, like that of composing verses in the shape of an axe or an egg: the walks and hedges may be agreeable, but in the form of a labyrinth they serve to no end but to puzzle; a riddle is a conceit not so mean, because the solution is a proof of sagacity, which affords no aid to tracing a labyrinth."

This was in his "Elements of Criticism," a work of which Dr. Johnson remarked: "Sir, this book is a pretty essay and deserves to be held in some estimation, though much of it is chimerical." The idea that sagacity affords no aid in tracing a labyrinth is certainly chimerical, as we shall see, but persons who incline to austerity in art will have little hesitation in agreeing with the other remarks of Lord Kames, even where, further on, he says: "The gardens of Versailles, executed with boundless expense by the best artists of the age, are a lasting monument of a taste the most depraved." Since Lord Kames's time, however, the gardens of Versailles have been subjected to considerable alteration, and at the present day form one of the greatest charms of the environs of Paris.

The contemporary French poet Delille, author of "Les Jardins, ou l'Art d'embellir les Paysages," was voicing the feelings of the times when he wrote:

" Des longs alignements si je hais la tristesse,
Je hais bien plus encore le cours embarrassé
D'un sentier qui, pareil à ce serpent blessé,
En replis convulsifs sans cesse s'entrelace.
De détours redoublés m'inquiète, me lasse,
Et, sans variété, brusque et capricieux,
Tourmente et le terrain et mes pas et mes yeux."

From that time onwards the hedge maze has been the object of much condemnatory criticism and contemptuous reference, sometimes grounded on a certain amount of reason, but often enough of the follow-my-leader type.

Even at the present time there are not wanting gardeners of influence who would view with equanimity the entire disappearance of this convoluted mass of evergreens which dares to offer its antiquated charms in competition with their latest floricultural triumphs.

And cannot one sympathise to some extent with their feelings in the matter? When one's whole career has been devoted to the creation of new forms of plant life or the improvement of existing forms, achievements which entail prolonged scientific training and patient experimenting, constant vigilance and careful selection of favourable variations, it *must* be rather galling to be asked to construct and maintain a meandering row of commonplace evergreens. One can imagine the case to be somewhat parallel to that of a highly trained musician who has just delivered himself of a great sonata and is asked by a member of his audience for "a descriptive battle-march!"

Mr. W. Robinson had perhaps experiences of this kind in mind when he wrote his observations about mazes in his well-known handbook, "The English Flower Garden." "The Maze," he says, is "one of the notions about gardening which arose when people had very little idea of the dignity and infinite beauty of the garden flora as we now know it." In the next sentence he refers to mazes as "ugly frivolities." They should be left, he says, "for the most part to places of the public tea-garden kind." Whatever we may think of the justice of these remarks, we must admit that there is some force in his objection that "one of its drawbacks is the death and distortion of the evergreens that go to form its close lines, owing to the frequent clipping; if clipping be neglected

144

the end is still worse, and the whole thing is soon ready for the fire."

A figure of a maze accompanies this criticism, but it can hardly be meant to typify the usual conception of a hedge maze, as it has the appearance of a seventeenth-century design, possibly intended for a floral labyrinth, for, apart from a few ornamental excrescences, it is entirely unicursal.

Although the strictures we have quoted would probably receive hearty support from a large proportion of modern gardeners, the maze is still not without its champions.

In Miss Madeline Agar's very practical book on "Garden Design," for example, it is treated as a wholly legitimate embellishment for large gardens, and the fact of its disfavour amongst present-day horticulturists is attributed to lack of patience.

A highly original design, with provision for seats, sundials, and statues, is likewise given, but it must be confessed that it conveys a flattering assumption of opulence on the part of the reader, for it certainly does not err on the side of simplicity.

Let us admit at once that, as a favourite of fashion, the maze has long since had its day. In every generation the craving is for novelty, for new forms of expression in all branches of art. Like every other defunct mode, the topiary labyrinth is liable to temporary revivals by lovers of the antique, but there is little reason to hope or to fear that it will ever again secure a position of any dominance in the affections of the gardener. The labour involved in its proper maintenance is alone a sufficient guarantee against that. The hedges require very frequent trimming, and sometimes partial renewal, the latter especially in those cases where unscrupulous visitors are not prevented, by barbed wire or other means, from short-circuiting the convolutions. The paths, too, of which there may be over half a mile, want regular attention

145

unless we are content to be constantly reminded of Tom Moore's punning conundrum:

> " Why is a garden's wildered maze
> Like a young widow, fresh and fair ?
> Because it wants some hand to raze
> The weeds which have no business there."

Deciduous plants such as hornbeam and lime give the maze a sorry appearance during the leafless months of the year, whilst the slower-growing conifers, yew and cypress, besides being expensive, necessitate a long waiting period before the hedges attain a presentable height and thickness. Box harbours slugs; juniper, holly, and the various thorn-bushes present inhospitable asperities which outweigh their other merits—in short, we may be certain that whatever material be suggested for the construction of a maze there will be no lack of objections wherewith the gardener may buttress his prejudice against the contrivance in any shape or form.

On the other hand, the maze has its own, almost indefinable, charms, and we need hardly tremble for its total extinction until we cease to bear children, even if we dismiss as decadent sentimentality that romantic instinct of which some of us cannot quite rid ourselves in maturer years.

CHAPTER XVII

In Chapter XII we noticed some of the principal suggestions which had been made up to a few years ago as to the origin of our turf mazes, and saw that the question was one which could not be settled by the study of remains found in this country alone. Several interesting facts have been brought to light in other lands since Dr. Trollope wrote the memoir which has for so many years been accepted as the standard authority on the subject, and we shall find that a little consideration of them will enable us to view the question in a new light.

As long ago as 1838, Dr. E. von Baer, whilst held up by bad weather on the uninhabited island of Wier, south of Hochland in the Gulf of Finland, observed a curious pattern (Fig. 124) formed in the ground by means of large pebbles. He also noticed several very similar arrangements on the southern coast of the peninsula of Lappland and presented a paper on the subject to the Academy of St. Petersburg.

In some of these figures the stones employed were small pebbles, in other instances they were as large as a child's head, and in one case they were so large that they required several strong men to lift them. Some of the figures had nearly disappeared through the action of moss, earthworms, etc.

In 1877, Dr. J. R. Aspelin, of Helsingfors, drew attention to the existence of similar figures in Finland

147

and on the east coast of Sweden. Fig. 125 shows a form found by him on an island not far from Borgo, Finland.

FIG. 124.—Stone Labyrinth on Wier Island, Gulf of Finland. (von Baer.)

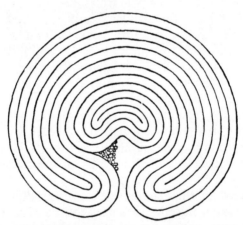

FIG. 125.—Stone Labyrinth on Coast of Finland.   (After Aspelin.)

He describes some of the figures as having one "centre," others two, and others again none at all. They are usually from ten to fifteen yards in diameter. One large specimen, nearly twenty yards across (Fig. 126), at Wisby, on

148

the Island of Gothland, is of a design very similar to the circular labyrinth which appears on certain coins of Knossos. They were generally found on islands or close to the sea-coast, and were known by various names in different localities (see p. 150).

The fishermen and peasants said that they were used for children's games, a girl standing at the centre whilst the boys raced for her along the winding paths; but

Fig. 126.—Stone Labyrinth at Wisby, Gothland. (Aspelin.)

Dr. Aspelin pointed out that they were in any case ancient remains, and thought that the idea might have originated in the Bronze Age.

Corresponding figures have been found in Iceland, and a somewhat similar arrangement, consisting of concentric circles of pebbles, with sometimes a cross at the centre, has long been known in the province of Brandenburg, Germany.

It seems to have escaped the notice of most writers on the subject that long before the nineteenth century these objects were described by the Swedish antiquarian

149

Rudbeck, from whose "Atlantica" (1695) we reproduce the sketch shown in Fig. 127.

The names given to these devices in the various localities in which they occur are of some interest. Around the Finnish coasts the names *Jatulintarha* (Giant's Fence) and *Pietarinleikki* (St. Peter's Game) predominate. Around Helsingfors the figures are more frequently spoken of as "Ruins of Jerusalem," "City of Nineveh," or "Walls of

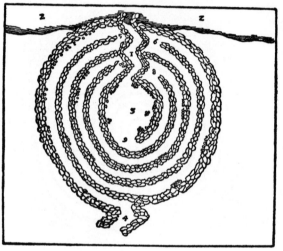

FIG. 127.—Scandinavian Stone Labyrinth. (O. Rudbeck, 1695.)

Jericho." In the neighbourhood of Viborg they are known as *Jätinkatu* (Giant's Street), *Kivitarha* (Stone-fence), or *Lissabon*.

In Lappland a common term is *Babylon*; in Iceland, where the mazes are sometimes formed of earth, the name applied is *Völundarhus* (Wieland's, or Weyland's, House).

In Norway and Sweden they are sometimes called *Nunnentarha* (Nun's Fence), *Jungfrudans* (Maiden's Dance), or *Rundborg* (Round Castle), and on an island in the Kattegat the name *Trelleborg* (The Troll's, or Giant's, Castle) is found; but more frequently they are known by

150

some name akin to our "Troy-town," such as *Trojin*, *Trojeburg*, *Trojenborg*, or *Tröborg*. Another name sometimes associated with them was *Steintanz* (Stone Dance). The Wisby labyrinth is named *Tröjeborg*.

FIG. 128.—Danish Runic Stone Cross, with Labyrinth Figure.
(O. Worm, 1651.)

That labyrinths of some kind were also known in olden Denmark appears from the works of the seventeenth-century Danish antiquary Olaf Worm, one of whose woodcuts (Fig. 128) shows the symbol engraved on an ancient cross.

We see then that John Aubrey (see p. 136) was not altogether speaking at random when he stated his belief that "we received these Mazes from our Danish ancestors." In fact, he based his observations on the works of the Danish and Swedish writers just referred to.

If, as the above considerations lead us to guess, the use of labyrinthine figures was a common feature of the northern peoples before the Norse invasion of Britain, we may wonder whether there is any evidence of the use of the symbol by earlier inhabitants of the same parts; are there any indications of this nature to be found among the relics of prehistoric man in the northern countries?

Well, there are certain remains which have been held to afford an affirmative reply to this question. The remarkable prehistoric rock engravings in Northumberland and the Borders, first noticed about a hundred years ago and described in detail by Mr. G. Tate in 1864, are very suggestive in this connection. They include many figures of a character closely approaching that of a circular labyrinth, but no actual design of the conventional Cretan type has been discovered. In Figs. 129 and 130 are seen examples found on rocks at Routing Linn and Old Bewick respectively. The engravings are as much as three or four feet in diameter, and in many cases are interconnected by grooves which terminate at their cup-like centres. They often coalesce and interconnect to form mazy patterns of great complexity. The greater number consist merely of a series of concentric circles around a central cup, the circles in some cases being interrupted along a radial line which is generally occupied by a straight groove. Their origin and purpose are very obscure.

Very similar rock engravings have been found, though not in such profusion, in other parts of Great Britain, as far north as the Orkneys, and as far south as Devonshire, and also in the south of Ireland. In other parts of Ireland the engravings have chiefly the shape of a simple spiral.

There is strong suggestion of the labyrinth idea in the

152

Fig. 129.   Rock Engravings, Routing Linn, Northumberland.
(G. Tate in Proc. Berwick Naturalists' Club, 1864)

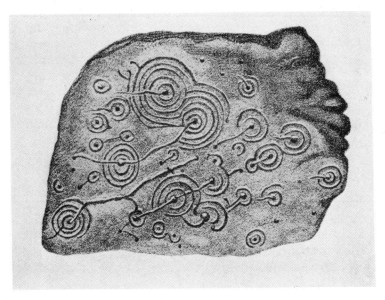

Fig. 130.   Rock Engravings, Old Bewick, Northumberland.
(G. Tate in Proc. Berwick Naturalists' Club, 1864)

elaborate series of engravings which adorn the stones of a cromlech on the island of Gav'r Innis, off the coast of Brittany. Here the surface of the stones is entirely covered with engraved concentric grooves, which never cross one another, but form systems of whorls very much like those on the skin of human finger-tips. There is, however, nothing that can be fairly compared with the designs of the turf mazes, the stone labyrinths or the coins of Knossos.

Amongst the remarkable assemblage of prehistoric engravings on the rocky surfaces of the Italian Maritime Alps is one which exhibits a spiral of five turns, with interruptions and blind branches, but the resemblance between this isolated figure and the conventional labyrinth form is rather too slender to support any useful deduction as to the ancestry of the latter.

The reader may perhaps wonder whether any traces of the labyrinths have been found in other continents, and, if so, whether any connection can be established between them and the labyrinth cult in Europe. An interesting discovery in this reference was made some years ago in the shape of a figure of the Cretan Labyrinth, of circular type, roughly engraved amid other pictographs on the wall of the ruined *Casa Grande*, an old Indian erection in Pinal County, Arizona, U.S.A.

An exactly similar figure, with the addition of some unknown symbol opposite its "entrance" (Fig. 131), was also found in a manuscript entitled "Rudo Ensayo" (Rough Essay), written by a Spaniard who visited the country—the home of the Pima Indians—in 1761 or 1762. According to this manuscript the diagram was scratched in the sand by an Indian and represented the plan of a building.

Dr. J. W. Fewkes, the Chief of the Bureau of American Ethnology, who investigated the matter about fifteen years ago, states that an old Indian living in the neighbourhood was asked whether he knew of any building, or remains of one, built on such a plan. He replied in the negative, but said the figure was commonly employed in a children's game called *Tcuhiki*, i.e. the House of Tcuhu. (Tcuhu is a mythical hero, probably identical with Gopher, who is supposed to have made the spiral hole through which the Pima Indians came up from the underworld.) A writer on this tribe of Indians has described another game played by them which seems to have much in common with that mentioned above. It is called *Tculikwikut*, and is played with rings and darts, count being kept by means of little stones which are moved along a series of small holes arranged in the sand in the form of a whorl, starting from a centre called *Tcunni Ki*, "the Council House."

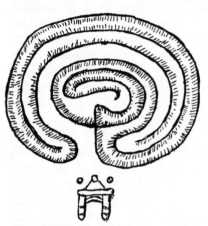

FIG. 131.—Indian Labyrinth Figure from Eighteenth-century Spanish Manuscript. (After Cotton.)

If it could be shown that these games were associated with the labyrinth figure in those regions before the date of the Spanish invasion of Mexico we should be forced to conclude either that, by an extraordinary coincidence, the figure became evolved independently in the Old World and the New, or that in both it had a common origin of astounding antiquity. However, there is a probability that it was introduced to the Indians by the early Spaniards, with whom it would have been a familiar symbol. The only other ancient Indian pictograph of labyrinthine type so far discovered appears to be that on a pebble found by Dr. Fewkes in 1919 in a ruin known as "Square Tower House," in Mesa Verde National

154

Park. This, it will be seen (Fig. 132), bears no likeness to the conventional design, but is merely an asymmetrical meandering groove somewhat similar in appearance to the braided designs often seen on modish feminine apparel at the present day. Its significance is unknown.

According to a short review in *Folk Lore* in 1913, a book entitled "Some Zulu Customs and Folk Lore," by L. H. Samuelson ("Nomleti"), 1912, contained a description of mazes made on the ground by Zulus. Unfortunately this book is out of print, and no copy,

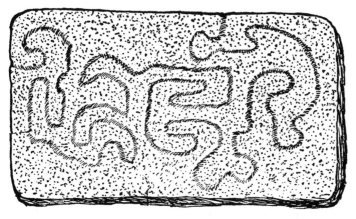

FIG. 132.—Labyrinthine Pictograph from Mesa Verde. (After Fewkes.)

strange to say, is to be found in the library of either the British Museum or the Folk Lore Society. It would be extremely interesting to know whether the mazes in question bear any similarity to the traditional Cretan figure.

So far, then, evidence of a definite labyrinth cult is confined to certain parts of Europe and the Mediterranean borders. It has, in fact, been shown that it corresponds roughly with the areas formerly occupied by the people that built the cromlechs. With regard to its origin and significance, many interesting speculations have been made, some of which we will now briefly review.

155

CHAPTER XVIII

THE DANCE OR GAME OF TROY

READERS of our previous chapters will have noticed the frequency with which the name "Troy" is associated with the idea of the labyrinth.

We find this association, for instance, in the case of the "Troy-towns" of Somerton and Hillbury, the "Walls of Troy" of the Cumberland Marshes and Appleby (Lincs), and the "Caerdroia" of the Welsh shepherds. In northern Europe we find it as "Troja" or in such combinations as "Trojeborg" or "Tröborg."

That this association is not of recent origin we have an interesting token in a reference which occurs in a fifteenth-century French manuscript preserved in the British Museum. This manuscript is the record of a journey made by the Seigneur de Caumont to Jerusalem in 1418, and is entitled "Voyaige d'oultremer en Jhérusalem." Calling at the island of Crete *en route*, the Seigneur, like most other travellers on similar occasions, takes occasion to make a few remarks about the famous legend associated with it. He speaks of the "mervelleuse et orrible best qui fut appellé Minotaur," who, he says, was confined within "celle entrigade meson faite par Dedalus, merveilleux maquanit, lequelle meson fut nommée Labarinte et aujourduy par moultz est vulguelmant appellé le cipté de Troie."

156

It would seem from the latter observation that the expression "Troy-town" or "City of Troy" was in general use 500 years ago as a title for the Cretan Labyrinth, and seeing that the renaissance of classical learning was as yet in embryo the inference is that the name was a popular tradition of some antiquity.

FIG. 133.—Etruscan Wine-vase from Tragliatella. (Deecke.)

We find the name of Troy definitely associated with the labyrinth long before this, however, in the crude engravings on the Etruscan wine-jar which we noticed in Chapter VIII., the *oinochoë* from Tragliatella.

The meaning of these figures (Figs. 133, 134 and 135) has been much discussed, but it is now generally agreed that the labyrinth shown has a close relationship with the operations which are being performed by the group of armed men, and it is obvious that it is also connected in some way with the

FIG. 134.—Etruscan Vase. "Troy Dance" Details. (Deecke.)

famous story of the wars of Troy, as we see by its label "*Truia*." What is this operation in which the warriors are engaged? We find a helpful clue in the story

157

related by Virgil (B.C. 70–19) in his great epic of the Aeneid, in which the poet has embalmed for us the legends current in his time concerning the wanderings of Aeneas, the reputed son of Anchises and Venus, after the fall of the city of Troy, which he had fought bravely to defend.

Aeneas, who escaped from the city carrying his father on his shoulders, led forth also his little son Iulus. It is this boy whom, in the fifth book of the poem, Virgil pictures as taking part with his companions in a sport called the *Ludus Trojae* or *Lusus Trojae* (Game of Troy), sometimes

FIG. 135.—Etruscan Vase. Details, showing Labyrinth and "retro-script" label—"TRUIA." (Deecke.)

simply *Troja*. According to the Roman tradition it was introduced into Italy by Aeneas, and his son Ascanius imparted it to the Alban kings and through them to the Romans. The game consisted of a sort of processional parade or dance, in which some of the participants appear to have been mounted on horseback. Virgil draws a comparison between the complicated movements of the game and the convolutions of the Cretan Labyrinth:

" Ut quondam Creta fertur Labyrinthus in alta
  parietibus textum caecis iter ancipitemque
  mille viis habuisse dolum, qua signa sequendi
  frangeret indeprensus et irremeabilis error."

(Aeneid, V. 585–591).

158

> " As when in lofty Crete (so fame reports)
> The Labyrinth of old, in winding walls
> A mazy way inclos'd, a thousand paths
> Ambiguous and perplexed, by which the steps
> Should by an error intricate, untrac'd
> Be still deluded."   (*Trapp's trans.*, 1718.)

The game is also mentioned as a well-established institution by other Roman writers of a century or so later, such as Suetonius and Tacitus, and appears to have assumed imposing dimensions at one time, as we see from a representation of it on the reverse of a medal of Nero, where it has more of the nature of a military review. It was generally performed by youths, and only those of good social standing took part.

It will be remembered that we have already had occasion to notice another ancient dance, or game, in which youthful notabilities were stated to have taken part, and in which the motions of the dances were supposed to represent the tortuous paths of the Cretan Labyrinth, namely, the dance performed by Theseus and his friends on the island of Delos. This dance was called the "Geranos," or Crane Dance, probably on account of the fancied resemblance of the attitude of the dancers to that of cranes in flight, or perhaps on account of actual adornments of the dancers. (An eighteenth-century German traveller in Russia relates that the Ostiaks of Siberia had an elaborate Crane Dance, the dancers being dressed up in the skins of those birds.)

Is there any connection between these two dances, both labyrinthine in character, the one traditionally based on the windings of the labyrinth of Knossos, the other compared by Virgil with the latter, but named after another city famous in ancient legend—to wit, Troy?

In regard to both these cities the events celebrated in the classic legends were of prehistoric occurrence (in so far as they occurred at all), and their recital was handed down orally for very many generations before they

159

became crystallised in the written record, and it is not therefore surprising if during that time various versions were evolved and discrepancies of person, place, and time were introduced.

The association of the labyrinth, by some of the Nordic Aryan peoples, with Troy instead of Knossos may perhaps be accounted for in this way.

The point with which we are most concerned at the moment, however, is the fact that the figure of the labyrinth, in each case, is connected with the idea of a ceremonial game or dance.

Another dance, possibly of similar character, associated with Knossos, is that mentioned in Homer's "Iliad" as having been invented by Daedalus for Ariadne. Youths with golden swords and maidens crowned with garlands performed it in ranks.

By analogy with a great number of myths, rites, and ceremonies of ancient and modern races, some anthropologists have been led to the conclusion that these Troy and labyrinth dances are only particular expressions of a very early and widely diffused ceremonial associated with the awakening of nature in spring, after its winter sleep, or the release of the imprisoned sun after its long captivity in the toils of the demon of winter.

In that marvellous compendium of universal folk-lore "The Golden Bough," and in the particular volume of it entitled "The Dying God," Sir James Frazer debates the significance of the classic legends we have mentioned, and draws the tentative conclusion that Ariadne's dance was symbolical of the sun's course in the sky, its intention being, "by sympathetic magic to aid the great luminary to run his race on high." (See also p. 92.) He draws attention to a practice observed by Chilcotin Indians, during eclipses of the sun, of walking around a circle leaning on staves, as if to help the sun around its course (much as a child pushes the partition of a railway compartment to help the train along).

160

Mr. A. B. Cook, the Cambridge classical archaeologist, points out in this connection a Knossian coin on which the Minotaur, or rather, a man with a bull's mask, is shown engaged apparently in a similar rite, the reverse being occupied by a "swastika" labyrinth.

All this appears highly speculative to the ordinary layman, but nobody who gives a little attention to the subject can avoid the conclusion that at any rate there must have existed in very early—possibly Neolithic—times an extremely widespread and important ceremonial, generally of a sacrificial type, in connection with the spring awakening. So deeply seated was this ancient tradition that traces of it have persisted, with various local modifications, right down to the present day.

The sword-dances and morris-dances of our own country, most of which but for the happy genius and industry of Mr. Cecil Sharp and his disciples would have passed away entirely by the next generation, are undoubtedly survivals of a ceremonial of this type, particularly the former. They were performed only on certain fixed annual occasions, and were treated with great reverence and meticulous attention to detail.

A correspondent writing to *Notes and Queries* in 1870 (Anne Silvester) laments the fact that "the old British game of *troy*, the vestiges of which are so rare," is becoming extinct, but does not describe it. No doubt the writer had in mind some game played in connection with earth mazes.

It is a pity that we have no record of the actual method of "running the maze" in this country in past generations. The idea that such ingeniously designed and carefully constructed works were made for the sole purpose of trotting along their convolutions to the centre and out again, without any symbolic or religious significance or any ceremonial observance, may be dismissed at once.

As regards their alleged use by the Christian Church

for purposes of penance, we have no reliable evidence, and even if we had we know that such a use would have been of a secondary character. Most probably they were appropriated to some seasonal observance, as in fact we know that several of them were within quite recent years, and were associated with some ritual dance similar in nature to the Crane Dance or the Dance of Troy. With regard to the word "Troy" itself there is a possibility that its connection with the dance and the labyrinth figure may have originated not with the name of a town, but with some ancient root signifying to wind, or turn; in the case of the Welsh "Caerdroia," as we have already seen, this suggestion was made long ago. It may also have some connection with the three-headed monster Trojano of the ancient Slavonic mythology, who appears in the Persian legends as Druja, or Draogha, and in the Rig-Veda of India as Maho Druho, the Great Druh, and who plays throughout the same part as the wintry demon Weyland Smith (or Wieland) of the northern traditions. In Iceland, as we have already seen (p. 150), the earth mazes are associated with the latter personage.

We find the word Troi, or Troi-Aldei, applied to certain ceremonial parades akin to the Troy-dance, in the writings of Neidhart von Reuenthal, in the early thirteenth century, the accompanying songs being termed "Troyerlais."

Quite recently a contributor to "Folk Lore" gave the airs of three popular dances which are performed by the Serbians at the present day under the names of Trojanka and Trojanac. The correspondent in question had thought that their names might have some connection with the root *tri* (= three), with reference to the rhythm of the dances, but the airs supplied by him certainly would not support this contention. It is far more probable, as he seems to conclude, that they indicate a connection with the Dance of Troy. Unfortunately he does not describe the dances themselves; it would be interesting to know whether they embody any movements suggestive of a labyrinthine origin or corresponding to the dances described by Homer and Virgil on the one hand, or to our morris and sword dances on the other.

Another point in this connection which might justify a little enquiry is the question of the origin of that maze-figure which forms, or used to form, part of the system of Swedish drill as taught to children in this country.

With regard to our native dances mentioned above, we may note that every care has been taken by competent investigators to discover and to preserve as much as possible of the pure tradition, and we have the satisfaction of knowing that, narrowly as they escaped oblivion, the English Folk-Dance Society will see to it that such a danger will not threaten them again for a very long time.

CHAPTER XIX

THE BOWER OF "FAIR ROSAMOND"

THE story of "Fair Rosamond" and her mazy Bower, though it cannot lay claim to that standard of authenticity which is generally required of historical data, has for so long occupied an honoured position in the realm of popular romance that, in a book professing to treat of mazes from a broad point of view, we cannot dismiss it quite as briefly as we might perhaps do in a book on English history.

"Fair Rosamond" has been stated, without very much foundation, to have been the daughter of Walter de Clifford, and is in consequence frequently referred to as Rosamond Clifford.

The story runs that King Henry the Second (A.D. 1133 to 1189) adopted her as his mistress, and that, in order to conceal his illicit amours from his Queen, Eleanor of Aquitaine, he conducted them within the innermost recesses of a most complicated maze which he caused to be made in his park at Woodstock. Rumours of her spouse's defections having reached the ears of Queen Eleanor, that indignant lady contrived to penetrate the labyrinth, confronted her terrified and tearful rival, and forced her to choose between the dagger and the bowl of poison; she drained the latter and became forthwith defunct.

Various trimmings, more or less scandalous in nature,

164

gathered around the central tale, as, for instance, that Rosamond presented Henry with the son who was afterwards known as William Longsword, Earl of Salisbury, but the main outline as indicated above was handed down intact for many generations.

The poisoning incident is not mentioned in the account given by a chronicler of that time, John Brompton, Abbot of Jervaulx (Yorks). It seems to have been first recorded by a French scribe in the fourteenth century.

Brompton's version, given under the year 1151 in his "Chronicon," is as follows:

"Sane idem rex *Henricus* quanquam multis virtutibus fuerat ornatus, aliquibus tamen viciis involutus personam regiam deturpavit. In libidine namque pronus conjugalem modum excessit. Regina enim sua *Elianora* jamdudum incarcerata factus est adulter manifestus, palam et impudice puellam retinens *Rosamundam*. Huic nempe puellae spectatissimae fecerat rex apud *Wodestoke* mirabilis architecturae cameram operi *Daedalino* similem, ne forsan a regina facile deprehenderetur. Sed illa cito obiit, et apud *Godestowe* juxta *Oxoniam* in capitulo monialium in tumba decenti est sepulta, ubi talis suprascriptio invenitur:

" Hic jacet in tumba Rosa mundi, non Rosa munda;
Non redolet, sed olet, quae redolere solet."

It would appear from this account that the "bower" was a labyrinth of an architectural kind, perhaps like that mentioned in Chapter XIV as having been built at Ardres by Louis of Bourbourg in the previous century, not, as popularly believed, a maze of evergreens. It will be seen, also, that Henry did not long enjoy his clandestine delights, for Rosamond shortly died and was buried before the high altar of the nunnery church of Godstowe. Her death is believed to have taken place about 1176. It is possible that she had entered the nunnery some time

165

before that. According to the contemporary annalist Roger de Hoveden her body was removed in 1191 by Bishop Hugh of Lincoln, on moral grounds, and was apparently re-interred in the chapter-house.

The imprisonment of Queen Eleanor, referred to by Brompton, was a consequence of her connivance at the rebellion of her sons in 1173–74.

Ranulph Higden, who lived in the thirteenth and fourteenth centuries, deals with the Henry and Rosamond story in the seventh book of his "Polychronicon," and tells us that visitors to Godstowe Abbey used to be shown a wonderful coffer which had belonged to Rosamond. It contained figures of birds, beasts, fishes and boxing men, which, by clockwork or springs, were endowed with apparently spontaneous motion (Cista ejusdem puella vix bipedalis mensura, sed mirabilis architectura ibidem cernitur; in qua conflictus pugilem, gestus animalium, volatus avium, saltus piscium, absque hominis impulsu conspiciuntur).

Most of the subsequent chroniclers seem to have followed Higden in their relation of the story. By Tudor times the romantic and tragic episode had become a favourite theme in popular lore; it was enshrined by the Elizabethan poet Drayton in his "Epistle to Rosamond," the bower being therein described as an arrangement of subterranean vaults. It achieved its greatest popularity, however, in the ballad form, and was printed, with several other "Strange Histories or Songs and Sonnets of Kinges, Princes, Dukes, Lords, Ladyes, Knights and Gentlemen, etc.," in a black-letter volume written or edited by Thomas Delone (or Delorney) in 1612. Two editions of the ballad were represented in the collection of Samuel Pepys, under the title of "The Life and Death of Rosamond, King Henry the Second's Concubine. And how she was Poysoned to Death by Queen Elenor."

John Aubrey, in his "Remaines," 1686, tells us that his nurse used to sing the following verses to him:

166

> " Yea, Rosamond, fair Rosamond,
>   Her name was called so,
>   To whom dame Elinor our Queene
>   Was known a deadly foe,
>   The King therefore for her defence
>   Against the furious Queene
>   At Woodstocke builded such a Bower
>   The like was never seen.
>
> " Most curiously that Bower was built
>   Of stone and timber strong.
>   An hundered and fifty dores
>   Did to this Bower belong,
>   And they so cunningly contriv'd
>   With turnings round about
>   That none but with a clew of thread
>   Could enter in or out."

The whole ballad will be found in the well-known "Reliques of Ancient English Poetry," collected by Bishop Percy and published by him in 1765.

Of a widely different nature was the version published in 1729 by Samuel Croxall in his "Select Collection of Novels," Vol. IV. "The Loves of King Henry II and Fair Rosamond." Here the attitude assumed is one of learned contempt for popular credulity. "What have we in this Story," says Croxall, "but a Copy of Ariadne's Clue and the Cretan Labyrinth? . . . Yet are we not to wonder that the monkish Historians should deliver down to us a Tale of such Absurdity, when the same Chronicles tell us that, in that King's Reign, a Dragon of marvellous Bigness was seen at St. Osyth's in Essex, which, by its very motion, set many Houses and Buildings on Fire."

As for the inscription on Rosamond's tomb, quoted by Brompton, our critic is equally scornful. "The conceit," he says, "is poor and common and, like the other Poetry of those times, depends on a certain Jingle and Play on the Words. The sense of them has been thus expressed in honest English Metre:"

(Whether the verse is in better taste when expressed in

honest English metre the reader must judge for himself.)

> " Rose of the World, not Rose the peerless Flow'r,
> Within this Tomb hath taken up her Bow'r.
> She scenteth now, and nothing Sweet doth smell
> Who earst was wont to savour passing well."

This rendering is perhaps preferable to that of Stowe ("Annals," 1631), which concludes with:

> " Though she were sweete, now foully doth she stinke,
> A mirrour good for all men, that on her thinke."

In any case the epitaph must be accounted a libel in one respect, for Leland, the Antiquary to Henry VIII, records that, on the opening of Rosamond's tomb, at the dissolution of Godstowe nunnery, the bones were found to be encased in leather, surrounded by lead, and that "a very swete smell came out of it."

An interesting point mentioned by Croxall is that in his time "a delightful Bower" was still in existence at Woodstock and was shown as the original of the story. Another reliable writer of the same period (Thomas Hearne, 1718) makes a similar observation, but in this case it is made clear that the remains are those of a large building, not, as we might have inferred, those of a hedge maze or arbour. These remains, whatever they may have been, have disappeared long since.

Woodstock Park, according to the historian Rouse of Warwick, was the first park to be made in England. Henry the First had a palace here, but the present great building, the masterpiece of Sir John Vanbrugh, was built for the first Duke of Marlborough and was named after the scene of his famous victory, Blenheim.

The traditional story of Fair Rosamond, in which she is made to figure as a cruelly wronged and guileless damsel of impregnable virtue and the victim of an unreasoning jealousy, formed the basis of many novels,

168

e.g., "Fair Rosamond," by T. Miller ("The Parlour Library"), 1847, and as late as 1911 it was cast into the form of a one-act tragedy by Mr. Oliver W. F. Lodge, under the name of "The Labyrinth," and was first performed by the Pilgrim Players on October 14 in that year. A little-known opera by Addison deals with the same theme; it is entitled "Rosamond" and is inscribed to the Duchess of Marlborough. The most poignant and beautiful version of the tragedy is that given by Swinburne in his "Rosamond" (not, of course, to be confused with his "Rosamund").

Tennyson, in his "Becket," makes that prelate rescue Rosamond from the Queen at the crucial moment and take her to Godstowe nunnery, whence she later escapes to intercede—ineffectually—with his murderers in Canterbury Cathedral.

No authentic portrait of Rosamond is known to exist, but in Hampton Court Palace, just outside Cardinal Wolsey's Room, there hangs a half-length female portrait by an unknown painter (No. 961 [937]), which is labelled Rosamond Clifford. The lady depicted, however, is attired in a fashion which did not obtain until considerably later than the time of Rosamond; in fact, there seems to be no justification whatever for assuming that the picture represents the fair Rosamond at all, except perhaps in the imagination of the artist.

CHAPTER XX

THE reader may be inclined to question the necessity for a whole chapter to be devoted to such a matter as this. "Surely anybody who has the curiosity to do so can look the words up in a dictionary!" Or he may object that the proper place to define and expound one's terms is in the opening chapter.

It will be found, however, that no clear-cut and simple definition of, for example, the word *labyrinth* itself is to be found in any dictionary, and that with regard to its derivation authorities are not even yet in complete agreement. With the facts recounted in the preceding chapters at his disposal the reader may possibly find a little informal discussion of these points more intelligible and interesting than the more rigid presentment afforded by even the best dictionaries. Moreover, most dictionaries have little or nothing to say about Julian's bowers or Troy-towns. On the other hand, of course, this chapter could not have been written without free recourse to Murray, Skeat, Webster, Wright, and other monuments of the lexicographer's toil.

We will consider such words as seem worth discussing in their alphabetical order, commencing with one which was prominent in our last chapter, viz., "bower."

We have here a word of which the early connotation has been rather obscured by poetical insistence upon one

170

of its extensions. As a convenient rhyme for "flower" and "shower" it has become one of the mainstays of the vernal poetaster, a circumstance which evoked one of the gems of Calverley's gentle satire:

> " Bowers of flowers encountered showers
>   In William's carol—(O love my Willie!);
> Then he bade sorrow borrow from blithe tomorrow
>   I quite forget what—say a daffodilly."
>   (*Lovers, and a Reflection.*)

The word has thus come to be chiefly employed to signify a leafy or shady arbour or a recess in a garden, a use quite consistent with, but narrower than, the principal and much older meaning, which was that of a dwelling, with particular reference to the character of privacy.

The common modern usage seems to have been first adopted by the Elizabethan poets. Hero, in "Much Ado about Nothing" (Act III, Sc. 1), sends by her attendant a message to her cousin Beatrice, bidding her

> " . . . steal into the pleached bower,
> Where honeysuckles, ripened by the sun,
> Forbid the sun to enter."

The Saxon form of the word was *búr* or *bure*, related to *búan*, meaning "to dwell," and it was always used to denote something of the nature of an inner chamber or sanctum.

In Chaucer's works (late fourteenth century) it has the same force, *e.g.*, in the "Wife of Bath's Tale":

> " Blissing halles, chambres, kitchines and boures."

Somewhat later we find a poetical extension of the word to include not only the dwellings of human beings but also of animals and birds. Thus William Dunbar, a Scottish poet who lived about 1465–1530, speaking of birds hidden within thickets, used the phrase "within their bouris." This usage gave rise to the idea that the word was derived from "bough," a notion that seems to

171

have first found expression in the anonymous "Letters of Junius," and shortly afterwards received the weighty sanction of Dr. Johnson. In Southey's "Curse of Kehama" the word in this sense is made to do duty as a verb:

> " And through the leafy cope which bowered it o'er
> Came gleams of chequered light."

The metaphorical use of the word in its original sense is seen in Moore's "Evenings in Greece":

> " Fancy, who hath no present home,
> But builds her bower in scenes to come."

The suggestion that Rosamond's Bower was of the nature of a hedge maze seems to be of rather late origin, probably arising in the seventeenth century, like the application of the term to the little hedge-box garden at Menteith (Queen Mary's Bower), to which we referred in Chapter XIII. In the earlier writers it is almost invariably spoken of as a building. Robert Fabyan, for instance, a historian of the late sixteenth century, speaks of it as a "house named Labyrinthus or Daedalus worke, or howse wroughte like unto a knot in a garden called a maze," and in some anonymous verses of the mid-fifteenth century it is stated:

> " Att Wodestocke for hure he made a toure
> That is called Rosemoundes boure."

It would appear that the Bower which is commemorated in the place-name of Havering-at-Bower, Essex, was also of the nature of a building, probably of large dimensions, for, according to an "Appendix on Bowers" annexed to an "Essay on Design in Gardening," by George Mason, 1795, there was a long-standing tradition to the effect that it was the site of a king's residence, and an old man of the locality could remember "many chimnies of the old bower standing." This may or may not be evidence, but it is at all events quite in keeping with the ancient use of the word. The royal residence in question would no doubt have been of the nature of a private retreat, not a court.

Writing in 1827, the Rev. H. J. Todd says, "In Cumberland, to this day, a back room or parlour is called a *boor*."

It will be seen from the remark of John Aubrey quoted on page 136 that he assumed "borough" to be identical in origin with "bower." The former is, however, derived from the Anglo-Saxon *burg* or *burh*, a city, allied to *beorgan*, to protect.

In any large dictionary there will be found detailed several other meanings for the word "bower"—including the sense in which it is used in Bret Harte's "Heathen Chinee"—but with these we are not here concerned.

Strange to say, the use of the word in the combination "Julian-bower" or "Julian's-bower" is usually overlooked or ignored.

The English Dialect Dictionary (Wright) gives the local variants *Gelyan-bower*, *Gillimber* and *Jilling-bo'or* as occurring in Lincolnshire, and *Jul-laber* as another form of the "Julaber's Barrow" or "Juliberry's Grave" which we have already noticed in Kent. Is the "bower" here the same as "barrow," which is derived from the Anglo-Saxon *beorg*, meaning, like the German *berg*, a hill? Or is it only the same word that we have met with in "Rosamond's Bower"? The former suggestion receives some support from the fact that turf mazes are often, though not always, constructed on the top of a hill or mound, but to the writer there is something more attractive in conceiving these works to be associated with the idea of a retreat, particularly if we consider, as we have some reason for doing, that the Julian referred to is the benign and hospitable Saint Julian of the mediaeval legends.

From Brand's "Popular Antiquities" it appears that there were three or four saints of this name, but the most well-known of these was the knight whose deeds are celebrated in the "Gesta Romanorum" and elsewhere, the reputed patron and protector of pilgrims and travellers. The chapel of Domus Dei at Southampton, now used as the French Protestant church, is dedicated to this St. Julian. The legend goes, that on returning home one day Julian discovered a man and woman asleep in his bed, jumped to the hasty conclusion that his wife had been untrue to him and slew the pair where they lay, only to find that they were his parents who had travelled from afar to visit him. In repentance and atonement he then founded a hospice for travellers and afterwards became known as *Hospitator*, or "the gude herbejour," in which capacity his renown is testified by many a reference in our early literature, *e.g.*, in the works of Chaucer:

> " Now up the heed ; for al is wel ;
> Seynt Julyan, lo, bon hostel !
> See here the Hous of Fame, lo ! "
>
> *(The Hous of Fame.)*

> " An housholder, and that a grete, was he
> Seint Julian he was in his contré."
>
> *(Canterbury Tales.)*

It seems to the writer just as likely that the name Julian's-bower commemorates this popular hero as that it has any connection, as some have maintained, with the invading Caesar or, as suggested by others (see Chapter XI), with his tribune, Quintus Laberius Durus. One can quite easily conjure up in imagination a game or ceremony in which the fatigues of the pilgrim treading the long course of the labyrinth's folds is rewarded by some form of refreshment on at length reaching the secluded retreat of the hospitable saint.

> " Surely they find St. Julians inn, which way-
> faring men diligently seek."
>
> *(The Ancren Riwle*—Thirteenth century.)

When we turn from our native bowers to the Aegean *labyrinthos*, transmitted practically intact from the ancient

174

Greek to most modern European languages, we are venturing on dangerous ground indeed, for the derivation of this word has been the subject of much disputation between rival schools of etymologists and philologists in recent years.

Down to a few decades ago we were content with the bald statement of most dictionaries that it was probably correlated with the word *laura*, meaning a passage, or mine,[1] though there was also a suggestion that it might be of Egyptian origin, viz., that it was derived from the name of Labaris (= Senusret III), erroneously conceived by the scribe Manetho to be the founder of the Hawara pile. Then Mr. Max Mayer put forward the suggestion that it might have some connection with *labrys*, a word which, in some of the early languages of Asia Minor, *e.g.*, Lydia and Caria, denoted an axe, the axe being the symbol associated with the god known as Zeus Labrandeus or Zeus Stratios, the worship of whom was known to have taken place at Labranda, in Caria. Coins from Mylasa, a neighbouring town, show this god holding in his hand a double axe.

The stir created by the discovery of double axes in abundance, with every indication of their religious and symbolic use, during the course of Sir Arthur Evans's explorations in the traditional home of the Cretan labyrinth, can therefore be well understood. As a consequence thereof every self-respecting dictionary nowadays gives pre-eminence to the *labrys* derivation of "labyrinth." At the same time it is well to bear in mind that many learned scholars have seen great difficulty in accepting this theory, mainly on account of the metathesis, or change-over, of the *r* and the *y* (*u* in Greek), which was stated to be unexampled, and to the addition of the termination *-inthos*. With regard to the latter it now seems to be generally agreed among scholars that this termination occurs only in words which were assimilated from the pre-existing

[1] "Coil-of-rope walk" according to Ruskin (*Fors Clav.*).

175

peoples of the Aegean lands, whom the Greeks, as northern invading hordes, overcame and superseded. The suffix is preserved only, however, in extremely few common nouns (*terebinthos* = the turpentine tree, *asaminthos* = a bathing-place), and in a similarly small number of place-names, such as *Tirynthos* (Tiryns) and *Corinthos* (Corinth). It is the equivalent of the ending *-nda* in certain place-names in Asia Minor, *e.g.*, *Labranda*.

The conjectures that the word was connected with *labros*, meaning "great," or that it was derived from the old Egyptian *la-pe-ro-hunt*, "the temple at the mouth of the reservoir," are hardly worth repeating.

The present position, then, is that the Labyrinth is the House of the Double Axe, the implication being that the Cretan example was not, as formerly believed, a miniature reproduction of the temple of Hawara, but that the latter was actually given the title by analogy with the building at Knossos.

As regards the use of the word in our own language, it was probably well known to most of the churchmen of the early and middle ages, through the medium of the classic authors accessible to them, but it never passed into common speech. In Chaucer's works, *i.e.*, in the fourteenth century, we find both *maze* and *labyrinth* employed; but whereas the latter evidently refers to the Cretan tradition, the English word seems to denote some figure familiar to the poet's readers—perhaps, we may conjecture, in the form of turf mazes.

Thus, in "The Hous of Fame" (line 826, etc.), he says:

> " Tho gan I forth with him to goon
> Out of the castel, soth to saye,
> Tho saugh I stoude in a valeye,
> Under the castel, faste by,
> An hous, that *domus Dedali*
> That *Laborintus* cleped is,
> Nas maed so wonderliche, y-wis
> Ne half so queynteliche y-wrought";

176

and in his "Legend of Ariadne," one of his minor poems, we read (line 125, etc.):

> " This wepen shal the gayler, on that tyde,
>   Ful privily within the prison hyde;
>   And, for the hous is krinkeled to and fro,
>   And hath so queinte weyes for to go—
>   For hit is shapen as the *mase* is wroght—
>   Thereto have I a remedie in my thought,
>   That, by a clewe of twyne, as he hath goon,
>   The same way he may returne anoon,
>   Folwing alway the thread, as he hath come."

Seeing that the "hous" here referred to is the Cretan labyrinth itself, the "mase" with which it is compared must be something sufficiently familiar to Chaucer's audience to furnish them with a ready illustration of the nature of the legendary structure which he is describing and which elsewhere he calls The Labyrinth or the House of Daedalus.

From very early times the classic authors used the word "labyrinth" metaphorically, and the mediaeval writers followed them. For instance Walter, a canon of St. Victor, towards the end of the twelfth century wrote a work which he called "A Treatise Against the Four Labyrinths of France," in reference to the great theological work in four books, known as the "Book of Sentences," a long and very metaphysical compendium of divinity, by Peter, Bishop of Paris.

In Renaissance times we find the word commonly used as a simile for the difficulties of life or the vagaries of love.

In Shakespeare's "King Henry VI" (Pt. I, V, Sc. 3) the Earl of Suffolk, after the exit of the gentle Margaret of Anjou, whose hand he has been soliciting on behalf of his royal master, exclaims:

> " O, wert thou for myself!—But, Suffolk, stay;
>   Thou mayst not wander in that labyrinth:
>   There Minotaurs and ugly treasons lurk."

177

We will notice further examples of this use of the word a little later, in connection with book-titles.

In "Troilus and Cressida" (Act II, Sc. 3) Thersites bursts into soliloquy before the tent of Achilles with:

" How now, Thersites!   What, lost in the labyrinth of thy fury!"

Milton says that "Lethe, the river of oblivion, rolls her watery labyrinth," and Pope that "Love in these labyrinths his slaves detains"; but the occurrence of such expressions in writings of all periods is too common to need further quotation. We might perhaps point out that a slight shade of difference may be assumed to exist between "labyrinth" and "maze," even when these words are used in their metaphorical sense. We may take "labyrinth" to signify a complex problem involving merely time and perseverance for its solution, "maze," on the other hand, being reserved for situations fraught, in addition, with the elements of uncertainty and ambiguity, calling for the exercise of the higher mental faculties—in short, we may regard the two words as having reference respectively to the unicursal and multicursal types of plan (see Introduction). A distinction of this kind adds point to a sentence like that which occurs, for instance, in Mr. Lytton Strachey's "Queen Victoria," where he tells us (p. 178) that the Prince Consort "attempted to thread his way through the complicated labyrinth of European diplomacy, and was eventually lost in the maze."

As a means of expressing complexities of outline or of inner structure, natural or artificial, the word has been adopted by various branches of science or art. Every student of anatomy knows the "labyrinth" of the inner ear, every geological tyro has heard of those gigantic amphibians of Carboniferous to Triassic times whose peculiarly lamellated teeth have earned for them the title of "labyrinthodonts." Zoologists are acquainted with

those lowly protoplasmic forms of life which, on account
of the mazy net-like appearance assumed at one stage in
their life-history, are called "labyrinthulidea." Even the
engineer finds it convenient to make use of the word, as,
for instance, when he speaks of a "labyrinth-packing"
for turbines, an arrangement which allows a certain
amount of lateral motion while ensuring steam-tightness.

We may remark in passing that the names of the
artificer Daedalus and of the winding river Meander
have also done duty in scientific nomenclature in some
cases where it was desired to commemorate labyrinthine
characteristics; for example, a pretty little fungus allied
to the *Stereum* so common on decaying wood has received
the generic title of *Daedalea*, on account of the mazy
pattern displayed by its spore-bearing surface, while the
beautiful "brain-stone" coral is known to the naturalist
under the name of *Meandrina*.

Compound words formed with "maze," on the other
hand, are usually of an old-fashioned or local character,
such as "Maze-Sunday," which in Devonshire dialect
signifies a Sunday given up to feasting; such compounds
are rarely formed for scientific or technical purposes.
The sheet glass which is obscured by a system of wrinkles
on its surface is, however, sometimes known as "maze-
glass."

The word *maze* is probably of Scandinavian origin.
Its oldest significance seems to be that of a state of bewilderment or confusion, or of being wrapped in thought
—a use which we nowadays regard as metaphorical. In
the Swedish and Norwegian languages are related words
which mean on the one hand to dream, or lounge, or to
move about in an idle or lazy manner, and on the other
hand to chatter or indulge in aimless talk.

Some dictionaries formerly stated that it was derived
from an Anglo-Saxon word *mase*, meaning "a whirlpool,"
but it has been shown that there was no such word.

In various dialects it is still used in its original sense.

One may often hear from the older type of country folk such expressions as "It fair mazed me to see it," giving one the feeling that the syllable "a-" has been dropped, whereas it was never there. In Shakespeare the expression frequently occurs. Titania, in "Midsummer Night's Dream" (Act II, Sc. 2), says:

> ". . . the spring, the summer,
> The childing autumn, angry winter, change
> Their wonted liveries ; and the maz'd world,
> By their increase, now knows not which is which."

Talbot of Shrewsbury, in his dire straits before the walls of Bordeaux ("King Henry VI," Pt. I, Act IV, Sc. 2), exclaims:

> " O, negligent and heedless discipline!
> How are we park'd and bounded in a pale,—
> A little herd of England's timorous deer,
> Maz'd with a yelping kennel of French curs!"

(See also "King Henry VIII," Act II, Sc. 4, line 185.)

That the word as here quoted has no identity with the word "amazed" is clear from a comparison of its context with that of the latter in the numerous instances of its employment by Shakespeare. The verb "to maze" is found in Chaucer:

> " 'Ye maze, maze, gode sire,' quod she,
> 'This thank have I for I have maad yow see.' "
> (*The Marchantes Tale*, l. 2387.)

In the sense of crazy, wild, or thoughtless, we find it in the dialect expressions "Mazed-antic" and "Mazegerry."

As a metaphor it is employed in like manner to its Greek equivalent. In "The Taming of the Shrew" Petruchio declares: "I have thrust myself into this maze, Haply to wive and thrive as best I may." "Let us," says Pope, in the "Essay on Man,"

> " Expatiate free o'er all this scene of man,
> A mighty maze! but not without a plan."

180

The term has no connection with the word which we see in, for instance, Mr. Hall Caine's novel "The Deemster":

> " Nine maze—not bad for the first night."

This is a variant of the word *mease* and denotes a measure of 500 herrings!

Of the etymology of the term "Troy-town" some indications have already been given in Chapter XVIII. We might, perhaps, in addition, hazard the guess that the Sanskrit root *dru* (= run) has some bearing on the origin of the word so widely associated with the idea of a dance or ceremonial, but the connection is too obscure to be very helpful.

We might further recall the ancient legend,[1] recorded in Welsh chronicles going back many centuries before the Christian era, to the effect that a great-grandson of Aeneas named Prydain, or Brutus, came over to this country with the Trojan prisoners of war whom he had helped to liberate from Greece, and with their aid built a city on the banks of the Temus (Thames), which he called *Caerdroi-Newydd* (New City of Troy). This name became corrupted into *Troinovant*—hence the "Trino-bantes" of Caesar's time—and was later discarded in favour of *Caerludd*, a name given in honour of Lludd, nephew of the Caswallon who fought against Caesar. The Saxons afterwards corrupted the name into *Lun-dun*.

As Spenser says ("Faerie Queene," iii, 9):

> " For noble Britons sprang from Trojans bold
> And Troy-Novant was built of old Troyes ashes cold."

If any reliance could be placed on this old story the Corporation of London might do well to embody the Labyrinth, or Troy-town, in their armorial bearings, for what symbol could better typify the complexities of our metropolis?

---

[1] Accepted as a historic fact by Mr. E. O. Gordon in his "Prehistoric London."

CHAPTER XXI

LABYRINTH DESIGN AND SOLUTION OF MAZES

THERE is no limit to the number of patterns which, without any metaphorical extension of terms, we may legitimately describe as coming within the scope of the words "maze" and "labyrinth." In common speech we use either word to describe any artificial design or natural pattern presenting a convoluted appearance, or any path or channel of an intricate nature, but when we come to consider the matter more carefully we feel the need for some definition. As we have seen, the dictionaries do not help us much in this respect. Let us, therefore, decide what limitations we feel compelled to observe in our use of the terms from the point of view of designers or unravellers of mazes and labyrinths.

In the first place we must limit ourselves to works of artifice, *i.e.*, we must exclude the "labyrinths" of nature, such as forests, caverns, and so forth, and agree that any application of our terms to such objects is to be regarded as strictly metaphorical.

Secondly, we must require, as a practical corollary to our first condition, that there shall be an element of purposefulness in the design. The purpose may be the portrayal of the imagined course of the sun through the heavens, the symbolisation of the folds of sin or of the Christian's toilsome journey through life, the construction of a puzzle, or the mere pleasure to be derived from packing the maximum of path into the minimum of space, but there must be an object of some sort. The aimless scribblings of an infant, like the trail of an ink-dipped fly, may in this connection be considered as the fortuitous meanderings of nature rather than the conscious design of man. By imposing this condition we exclude the Indian pictograph shown in Fig. 132, which, in the absence of any indication as to its significance, can only by a loose extension of the term be called a labyrinth.

(Our use of the words "aim," "design," and "purpose" will be quite clear to everybody but the sciolist dabbling in metaphysics.)

Thirdly, there must be a certain degree of complexity in the design, a degree which it is manifestly impossible to define as it must be considered in conjunction with other characteristics in any particular case. In the case of a unicursal labyrinth, *i.e.*, one in which there is only one path, the complexity lies in the multiplicity of turnings and the extent of the departure from pure geometrical figures such as the meander, the zigzag, and the spiral; in the case of a puzzle-figure it lies partly in this but partly also in the number and disposition of branch-paths. It naturally follows that in a unicursal design there cannot be absolute symmetry, although, with a little ingenuity, a very pleasing *appearance* of symmetry may be obtained.

Fourthly, there must be communication between the component parts of the design; in other words, the path must be continuous. This does not preclude the occurrence in the design of closed "islands," but only makes it clear that such inclusions do not form part of the labyrinth proper.

Fifthly, there must be communication between the interior and the exterior. We might not altogether withhold the application of the term "labyrinth" or "maze" in the case of a closed design, but we should have to qualify it, *e.g.*, by prefixing the word "closed." In the

183

case of the beautiful and intricate mosaic pavement found in the *Casa del Labirinto* at Pompeii mentioned on page 46, for example, although we know that the pattern was intended to convey an allusion to the Cretan labyrinth, we cannot look upon it as a true labyrinth design; not only is there no communication with the exterior, but by its repetition of purely geometrical design it fails to satisfy our third condition.

If the reader chooses to formulate for himself a working definition based on the above remarks he is at liberty to do so, but he may take for granted that nobody else will accept it. However, he will have gained, at any rate, a clearer conception of the matter than he would perhaps have gathered from any dictionary.

We have seen that mazes and labyrinths may be roughly divided into two types as regards the principle of their design, namely, into *unicursal* and *multicursal* types, or, as some say, into "non-puzzle" and "puzzle" types respectively. The word "unicursal" has hitherto been chiefly used by mathematicians to describe a class of problems dealing with the investigation of the shortest route between two given points or of the method of tracing a route between two points in a given figure without covering any part of the ground more or less than once (*e.g.*, the well-known "bridge" problems), but there is no reason why we should not apply the adjective "unicursal" (="single course" or "once run") to denote those figures which consist of a single unbranched path, using the term "multicursal" as its complement, or antonym. We must not draw too hard a line between these two types; for instance, we could not reasonably insist that the turf maze at Wing (Fig. 60) is multicursal simply on account of the dichotomy of its path to form the central loop. Where the loop is itself relatively large and complex, as in the Poitiers example (Fig. 55), there are better grounds for doing so, but it is plain that in such cases the point is one to be decided by common-sense.

184

Let us consider a little further the various *forms* of labyrinth design and make some sort of a classification.

In the first place we may observe that a labyrinth (using this word, for convenience, as embracing "maze") may be arranged in one plane, as we commonly see it on a sheet of paper, or it may be disposed in two or more intercommunicating planes, like the Egyptian labyrinth or a block of flats. We may thus classify all labyrinths, for a start, as either two-dimensional or three-dimensional. As the vast majority belong to the first class and as, moreover, every subdivision of the first class may be applied equally to the second, we need say no more concerning the latter except to remark that the complexity of a garden maze may be greatly increased, if desired, by introducing tunnels or bridges, thus converting it into a three-dimensional maze.

Another general grouping of labyrinths would be into "compact" and "diffuse" types, the former having, in a typical case, the whole of its area occupied by the convolutions of its path and its bounding walls, the latter having spaces between the bounding walls of the various sections of the path, such spaces having no communication with the path itself. Amongst unicursal labyrinths the Alkborough specimen (Fig. 59) exemplifies the compact type and the Pimperne maze (Fig. 63) the diffuse type.

The Hampton Court maze (Fig. 111) may serve as the type of a compact and the Versailles example (Fig. 88) that of a diffuse multicursal labyrinth.

With regard to the nature of the path itself, we may distinguish broadly between labyrinths with curved and those with straight paths, allowing for an intermediate "mixed" group in which part of the path is curved and part straight. Examples of each kind will be found amongst the figures given.

Multicursal mazes, again, may be subdivided according to the manner of branching of the path, *e.g.*,

185

according to whether the branches are simple or sub-divided (the occurrence of more than one branch at any point may be considered as the case of a subdivided branch), whether the branches do or do not rejoin the main path, forming "loops," and whether—a rather important point as regards the solution of the maze—the "goal" is or is not situated within a loop.

Finally we may create separate classes for those mazes in which there are two or more equivalent routes between the entrance and the goal, those which have two or more entrances, and those in which there is no distinct goal (*e.g.*, the Versailles maze) or in which there are two or more equivalent goals.

We can represent the branch system of any labyrinth whatever in a very simple manner by means of a straight-line diagram, wherein the paths of the labyrinth are represented by lines, to scale if need be, branches being shown to the left or right respectively of the main straight line representing the shortest path from the entrance to the goal. It will be seen that no account is taken of the actual orientation or of changes of direction of any part of the path.

A unicursal labyrinth will thus be represented by a single straight line. Figs. 136 and 137 represent, roughly to scale, the Hampton Court and Hatfield mazes respectively and should be compared with those shown in Figs. 111 and 87. Triangles and discs may be used, as shown, to indicate entrances and goals respectively.

Such diagrams as these are just as useful as the actual plans of the mazes for the purpose of serving as a clue for the visitor; in fact, they are really more easily followed.

Amongst the many speculations that have from time to time been made regarding the origin and significance of the design on the Knossian coins, the suggestion was made by a contributor to *Knowledge* about thirty years ago—somewhat similar theories having been expounded by a German writer a decade earlier—that this figure

186

was a simplified diagram comparable with the diagrams described above. According to this conception the figure was intended as a clue to the actual labyrinth, the designs on the coins being perhaps copied from those on "souvenir" tokens issued by the priests or curators of the edifice, and indicated the right path to be taken, all other paths being omitted. By splitting the circular dividing walls so as to form a passage of the same width as the path shown in the figure, a maze of much more intricate appearance was arrived at, which, it was thought, might

FIG. 136.—Straight-line Diagram, Hampton Court Maze.

FIG. 137.—Straight-line Diagram, Hatfield Maze.

bear some resemblance to the form of the original labyrinth.

On the other hand, Dr. E. Krause, in a book of about the same date, showed how the Knossian design and certain other unicursal figures might be derived from a series of concentric circles, with interruptions along a radial line like the figures in the northern rock engravings described in Chapter XVII, by means of one or two simple methods of cross-connection (Figs. 138 and 139).

Such speculations give food for thought, but we must remember that so far they *are* speculations and not statements of fact.

The use of the straight-line diagrams suggested above may be found helpful not only as a means of facilitating the study of an existing labyrinth, but also to some extent in designing a new one. It is not necessary to describe here in detail how to design a maze:

> " It is purely a matter of skill,
> Which all may attain if they will,"

and, like most tasks requiring simply common-sense, patience, and practice, it is much more trouble to explain than to perform. As regards the design of hedge mazes,

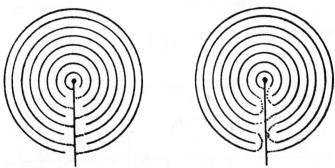

FIGS. 138 and 139.—Derivation of Labyrinth Types from Rock-engraving Figures. (After Krause.)

the fact that the circumstances are hardly ever alike in any two actual cases gives plenty of scope for individuality and ingenuity. The space allowed may be strictly limited, or it may be of an awkward shape. The materials available for the walls may vary widely in character according to the space they require for their proper growth and maintenance, and thus affect the amount of path-area.

There are one or two points which are of general application and should be borne in mind. For instance, if the object of the designer is to provide a maze which shall offer a fair amount of puzzledom without imposing undue fatigue on the visitor, he must take care that the nearest route from the centre to the exterior be neither too long nor too short. If the space to be covered by the maze is large the tendency to over-elaboration of the design must be avoided.

Another feature which is likely to spoil an otherwise good design is the inclusion of long stretches of path without bend or branching; these are tedious and annoying, especially when they have to be retraced by reason of their leading into a *cul-de-sac*.

In a large maze it is well to relieve monotony by means of occasional variations in the mode of treatment of the hedge, the introduction of arbours, statues, etc.; but these should not be of such a character as to defeat one of the main objects of the design by providing easy clues.

If the maze is intended to be seen at all from above, some attempt should be made to introduce a symmetrical and artistic element into its design. Usually some vantage-point is available from which an attendant or expert can observe and direct over-bewildered visitors, but if this point be accessible to the visitors themselves the hedges should be provided with pinnacles or balks, here and there, to prevent the observer from solving the puzzle by unfair means. This is the case with, for instance, the Saffron Walden maze; at Hampton Court, where there are no balks, only the attendant is permitted to mount the rostrum.

The "solution" of mazes means the discovery of a route to their "goal." (This word is preferable to "centre," as the object of quest is not necessarily at the geometrical centre of the maze, but may be considerably removed from it.)

It would be going too far to say the *shortest* route, as this would be discoverable only from the plan or by prolonged experience, but the goal in any maze will on the average be reached more certainly and quickly by observing a little method than by fortuitous wandering.

The subject of the solution of mazes has been examined by various mathematicians, in their lighter moods, but we need not burden ourselves with more than a few simple considerations.

In most cases it is not practicable to adopt a system of marking the various paths as we reach them, but if this be permitted we can so arrange our marks that we need never traverse any portion of the path more than twice—*i.e.*, once in each direction—so that in any finite maze we must eventually arrive at the goal, though not necessarily by the shortest route.

Using the word *node* to signify a point of branching, and the terms *odd* and *even* to describe respectively those nodes at which odd or even numbers of paths are to be found, we see that there must be at least three paths meeting at a point to form a node, for two paths meeting at a point constitute only a change of direction of the path without formation of branches, whilst the arrival of one path only at a point also precludes the idea of "branching" at that point, and can only occur at the end of a blind alley, at the entrance of the maze, or at the goal. We find it convenient, however, to regard the latter arrangement as an odd node of the lowest order, the lowest possible order of even nodes being, of course, that at the meeting of four paths.

It will be clear that if the entrance and the goal are the only odd nodes the maze will either be unicursal, in the sense in which we have been using the term, or any branches must form loops on the main route; in either case it will be possible to traverse the maze unicursally, *i.e.*, to thread every portion of the path without going over any part twice.

Supposing that we are able to make what marks we like, without danger of their removal in our absence, we can adopt the following plan:

On arriving at a node which, by the absence of marks, you know you have not already visited, mark the path by which you have just arrived by three marks; if you see by marks on other paths that you have already been to that node, mark the arrival path with one mark only. If now there are no unmarked paths at this node, it means that you have explored this particular branch-system and must retrace your steps by the path by which you have arrived. If, however, there are one or more unmarked paths leading from the node, select one of them, and, as you enter it, mark it with two marks.

We can now make certain of visiting every part of the maze if we make it a rule that, on arrival at a node, we shall never take a path with three marks unless there are no paths unmarked or with one mark only. When we enter a one-mark path, we of course add the two marks which we always make on leaving a node, and thus it becomes a three-mark path at that node.

When it is impracticable to place marks, or even to use, like Theseus, a clue of thread, it is still possible in the majority of cases to make certain of finding the goal by the simple expedient of placing one hand on the hedge on entering the maze, and consistently following the hedge around, keeping contact all the time with the same hand. Blind turnings present no difficulty, as they will only be traversed first in one direction and then in the other. The traveller being guided by his contact with the hedge alone is relieved of all necessity for making a choice of paths when arriving at the nodes.

The only case in which this method breaks down is that in which the goal is situated anywhere within a loop. Where this occurs the explorer adopting the method described will discover the fact by finding himself eventually back at the starting-point without having visited the goal. He must then adopt different tactics, but unless it is practicable to use a clue or a system of marks like that detailed above there is no rule that will help him. One may, of course, thread the maze by remembering a formula of some sort applicable to that particular maze, *e.g.*, in the case of Hampton Court, "Left, right, right, left, left, left, left," but this is equivalent to having a plan of the maze. Such mnemonics, unless perfectly retained, are apt to prove more of a nuisance than a help.

Can anybody who has once yielded to the exuberant mirth of "Three Men in a Boat" forget the predicament of the over-confident Harris when he volunteered to conduct a party, strangers as well, through the Hampton Court maze? "We'll just go in here," he said, "so that you can say you've been, but it's very simple. It's absurd to call it a maze. You keep on taking the first turning to the right. We'll just walk round for ten minutes and then go and get some lunch." Poor Harris!

CHAPTER XXII

THE LABYRINTH IN LITERATURE

THE romantic and mysterious flavour of the words "maze" and "labyrinth" has induced many a writer of fiction to adopt one or the other as the theme of a story, or as the setting of some of the action in a story, or else to use the name as an attractive symbolical title for a work.

We have several times already had occasion to refer to instances of this kind in the course of our survey, but the reader may have sufficient patience to support the enumeration of a few more, not by any means exhaustive, examples.

In most cases where the words are used in book-titles it is perhaps the allegorical rather than the romantic element which is in requisition, though truly the two are never far apart.

The Spanish poet Juan de Mena, in the fifteenth century, was inspired by Dante's "Divina Commedia" to compose a ponderous allegorical poem which he named "El Laberinto." This was published in Seville in 1496 and was a queer mixture of theology, astrology, and universal history. In it the poet is shown as being guided by a beautiful woman, symbolising Divine Providence, through three vast concentric circular regions, representing respectively the past, the present, and the future. These are somehow involved with the seven planets, after which the seven divisions of the poem are named.

193

No doubt there were at that time many folk to whom such a work made a strong appeal, but it was evidently not the kind of book that we should nowadays choose to take away for a holiday.

A few years after its publication a French bard, Jean Bouchet by name, jealous perhaps for the reputation of his native art, cast upon the astonished world a mythical epic of between four and five thousand verses, entitled "Le Labyrinthe de Fortune." In this case the guide is a female representing Illusion, and her aim seems to have been to impress the poet, and through him the less gifted mortals, with the total instability and evanescence of everything pertaining to humanity.

An "allegorical labyrinth" printed at Lyons in 1769 —the period, it will be remembered, at which some of the finest cathedral labyrinths were destroyed—must have been the ancestor of some of the Sunday School pictures of our early youth. It depicted "the spiritual labyrinth ornamented with four channels of grace representing (*a*) the four rivers of the Earthly Paradise and the happy state of Man before the Fall; (*b*) by divers convolutions, the various miseries with which human life has since been beset; (*c*) by the fact of the labyrinth terminating at the same point as that from which it starts, we see how Man, being formed of earth, returns, as to his first principle, by the decay of the body; (*d*) the health-giving waters of these channels represent the grace of God in which the depraved soul finds its remedy." This pious chart is signed "BELION *fecit*."

The curious jumble of crude imagery shown in Fig. 140 is reproduced from the heading to a long set of allegorical verses in German, published about 1630. The King referred to in the title is thought to be Frederick I of Bohemia.

When touching upon the question of etymology we made reference to the theological "Treatise against the Four Labyrinths of France," by Walter of St. Victor.

194

Gerechter Wegweiſer deß irrländiſchen Königs auß dem
Prageriſchen Thiergarten.

Fig. 140.   Allegorical Labyrinth.   (German Print, *circ.* 1630)

We find the word used in this sense of verbal or mental entanglements in theological matters as the title of a book written some five centuries later by Thomas Carwell (*alias* Thorold). The full title of this work, which was printed in Paris in 1658, is: "Labyrinthus Cantuarensis; or Doctor Lawd's Labyrinth. Beeing an answer to the late Archbishop of Canterburies relation of a conference between himself and Mr. Fisher, etc. Wherein the true grounds of the Roman Catholique religion are asserted, the principall controuersies betwixt Catholiques and Protestants thoroughly examined, and the Bishops meandrick windings throughout his whole worke layd open to publique view."

"Labyrinthus," according to Hazlitt's Bibliographical Collections, was the name of a Latin comedy performed at Cambridge before King James I. Perhaps this had some connection with that play which Pepys mentions in his Diary on May 2, 1684: "By coach to the King's Playhouse to see 'The Labyrinth' . . . the poorest play, methinks, that ever I saw, there being nothing in it but the odd accidents that fell out, by a lady's being bred up in man's apparel and a man in a woman's."

In some cases the use of the word "labyrinth" in a book-title seems to suggest that the term was regarded as an equivalent for "Thesaurus" or "Compendium of Knowledge" in respect of any particular branch of learning. This is the case in the "Gardener's Labyrinth" of Didymus Mountayne (Thomas Hill), to which we referred in Chapter XIII. The title has no reference to the discourse on mazes which occupies a small section of the book, but simply means the gardener's book of instructions or *vade mecum*. Much the same meaning is conveyed also by the title of a rather earlier book, the "Labyrinthus Medicorum Errantium" or "Labyrinth of Lost Physicians," which was one of the last works of the great Swiss doctor and alchemist Paracelsus, and was published in 1553, twelve years after his death. The

195

Polish educational reformer Komensky, better known as Comenius (1592–1671), likewise published a "Labyrinthus" of this kind. An English translation of it was printed early in the present century under the title of "The Labyrinth of the World and the Paradise of the Heart."

The "Labyrinthus" or "Laborintus" ascribed to the monk Eberhard of Bethune, who wrote in A.D. 1212 or thereabouts, is an elaborate and critical treatise on poetry and pedagogics; it is alternatively entitled "De Miseriis Rectorum Scholarum," and its reiterated plaints on the woes of the schoolmaster should find an echo in the heart of many a present-day instructor of youth.

"*Love* in these labyrinths his slaves detains," sang Pope; but he was only making use of an old and well-worn metaphor, which we mention at the moment because it has so often figured in book-titles. In 1593 Dr. G. Fletcher, uncle of the dramatist, wrote a poem of ingenious form entitled "A Lover's Maze." A similar title, "Love in a Maze," was given by Shirley to one of his plays, a performance of which was witnessed by Pepys on May 22, 1662. "The play hath little in it," says Pepys, "but Lacy's part of a country fellow, which he did to admiration." In 1611 a suite of poems entitled "Le Labyrinthe d'Amour" was published by a French poet, who modestly veiled his identity behind the initials "H. F. S. D. C." A century and a half later another French writer, equally retiring—his initials were "T. M."—wrote an *opéra comique* of the same name.

One would almost think that there was something shameful or dangerous in allowing one's identity to be revealed in connection with works bearing such titles, for we find the same desire for anonymity in the writer of some poems entitled "The Maze" which appeared in 1815, headed by a quotation from Cowper:

> " . . . to and fro,
>   Caught in a labyrinth you go."

That the maze or labyrinth has not lost its favour as either a descriptive or a metaphorical book-title is testified by the numerous modern examples of its use, amongst which we may mention Mrs. Henry Wood's "Within the Maze," "The Maze of Scilly," by E. J. Tiddy, "The Maze," by A. L. Stewart, "The Labyrinth," by R. Murray Gilchrist (perhaps in this case the reference is to the rambling old House with Eleven Staircases which features largely in the book), and finally, as an instance of undeniable descriptiveness, "The Physiology of the Human Labyrinth," by S. Scott. We have already made mention of O. W. F. Lodge's play, "The Labyrinth," when speaking of Fair Rosamond (Chap. XIX). The same title has recently been bestowed on one of a series of fanciful prose sketches by Mr. Martin Armstrong published collectively as "The Puppet Show."

The Italian aviator-poet Gabriele d'Annunzio, whose inconvenient conception of patriotism has proved such a source of embarrassment to his country since the war, has adopted as a most attractive and appropriate cover-design for his novel "Forse che si, forse che no" ("Perhaps yes, perhaps no") a conventional square unicursal labyrinth, the path of which is occupied by several repetitions, in block capitals, of the title of the book. The title on the wrapper of a recent novel by Miss Isabel Ostrander is accompanied by an effective design in which a female figure is seen against a background consisting of a plan of the Hampton Court maze.

Mr. Rudyard Kipling, in that curious collection of inconsequential whimsicalities which he calls the "Just so Stories," shows a queer sort of labyrinthine contrivance in his illustration to the story of "The Crab that Played," referring to it in the text as "the Big Miz-Maze."

Lest any reader who happens to be unacquainted with Sir A. T. Quiller-Couch's novel "Troy Town" should be misled by the title into antiquarian expectations, we

197

may as well remark that it has no more connection with "turf mazes" than had the famous racehorse of the same name that came to a sad end in 1920—even less, in a manner of speaking. It has reference to the same Cornish seaport as his "Mayor of Troy," that Mayor who was so popular with the townsfolk that in the next year they made him an Ex-Mayor.

The vogue of allegory and extravagant symbolism which flourished in the sixteenth and seventeenth centuries was evidenced by the appearance of numbers of little books of "emblems," mainly based upon those of Andrea Alciati (1492–1550), and, as might well be expected, the labyrinth furnished many an inspiration to the compilers of these works. The emblem books of the Dutchman Jacob Cats, for example, and of our own poet Francis Quarles (1592–1644), were, like those of Alciati himself, enormously popular and ran through very many editions, not only in the native tongues of their authors but in most of the languages of Europe.

We have already, in Chapter XII, drawn attention to a labyrinth-emblem in the collection of the French writer Claude Paradin. A labyrinth of a different type appears in the "Emblems" of Quarles (e.g., in the 1635 edition, bk. iv, no. 2). In this case we are shown a woman walking away from the centre of what looks like a tall hedge maze, which has its path on the top of the hedge! With one hand she holds a staff and in the other a cord, the distant end of which is held by an angel located at the summit of a round tower some way off. A winding path proceeds from this tower to the gateway of the labyrinth. Here and there one sees unfortunate beings who are slipping from the wall into the deep crevasses below. A quotation from the Psalms, in Latin and in English, accompanies this figure: "Oh that my Wayes were directed to keep Thy Statutes." The labyrinth shown in most of the other emblem-books, where one occurs at all, is a very poor affair and looks rather like a low, flat fortress or an

198

inverted cake-tin. A more realistic arrangement, however, appears in the collection of Jacob Cats.

The Hampton Court maze has more than once figured in literature. One appearance we have already noticed at the end of the preceding chapter; another, of a totally different character, we cull from the *British Magazine* for 1747. Few people, one would imagine, look upon a visit to this popular resort as an occasion for melancholy meditations, or for chanting moral dirges, but a foreigner might well be excused for reading the following lines as a justification of the reproach that Englishmen take their pleasures sadly.

Reflections on Walking in the Maze at
Hampton Court.

" What is this mighty labyrinth—the earth,
   But a wild maze the moment of our birth ?
   Still as we life pursue the maze extends,
   Nor find we where each winding purlieu ends;
   Crooked and vague each step of life we tread,—
   Unseen the danger, we escape the dread!
   But with delight we through the labyrinth range,
   Confused we turn, and view each artful change—
   Bewildered, through each wild meander bend
   Our wandering steps, anxious to gain the end;
   Unknown and intricate, we still pursue
   A certain path, uncertain of the clue;
   Like hoodwinked fools, perplex'd we grope our way
   And during life's short course we blindly stray,
   Puzzled in mazes and perplex'd with fears;
   Unknown alike both heaven and earth appears.
   Till at the last, to banish our surprise,
   Grim Death unbinds the napkin from our eyes.
   Then shall GAY's truth and wisdom stand confest,
   And *Death* will shew us *Life* was but a jest."

This genial gem should be engraved on brass and stuck up at the entrance to ensure that visitors, especially those of tender age, may enter the maze in the right spirit!

Scarcely more cheerful is the view regarding mazes taken by "The Poet" in Alfred Austin's "The Garden that I Love," where he speaks of

"tragic gardens, with dark avenues of intertwisted ilexes immeasurably old, where there might be lurking the emissary of an ambitious d'Este; gloomy labyrinths of mediaeval yew concealing the panther-spring of a vindictive Sforza or the self-handled stiletto of a fratricidal Borgia. . . ."

And again:

> "Had I a garden, claustral yews
> Should shut out railing wind,
> That Poets might on sadness muse
> With a majestic mind."

If space permitted, or if any useful purpose were served, a good deal more might be written concerning the Labyrinth in relation to Literature. Similarly, the Labyrinth in Art might form the subject of a fairly bulky volume. A considerable amount of space could be taken up with the speculations that have been made as to the probable relationship of the Knossian design to the Cross, the Swastika—with its variants, the Triskelion and the Tetraskelion—the Circle, the Spiral, and so forth; but the reader who thirsts for discussions of this nature must be referred to more specialised archaeological literature. The main points of interest with regard to the use of the labyrinth figure in Art have already been presented, and most of the lines along which the labyrinth idea has been elaborated have been indicated, either in the text or in the illustrations. Before finally taking leave of our theme, however, there are yet a few miscellaneous aspects of it at which we may take a glance.

CHAPTER XXIII

MISCELLANEA AND CONCLUSION

In the *Annales Archéologiques* for 1857 it was stated that M. Bonnin, of Evreux, had collected no less than 200 designs of mazes or labyrinths, representative of all sorts of nations and periods, and the editor promised to make a selection of these for reproduction as soon as the text to accompany them should be ready. The editor of the *Annales* incidentally referred to an early sixteenth-century painting on wood, in the palace of the Marquis Campana, which represented the legend of Theseus and showed a labyrinth similar to that of St. Maria in Aquiro at Rome. This also was to have been illustrated at the same time. The matter seems to have rested there, however, for no subsequent reference appeared.

As an instance of the unlikely places in which the employment of labyrinth figures for decorative or symbolic purposes are sometimes found, we may quote an entry which occurs in an inventory of the contents of a house at Duffus, Morayshire, dated May 25, 1708, from which it would appear that household napery, at that time, was sometimes patterned with the labyrinth:

"*In the Nurserie.* A large neprie press, wherein there is six pair Scots holland sheits . . . three fyn towels and five of the walls of troy."

Mr. Albert Way, in his notes to Dr. Trollope's memoir on Labyrinths in 1858, after referring to the popularity of mazes and "Troy-towns" in Scotland, mentions a labyrinth incised on the stone bench in one of the window recesses of the hall at Craigmillar Castle.

According to a Swedish publication of 1877, labyrinths have been found in West Gothland engraved on church bells!

The hedge maze is, of course, the chief embodiment of the labyrinth idea as a medium of amusement, but it is far from being the only form in which the principle subserves this purpose.

We have already referred to the practice, noted in various parts of England and Wales, of cutting "Troy-towns" in the turf. Most of us are, moreover, familiar with the schoolboy pastime of drawing mazes on paper, or on slates in the days before they were banished on hygienic grounds; the object of the designer in this case differing from that of the Troy-town constructors in that it consists of providing as difficult a puzzle as one's ingenuity at the moment can devise, whereas the latter merely laid out a conventional unicursal figure for the purpose of performing a ceremonial or playing a game thereon, like the squares for nine-men's morris or the diagram for hop-scotch.

An ingenious development of the hedge maze principle is the construction of indoor mazes lined with mirrors, by means of which the perplexity of the visitor is very greatly increased. Such "mirror mazes" often find a place in fairs and exhibitions.

Another method of utilising the puzzle-maze idea, and one which constitutes a valuable asset to the parent or nurse in charge of young children at the sea-side, is that of scratching maze-figures on the sands, of sufficient dimensions to enable little feet to perambulate the paths. Figures 141 and 142 show some of the mazes constructed on the sands of a well-known southern resort in the summer of 1920. The examples shown were made in a quiet corner of the beach and were "snapped" before

[Photo: W.H.M.

Fig. 141.　Sea-Side Sand Maze.

[Photo: W.H.M

Fig. 142.　Sea-Side Sand Maze.

the children had discovered them; otherwise, although no doubt prettier pictures would have resulted, the mazes would have been invisible.

Figure 143 shows the plan of a small temporary maze constructed by the writer for a garden fête held in aid of local church funds in the grounds of Mr. Kenneth Goschen, at Eastcote, Middlesex, on May 25, 1921. It was formed of galvanised-wire netting supported on six-foot fir stakes and thickened with elm foliage. At the entrance was displayed a conventional labyrinth design,

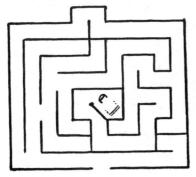

Scale |⌐⌐⌐⌐⌐⌐⌐| yards.

FIG. 143.—Temporary Maze at Village Fête. (W. H. M.)

slightly modified to convey the misleading suggestion that it was a key to the maze, and below this were the following lines :

Beware the dreadful Minotaur
That dwells within the Maze.
The monster feasts on human gore
And bones of those he slays.
Then softly through the labyrinth creep
And rouse him not to strife.
Take one short peep, prepare to leap
And run to save your life !

At the goal was placed a chair facing an embowered mirror.

203

Some readers may remember the publication many years ago of highly coloured lithographs of mazes, of bizarre design, generally emanating from the Continent and sold for a penny or twopence. An old scrap-book seen by the writer contains some specimens of this nature, published in Brussels. In some the "nodes" are occupied by various objects which, according to the printed instructions, have to be visited in a given order. One design, generously tinted in all the colours of the spectrum, is labelled "Le Jardin Chinois," although there is nothing distinctively Chinese about it except the absence of all resemblance to anything European. One may still purchase in the toy-shops coloured labyrinths of this kind, mounted on cardboard, with spaces at various points of the path for the accommodation of counters, which are moved progressively in accordance with the throws of dice by the competing players.

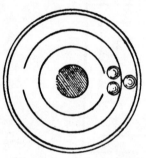

FIG. 144.—Maze Toy by A. Brentano. (After Patent Specification.)

Some very ingenious applications of the labyrinth idea have been evolved by modern designers of toys and games.

Perhaps the most popular toy of this nature on the market is that of the "Pigs in Clover" type, consisting of a series of concentric interrupted circular walls, the innermost of which constitutes the goal into which the player strives to roll all the marbles—usually three in number —which are seen through the glass cover (Fig. 144). This toy was patented by A. Brentano in 1889. Some skill is required to get all the marbles into the central compartment at the same time. Another toy of this character is seen in Fig. 145. It consists of a rather complicated maze formed of ridges, between which the player

204

rolls a ball or a globule of mercury from the point marked A to that marked B, or *vice versa*. This was patented by S. D. Nix in 1891.

A somewhat similar arrangement, but with the addition of magnetism as the motive force, is that devised by J. M. Arnot in 1894, and shown in Fig. 146. In this

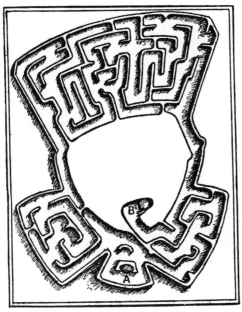

FIG. 145.—Maze Toy by S. D. Nix. (After Patent Specification.)

case the maze is not flat but is in the form of a shallow dome; the balls are of iron and are rolled not by tilting the box but by moving a magnet beneath it.

R. A. Cuthbert and W. Bevitt patented in 1889 a toy in which a ball, called "The Man in the Maze," is rolled about inside a small closed box, the internal partitions of which cannot be seen but are indicated on the outside of the case. The "Man" is invisible during his journey.

At about the same time a somewhat similar toy was brought out by J. Proctor, in which, however, the travelling ball can be watched through the glass top, the puzzle element in this case consisting of the use of circular holes of two sizes for communicating between adjacent compartments, one size being just large enough to permit of the passage of the ball, the other just too small (Fig. 147).

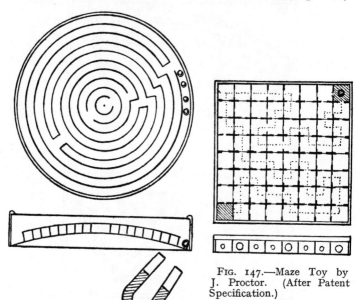

FIG. 147.—Maze Toy by J. Proctor. (After Patent Specification.)

FIG. 146.—Maze Toy by J. M. Arnot. (After Patent Specification.)

The most complex puzzle of the kind so far produced is that patented by H. Bridge in 1906 and shown in Fig. 148. The ball in this case is made to pass through channels formed between projections of labyrinthine pattern fixed to a base and others fixed to the transparent top, which can be moved relatively to the base. The toy may be of a circular pattern or rectangular. In the former case the top is rotated, in the latter it is slid from side to side. The patent also covers cases in which the toy is constructed on the "skeleton" principle, the use of

FIG. 148.—Maze Toy by H. Bridge. (After Patent Specification.)

207

a ring in place of a ball, and the combination of more than two mazes.

It now remains for some inventor of Einsteinian proclivities to devise one in several dimensions!

An interesting little study in what one might call "Labyrinth Psychology" was carried out by an Austrian biologist in connection with his researches on "The Evolution of Efficiency in the Animal Kingdom," in 1917. This was a series of experiments to test the efficiency of animals in learning to thread a labyrinth in search of food. Figs. 149, 150 and 151 show three stages in the

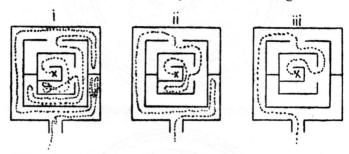

FIGS. 149, 150 and 151.—Path of Rat in Labyrinth ; three stages.
(Szymanski.)

education of a rat in this respect, the dotted line representing the track followed by the animal from the entrance to the food-containing centre of a simple form of labyrinth.

Some sort of game, known as "Labyrinthe," enjoyed a passing favour in France in the eighteenth century. An advertisement of May 8, 1869, referring to one offered for sale by a Parisian upholsterer named Lechevin, describes it as "un jeu de labyrinthe a 11 cases doré d'or moulu, avec tableau dans chaque case," but this does not tell us much concerning the nature of the pastime.

A card game of similar name was played in this country half a century ago; it was a kind of bezique.

In France the name "Labyrinthe" is also given to a
208

children's game in which the majority of the players hold hands so as to form a chain of arches which are threaded by two runners called respectively *le tisserand* and *la navette*—"the weaver" and "the shuttle."

A visitor to the Latin Convent on the summit of Mount Carmel, Palestine, in 1874, described a "verbal labyrinth" which he saw displayed on a board hanging on the wall of an inner staircase. It was called "The Labyrinth of St. Bernard," and consisted of a number of words or short phrases arranged in a square, as shown below. By selecting the words in the proper order five maxims are obtained "by which man may live well." The first of these maxims, commencing with the word at the foot of the left-hand column, is: *Noli dicere omnia quae scis quia qui dicit omnia quae scit saepe audit quod non vult.*

The remaining four injunctions may be read by similarly utilising the words in the bottom row with those in the second, third, fourth, and fifth rows respectively:

LABYRINTHUS A DIVO BERNARDO
COMPOSITUS QUO BENE VIVIT HOMO

DICERE	SCIS	DICIT	SCIT	AUDIT	NON	VULT
FACERE	POTES	FACIT	POTEST	INCURRIT	NON	CREDIT
CREDERE	AUDIS	CREDIT	AUDIT	CREDIT	NON	EST
DARE	HABES	DAT	HABET	MISERE QUAERIT	NON	HABET
JUDICARE	VIDES	JUDICAT	VIDET	CON-TEMNIT	NON	DEBET
NOLI	OMNIA QUAE	QUIA QUI	OMNIA QUAE	SAEPE	QUOD	

As a sample of a verbal labyrinth this seems to be very simple and straightforward in comparison with the average Act of Parliament.

Let us turn now, for a brief space, to a question which, although bearing upon matters dealt with earlier in the book, has been too little investigated to warrant more than a nodding reference in our more serious chapters— the question of place-names.

The occurrence of a suggestive place-name is, as previously hinted, very slender evidence by itself on which to form an opinion of the former existence of a maze in the locality. There is always the possibility that the name may be a corruption of some ancient word of very different significance, perhaps the name of some person, or that it may have been bestowed fancifully or in respect of some resemblance to another place.

In the absence of fuller information we will limit ourselves to the bare mention of such names as convey a suggestion of possible maze sites, merely remarking any cases in which evidence in one direction or the other has come to notice.

The district known as Maze Pond, familiar to Londoners in the neighbourhood of the Borough, and to which we made reference in Chapter XV, takes its name from the ancient manor of the Maze, which was in the holding of Sir John Burcestre in the fifteenth century. An old token bears the inscription, "Michael Blower, at ye Maze, Southwarke." What kind of maze, if any, formerly existed in the locality we do not know.

Maze Hill has sometimes been assumed to derive its name from a maze which is supposed to have existed in the park of the former royal palace of Greenwich (see p. 136), but the name was formerly spelt in a different manner and may have quite another origin. In Hasted's "History of Kent," 1778, it is referred to as Mease Hill, and it has been suggested that this may have come from the Celtic word *Maes*, meaning "field." There is a Maze Green in Hertfordshire, near Bishops Stortford. Possibly there was formerly a turf maze in the vicinity like that on

Saffron Walden common, not very far away, but we have no evidence to that effect.

A few miles west of Lisburn, in Ireland, are two places named respectively "The Maze" and "Mazetown," the former a small village in Antrim, the latter a racing centre just over the county border in Down.

"Troy-town," as we have seen, also occurs as a place-name. In Dorset there is one near Dorchester and another near Bere Regis. These are alleged to be the sites of former turf mazes, of which, however, there are no authentic records. In Kent there is one near Hasting-leigh, and the name also occurs at Rochester.[1] The latter is said to commemorate a former owner or builder of property in that part of the town, whose name happened to be Troy. A part of Peckham also used to be known as Troy-town.

The word "Troy" alone is also of fairly frequent occurrence, as for instance near Stalybridge, Lancs, and near Londonderry; Troy Michell and Troy Hall are found in Monmouthshire, and the latter name also at Blackburn, Lancs, but such names are no more likely to have any connection with ancient maze sites than is the flourishing city of similar name in the United States, the probability being that in all these cases it is the famous Troy of the Iliad that furnished the inspiration. The name of Troy-town may in some cases have been given on account of irregularity or intricacy of design, for the word is found in certain local dialects as a synonym for a state of confusion, an untidy house being said to be "just like Troy-town."

It is surely uncommon for the word "Labyrinth" itself to be found as a place-name, but in February 1911 Captain Scott pitched his camp in an Antarctic spot which, on account of the fantastically sinuous nature of its surroundings, he decided to name "Labyrinth Camp."

[1] See also p. 91.

We must now draw to a close.

Enough has perhaps been said to give some idea of the variety and extent of the different ways in which the labyrinth idea has developed and in which it has been employed, but it would obviously be wrong to assume that the last word on the subject has now been pronounced.

As regards the early history of the idea and of the terms associated with it we have seen that the boundaries of our knowledge are still misty and ill-defined, a circumstance that only gives zest to the study of the subject.

We see that our enquiry has taken us into realms far removed from everyday experience and in which we feel the need of special training in order to weigh the facts presented. It has given us glimpses of the workshop of the archaeologist, the anthropologist, and the etymologist.

The study of later developments has led us into curious by-paths of art and literature—classical, mediaeval, renaissance, and modern—and we see that even now the labyrinth idea has not entirely ceased to exercise its allurements or to evoke the spirit of invention.

There is still room for a good deal of research and for the possibility of highly interesting discoveries in respect of almost every phase of the labyrinth's past history.

With regard to its future developments, much as we should have liked to close our review with a vindication of utilitarian interest, and although one can never safely prophesy to what uses the ingenuity of men may put any given principle, we could not hope to sound an expectant note without creating an impression of fatuity. Lest this statement be taken to mean that our enquiry has, therefore, had no practical aim, let us hasten to repeat once more the hope expressed in our introductory chapter to the effect that a perusal of this little book will at least ensure a revival of interest in, and consequently the preservation of, those few relics of rustic revelry and prehistoric magic which yet remain with us in the shape of the turf labyrinths.

As Mr. A. H. Allcroft, in his "Earthwork of England" (1908), has truly remarked, when speaking of the Asenby maze: "It is marvellous that the memory of such things, once prominent features of rural life, can die out so rapidly as it does." And yet, who can deny that they are worthy of at least as much care and interest as many of the obvious and commonplace antiquities upon which the guide-books lavish their encomiums?

We need not emulate the misguided enthusiasm of those who are unable to discover a merit in a bygone practice without plunging into an indiscriminate advocacy of its revival—an enthusiasm which inevitably brings discredit upon its object—but let us at any rate see to it that no more of these rare and interesting heirlooms are lost to us through ignorance or neglect.

APPENDIX

BIBLIOGRAPHY OF MAZES AND LABYRINTHS

(TOGETHER WITH NAMES OF PERSONS WHO HAVE FURNISHED THE WRITER WITH FIRST-HAND INFORMATION)

NOTE.—*Names of Authors are also arranged alphabetically in the Index, which contains detailed references to the sections of the Bibliography.*

I. GENERAL

TROLLOPE, E. "Ancient and Mediaeval Labyrinths," with notes by ALBERT WAY, in *Archaeological Journal*, Vol. XV, 1858. Also in *Reports of the Associated Architectural Societies* in 1858, and appended to a paper on the Caerleon mosaic in the *Proc. Monmouth and Caerleon Antiquarian Association*, 1866.

(Mainly concerned with church labyrinths and British turf mazes.)

DE LAUNAY, R. "Les Fallacieux Détours du Labyrinthe" in *Révue Archéologique*, Series V, 1915-16.

(A bold and striking essay, chiefly concerned with the labyrinth as the architectural expression of a sun-myth.)

FRAZER, Sir J. G. "The Golden Bough," Pt. III, "The Dying God," 1911.

(In the section dealing with the octennial tenure of the kingship the labyrinth is treated from the point of view of the anthropologist and folk-lorist.)

Cook, A. B. "Zeus. A Study in Ancient Religions," 1914.
(The labyrinth, particularly that of Crete, is studied from the point of view of the classical archaeologist.)

Krause, Ernst. "Die Trojaburgen Nordeuropas" and "Die Nordische Herkunft der Trojasage," Glogau, 1893. Also "Tuiskoland der Arischen Stämme und Götter Urheimat," 1891.
(A study of classic and northern mythologies with special reference to solar rites. The labyrinth is held to be distinctively northern, the classic legends being derivative.)

Massmann, H. F. "Wunderkreise und Irrgarten," Leipzig Basse, 1844.
(This work is mentioned in a German encyclopaedia, but the writer has not been able to obtain access to a copy. Written by a mathematician, it probably deals with the subject from a corresponding aspect.)

Daremberg, Saglio & Pottier. "Dictionnaire des Antiquités," 1904, Vol. III.
(The article "Labyrinthe" gives very full references to the occurrence of labyrinth figures on ancient monuments.)

Dictionary of Architecture (1867). Arts. "Maze" and "Meander."

Encyclopaedia Britannica. Art. "Labyrinth." By Thos. Moore, F.L.S. (1821–87) (with especial reference to hedge mazes).
(Several other encyclopaedias, American, French, German and Italian, also contain good articles on the subject, notably Larousse, La Grande Encyclopédie, The New International Encyclopaedia, and Roscher's Lexikon de Mythologie, Vol. II, 1894–7.)

"Country Life." Two well-illustrated anonymous articles in issues of January 24 and March 14, 1903.

There is a popular article on Mazes by G. S. Tyack in W. Andrews's "Ecclesiastical Curiosities," 1897 ; and a chapter of E. O. Gordon's "Prehistoric London," 1914, treats of the matter in so far as it supports the theory of the Trojan origin of London (Troy-Novant).

216

II. FORM, AND MATHEMATICAL PRINCIPLES

BALL, W. W. R. "Mathematical Recreations and Essays," 1905, pp. 174–80.

TARRY, G. "Le Problème des Labyrinthes," in *Nouvelles Annales de Mathématiques*, Vol. XIV, 1895, pp. 187–90.

LUCAS, E. "Récréations Mathématiques," 1882–94.

WOLTERS, P. "Darstellungen des Labyrinths," in *Sitzungsberichte der phil.*, *&c., Classe der k.b. Akademie zu München*, 1907.

MEYER, W. "Ein Labyrinth mit Versen" in *Sitz. der phil.*, *&c., Classe der k.b. Ak. zu München*, 1882, Bd. II, Heft. I, pp. 267–300, and *Nachtrag* on p. 400.

KRAUSE, E. "Die nordische Herkunft der Trojasage," 1893. (Shows how typical labyrinth figures may be derived from Northumbrian rock engravings.)

REINACH, S. "Cultes, Mythes, et Réligions," 1906, Vol. II, pp. 234, etc.
(Derivation of swastika, triskelion, etc.)

DUDENEY, H. E. "Amusements in Mathematics," 1917, pp. 127–37.

INWARDS, R., on the Labyrinth on the Coins of Knossos in *Knowledge*, October 1892.

III. THE CLASSIC LABYRINTHS

(i) THE EGYPTIAN LABYRINTH

HERODOTUS. ii. 148–9.

DIODORUS SICULUS. I. iv. 61, 66.

STRABO. XVII. i. 37.

POMPONIUS MELA. "De situ orbis."

PLINY. "Hist. Nat." xxxvi. 19.

PETRIE, W. M. FLINDERS. "The Labyrinth, Gerzeh, and Mazghuneh" (London School of Archaeology in Egypt, University College, Gower St.), 1912. Also "Kahun, Garob, and Hawara," 1890, and "Hawara, Biahmu, and Arsinoë," 1889.

217

How, W. W., and WELLS, J. "A Commentary on Herodotus," 1912, Vol. I. p. 240, etc.

MYRES, J. L., in *Annals of Archaeology and Anthropology*, III.
p. 134.

PERROT & CHIPIEZ. "Histoire de l'Art dans l'Antiquité"
I. ("Egypte").

FERGUSSON'S "History of Architecture," 1893, Vol. I.
pp. 110-12.

LEPSIUS, K. R. "Denkmäler," 1859, Vol. I. pl. 46-8.

EBERS, G. M. "L'Egypte, du Caire à Philae," 1868, p. 174.

WIEDEMANN, A. "Herodots Zweite Buch," 1890, p. 522, etc.

CANINA, L. "L'Architettura Antica," 1839-44, Sec. I.
(Egiziana), Tav. 122.

JOMARD, E. F. "Description de l'Egypte," 1807. Vol. IV.
p. 478.

   (Embodies results of Napoleon's expedition.)

POCOCKE, R. "A Description of the East," 1743, p. 61, etc.

LUCAS, P. "Voiage de la Haute Egypte," 1705. Vol. II. p. 261,
etc.

CARERI, J. F. GEMELLI. "A Voyage round the World,"
1699. Bk. I. Ch. vi. (in Churchill's Collection, 1732,
Vol. VI).

(ii) THE CRETAN LABYRINTH

VIRGIL. "Aeneid," V. v. 588.

PLINY. "Hist. Nat." xxxvi. 19.

OVID. "Metamorphoses," VIII. v. 159.

DIODORUS SICULUS. IV. iv. 77.

APOLLODORUS. III. i. 3, xv. 8.

PLUTARCH. "Life of Theseus."

MEURSIUS, J. (GRAEVIUS, J. G.). "Creta, Cyprus et Rhodus."
Amsterdam, 1675.

   (Gives very comprehensive references to the Cretan
Labyrinth in classical and mediaeval literature.)

EVANS, Sir A. J. "Excavations at Knossos," in *Annals of the
British School at Athens*, Vol. VIII, 1902. "Mycenaean
Tree and Pillar Cult" in *Journal of Hellenic Studies*,
Vol. XXI, 1901. "The Tomb of the Double Axes at
Knossos" in *Archaeologia*, Vol. LXV, 1914. "The Palace

of Minos at Knossos," Vol. I, 1921. Article in *The Times* of July 14, 1922, p. 11.

Rouse, W. H. D. "The Double Axe and the Labyrinth" in *Journal of Hellenic Studies*, Vol. XXI, 1901.

Hall, H. R. "The Two Labyrinths" in *Journal of Hellenic Studies*, Vol. XXV, 1905. "Aegean Archaeology," 1912.

Burrows, R. M. "Discoveries in Crete," 1907.

Glasgow, G. "The Discoveries in Crete" in *"Discovery,"* Vol. I, 1920.
    (A general review to date.)

Mosso, A. "The Palaces of Crete," 1907.

Hawes, C. H. and H. B. "Crete the Forerunner of Greece," 1909.

Cook, A. B. *Op. cit.,* 1914.

Baikie, J. "The Sea-Kings of Crete," 1920.

Frazer, Sir J. G. *Op. cit.,* 1911.

Spratt, T. A. B. "Travels in Crete," 1865.

Sieber, F. W. "Reise nach der Insel Kreta in 1817," 1823.

Hoeck, C. "Kreta," 1823–29.

Cockerell, C. R., R.A. "Travels in Southern Europe," 1810–17. Edited by his son, S. P. Cockerell, 1903. Ch. xi.
    (Cavern of Gortyna.)

Savary, C. E. "Lettres sur la Grèce," 1788 (Trans. in *Annual Register,* 1789, Pt. II. pp. 90–98).

Tournefort, G. P. de. "Voyage du Levant," 1717 (Trans. by J. Ozell, 1718).

Caumont, Le Seigneur de ("Nompar II"). "Voyage d'oultremer en Jhérusalem," 1418, Brit. Mus. Egerton MSS. 890, fol. 2, ed. by Marquis de la Grange and printed Paris, 1858, p. 42.

Florentine Picture Chronicle, XV. Century. Brit. Mus. Prints 197d 3 fol. 50–51.

Italian Engraving, School of *Maso Finiguerra.* Brit. Mus. A. II. 10b.

(iii) The Etruscan, Lemnian, etc., Labyrinths.

Strabo. VIII. vi. 369.
    (Labyrinth of the Cyclops, Nauplia.)

Pliny. "Hist. Nat." xxxvi. 19, 4.

Dennis, G. "The Cities and Cemeteries of Etruria," 1848.

Canina, L. "L'Architettura Antica," 1839–44, Sec. II. Tav. 159.

Quatremère de Quincy, A. C. "Restitution du Tombeau de Porsenna," 1826.

Müller, K. O. "Die Etrusker," 1828, Vol. IV. 2, 1.

IV. THE LABYRINTH IN ANCIENT ART

(i) Coins

Wroth, W. W. "Catalogue of Greek Coins," 1886, Pl. IV., V., VI.

Head, B. V. "Historia Nummorum," 1887, pp. 389–91.

(ii) Pottery

Deecke, W., in *Annali dell' Instituto di Correspondenza Archeologica*, 1881.
    (Tragliatella Vase.)

Reinach, S. "Vases Peints," 1899, p. 345.

Perrot et Chipiez. "Histoire de l'Art dans l'Antiquité," Vol. VII. p. 118.

Walters, H. B. "History of Ancient Pottery," 1905, Vol. I.
    (Frontispiece shows Theseus kylix, by Duris.)

Elderkin, G. W. "Meander or Labyrinth" in *Journ. Amer. Arch.* XIV, 1910, pp. 185–190.
    (Meander figures on Theseus Vases.)

(iii) Mosaic Pavements, etc. (*See also* Church Labyrinths, *Appendix V.*)

Arneth, J. C. von. "Archäologische Analekten," 1851–3, Tafel V. (Salzburg mosaic.)

Archäologische Zeitung, 1848, p. 99.
    (Mosaics at Orbe and Bosséaz, Switzerland.)

Millin, A. L. "Voyage dans le Midi de la France," 1807, Pl. 34.
    (Mosaic at Aix, near Marseilles.)

Mittheilungen der Antiquarischen Gesellschaft zu Zurich. Bd. XVI, 1841, etc., Pl. 29.
    (Mosaic at Cormerod, Switzerland.)

Creuzer, G. F. "Abbildungen zu Symbolik und Mythologie der älter Volker," 1819, Taf. LV, No. 1 (Salzburg).

CAUMONT, A. DE. "Abécédaire d'Archéologie." 1886 Ed.
Vol. III. (Mosaic at Verdes, Loir-et-Cher.)

ZAHN, W. "Schönsten Ornamente aus Pompeji, etc.," 1828,
Vol. II, Taf. 50.
(Mosaic in Casa del Labirinto, Pompeii.)

COMARMOND, A. "Description du Musée Lapidaire de la
Ville de Lyons," No. 273.
(Inscription relating to a labyrinth.)

GUÉRIN, V. "Voyage Archéologique dans la Régence de
Tunis," 1862, Vol. I, p. 109.
(Mosaic at Susa.)

DOUBLET, G., in Comptes Rendus de l'Académie des Inscriptions,
1892, pp. 318–329. (Mosaic at Susa.)

Révue Archéologique, 1884, p. 107. (Mosaic at Brindisi.)

CAETANI-LOVATELLI, E. "Miscellanea Archeologia," 1891,
and in Nuova Antologia, Vol. XXVIII, 1890.
(General review.)

COLLIER, C. V., in Proceedings of the Society of Antiquaries,
Vol. XX, No. II, February 9, 1905, pp. 215–19.
(Mosaic at Harpham, Yorks, and mention of one in
Northants.)

MORGAN, O., in Proceedings of Monmouth and Caerleon Antiquarian Association, 1866.
(Mosaic at Caerleon.)

RICH, A. "A Dictionary of Roman and Greek Antiquities,"
1893, pp. 481–2.

(iv) MISCELLANEOUS

EVANS, Sir A. J. "The Palace of Minos," 1921, Vol. I,
pp. 121 et seq. and p. 357.
(Origin of Labyrinth Figure.)

PETRIE, W. M. F. "Egyptian Decorative Art," pp. 42, 43.
(Meanders.)

Real Museo Borbonico, XIV, 1852, Tav. a.
(Labyrinth graffito on pillar of house at Pompeii.
This figure is reproduced in E. Breton's "Pompeia," and
elsewhere.)

OZANAM, A. F. "Documents inédits," 1850, Section
"Graphia aurae urbis Romae."
(Labyrinth embroidered on emperor's robes.)

De Launay, R. *Op. cit.*
    (Interpretation of *tholos* of Epidauros, etc.)
Kabbadias, P. "Fouilles d'Epidaure," 1893.
    (*Tholos* of Temple of Aesculapius.)
Müller, K. "Tiryns Vorbericht über die Gräbungen, 1905–
    1912," in *Athen. Mittheilungen*, XXXVIII, 1913,
    p. 78, etc. (Labyrinth-like structure in masonry.)
Maffei, P. A. "Gemmae Antiche," 1709, Pt. IV, pl. 31.
    (Labyrinth engraved on a gem.)

V. LABYRINTHS IN CHURCHES

(i) General

Amé, E. "Les Carrelages Émaillés du Moyen Age," 1859.
    (Has a good chapter on the French church labyrinths,
    with coloured plates.)
Gailhabaud, J. "L'Architecture du Vme au XVIIme siècle,"
    1858.
Durand, J. "Les Pavés Mosaïques en Italie et en France," in
    Annales Archéologiques, XIV–XVII, 1855–7.
Deschamps des Pas, L. "Le Pavage des Églises," in *Ann.
    Arch.* XII, p. 147.
Viollet-le-Duc, E. E. "Dictionnaire Raisonné de
    l'Architecture Française du XIe au XVIe siècle," Art.
    "Labyrinthe."
Walcott, M. E. C. "Sacred Archaeology," 1868.
Müntz, E. "Etudes Iconographiques," 1887, p. 15 *et seq.*
    (Italian examples.)

(ii) Particular Localities

Campi, P. M. "Dell' Hist. Eccles. di Piacenza," 1651–62.
    (S. Savino, Placentia.)
Ciampini, G. G. "Vetera Monimenta," 1690–9, Vol. II,
    pl. 2.
    (S. Michele Maggiore, Pavia.)
Géruzez, J. B. F. "Descrip. Hist. et Stat. de la Ville de
    Rheims," 1817, Vol. I, p. 316.
    (Rheims Cathedral. "Penitential" theory of church
    labyrinths.)
Debray, M. "Notice sur la Cathédrale d'Arras," 1829.

WALLET, E. "Descrip. d'une Crypte et d'un Pavé mosaïque de l'Église Saint Bertin à St. Omer," 1834.

DAIRE, L. F. "Histoire de la Ville d'Amiens," 1782, Vol. II, p. 92.
(Amiens Cathedral.)

TURNER, DAWSON. "Tour in Normandy," 1820, Vol. II, pp. 206–7.
(Caen. Guard-Chamber of Abbey.)

AUBER, C. A. "Histoire de la Cathédrale de Poitiers," 1849, Vol. I, Pl. I, Fig. 6.
(Poitiers Cathedral. Mural sketch.)

DIDRON, A. N. "Voyage Archéologique dans la Grèce chrétienne," in *Annales Archéologiques*, Vol. I, 1844, p. 177.
(Labyrinth figure in Convent of St. Barlaam.)

ROBOLOTTI, F. "Dei Documenti Storiei Litterarj di Cremona," 1857, Tav. II.
(Cremona Cathedral.)

PRÉVOST, M., in *Révue Archéologique* IV, 1848, and VIII, 1851–2, pp. 566–7.
(Church of Reparatus, Orléansville, Algeria.)

DOUBLET DE BOISTHIBAULT, in *Révue Archéologique*, VIII, 1851–2, pp. 437–47.
(Chartres Cathedral.)

AUS'M WEERTH, E. "Mosaikboden in St. Gereon zu Cöln," 1874.
(Churches in Cologne and Pavia.)

RUSKIN, J. "Fors Clavigera," Fors 23. (Lucca.)

Proceedings of Architectural Societies of Northampton, York, etc. Vols. XIX–XX, 1887–8.
(Church at Alkborough.)

The Builder, Vol. XVI, 1855, p. 90.
(Notre Dame de la Treille, Lille.)

Annales Archéologiques, Vol. XVI, 1855, p. 211.
(Notre Dame de la Treille, Lille.)

Manuscript. Bibliothèque Barberini, XLIV, p. 35.
(Pavia.)

Manuscript. Villard de Honnecourt. "Album," ed. by J. B. A. LASSUS, 1858, Plate XIII.
(Chartres.)

223

VI. HEDGE MAZES, FLORAL LABYRINTHS, ETC.

(i) CLASSICAL REFERENCES
(Roman Topiary Work and Ornamental Gardening)

PLINY. "Hist. Nat.," XV. 30; XVI. 33; XXXVI. 13.
PLINY THE YOUNGER. Epist. V. 6.

(ii) GREAT BRITAIN (GENERAL)

HYLL, T. (*Didymus Mountayne.*) "The Profitable Art of Gardening," 3rd edition, 1579, pp. 9, 15.

ISLIP, A. "The Orchard and the Garden," 1602, p. 48.
(Gathered from Dutch and French sources.)

LAWSON, W. "A New Orchard and Garden," 1631.
(Afterwards embodied in K. MARKHAM's "A New Way to Get Wealth," 1648, etc.)

PARKINSON, J. "Paradisus in soli," 1629, Ch. II.

MEAGER, L. "The Compleat English Gardener," *circ.* 1685.

Harley Manuscripts. Brit. Mus. Harl. 5308 (71, a, 12).
(A seventeenth-century gardener's manuscript book, with two mazes.)

LONDON, G., and WISE, H. "The Compleat Florist," 1706 (afterwards published by J. CARPENTER as "The Retir'd Gardener." (Primarily a translation of French works by L. LIGER and F. GENTIL.)

LANGLEY, BATTY. "New Principles of Gardening," 1728.
(Numerous maze designs.)

SWITZER, S. "Ichnographia Rustica," 1742, Vol. II, p. 218.

FULLMER, S. "Gardener's Companion," 1781, p. 105.

HOME, H. (Lord KAMES.) "Elements of Criticism," 1796, Vol. II, p. 348.
(Criticism of mazes in gardens.)

WALPOLE, H. "Essay on Modern Gardening," 1785.

ROBINSON, W. "The English Flower Garden," 1921.

MACARTNEY, MERVYN. "English Houses and Gardens of the Seventeenth and Eighteenth Centuries," 1908.
(Article on hedges and mazes.)

BROWN, A. J., in *American Homes and Gardens*, VII, November 1910, pp. 423–5.

(iii) Great Britain (Particular Localities)

Law, E. "History of Hampton Court Palace," 1900,
Vol. III, pp. 74–7.

Rocque, J. "Engraving of Hampton Court," 1736.
(Shows the "Troy-town," as well as the Maze and
a spiral garden.)

Defoe, D. "Tour through Great Britain," 1738.
(Hampton Court "Wilderness.")

Daily Chronicle, February 22, 1921.
(Revenue from Hampton Court Maze.)

Parliamentary Surveys. Survey No. 72, 1649. Transcribed
by John Caley, F.R.S., in *Archaeologia*, Vol. X, 1792.
(Maze at Wimbledon.)

Kip, J. "Britannia Illustrata," 1720.
(Mazes at Wrest House and Badminton.)

Williams, W. "Oxonia depiĉta," 1732.
(Trinity College labyrinth.)

Vallance, Aymer. "The Old Colleges of Oxford," 1913,
p. 77.
(Trinity College labyrinth.)

Aubrey, J. "Remaines of Gentilisme and Judaisme," 1686–7.
(Mazes in Southwark and Tothill Fields, Westminster.
The 1881 edition has an editor's note *re* maze on Putney
Heath.)

Churchwardens' Accounts, St. Margaret, Westminster, 1672.
(Tothill Maze.)

Colleĉtanea Topographica, Vol. VIII, 1843, pp. 253–62.
(Maze in Southwark.)

Strickland, A. "Lives of the Queens of England," 1851,
Vol. I, p. 264.
(Southwark.)

Wroth, W., and A. E. "The London Pleasure Gardens of
the Eighteenth Century," 1896.

Crisp, Sir F. "Guide for the use of visitors to Friar Park,"
1914.
(Maze and Dial Garden at Henley-on-Thames.)

Nesfield, W. H. "Estimate and Plan for R.H.S. Gardens,"
1860 (S. Kensington). Also plan in R.H.S. "Official
Guide," 1864.

Hutchison, A. F. "The Lake of Menteith," 1899.
  (Queen Mary's Bower.)
Triggs, H. Inigo. "Formal Gardens in England and Scotland," 1902.
  (Mazes at Arley Hall and Belton House figured.)
Elgood, G. S., and Jekyll, G. "Some English Gardens," 1904, p. 127.
  (Maze at Arley Hall.)

(iv) France

Androuet du Cerceau, J. "Les Plus Excellents Bastiments de France," 1576, and other architectural works.
  (Mazes at Charleval, Gaillon, etc.)
Estienne, C. "La Maison Rustique," 1573, Vol. II, ch. vi, p. 68.
  (Translated by R. Surflet as "The Country Farme," 1600.)
Betin, P. "Le Fidelle Jardinier," 1636, p. 24.
Perrault, C. "Labyrinte de Versailles," 1677.
  (With plan and many illustrations by S. Le Clerc.)
Panseron, S. "Receuil des Jardins Français," 1723.
  (With many plates.)
Blondel, J. F. "Cours d'Architecture," 1771–7, Vol. I, p. 17 ; Vol. IV, p. 72 ; Vol. VIII, Plates 18, 19.
  (Mazes at Choisy and Chantilly.)
Havard, H. "Dictionnaire de l'Ameublement," etc., 1887–90. Art. "Labyrinthe."
  (Mazes at Baugé and Les Rochers.)
Stein, H. "Les Jardins de France," 1913, Plates 88, 89.
Triggs, H. Inigo. "Garden Craft in Europe," 1913, pp. 21, 81, 141.
  (Mazes at the Tuileries, Hôtel St. Paul, and Sceaux.)

(v) Italy

Serlio, S. "Libri Cinque d'Architettura," 1537 ; English edition, 1611.
Dupérac, S. "Vues et Perspectives des Jardins de Tivoli," 1573.
  (Labyrinths at Villa d'Este.)

Evelyn, J. "Memoirs," *s.a.* 1646.
    (Labyrinth at Vicenza.)
Triggs, H. Inigo. "The Art of Garden Design in Italy,"
    1906, p. 51.
    (Mazes at Castellezo dei Arconati, Milan.)
Skippon, Sir Philip. "A Journey through part of the Low
    Countries, Germany, Italy, and France," 1663.
    (Labyrinth at Vicenza.)

(vi) Holland and Belgium

De Vries, J. V. "Hortorum Viridariorumque Formae,"
    1583, Plates 14–16, 22–7.
Commelyn, C. "Nederlantze Hesperides," 1676.
    (Several designs for mazes.)
Harris, W. "A Description of the King's Royal Palace and
    Gardens at Loo," 1699.
Visscher, N. "De Zegepraalende Vecht," 1719.
    (Maze at Gunterstein.)
Triggs, H. Inigo. "Garden Craft in Europe," 1913,
    pp. 173, 192.
    (Mazes at Sorgvliet and Enghien.)
Fouquier, M. "L'Art des Jardins," 1911, p. 120.
    (Maze at Enghien.)

(vii) Other Countries

Boeckler, G. A. "Architectura Curiosa," 1664, Pt. IV.
    (Numerous plates contain labyrinth designs.)
Lauremberg, P. "Horticultura," 1632, Plates 15–22.
Daily Mail, September 23, 1899.
    (Art. on "Puzzle Gardens" gives account of curious
    allegorical labyrinth at Anhalt ; also describes mazes at
    Barcelona.)
Mollet, A. "Le Jardin de Plaisir," 1651.
    (Sweden.)
Triggs, H. Inigo. "Garden Craft in Europe," 1913, p. 280.
    (Maze at the Alcazar, Seville.)
Skippon, Sir P. "A Journey through part of the Low
    Countries," etc., 1663.
    (Munich.)

Moulton, R. H., in *Architectural Record* (*New York*), October 1917, p. 400.
  (American replica of the Maze at Hampton Court.)
Warren, C., in *Country Life* (*Garden City*), VIII, September 1905, pp. 527-8.
  (Cedar Hill Maze, U.S.A.)
The following kindly furnished the writer with recent information regarding the mazes at the localities indicated:
  H. Collar, Esq., Curator, Museum, Saffron Walden (Saffron Walden); H. Wallis Chapman, Esq., Jordans, Bucks (Sudeley Castle); W. Emerton, Esq., Grantham (Belton House); E. M. Jackson, Esq., M.A., Manningtree (Mistley Place); G. Kerry Rix, Esq., Somerleyton (Somerleyton Hall); R. Pogmore, Esq., Mansfield (Debdale Hall).

VII. TURF LABYRINTHS

(i) General

Trollope, E. *Op. cit.* 1858.
Aubrey, J. "Remaines of Gentilisme and Judaisme," 1686-7. Ed. by J. Britten, F.L.S., 1881.
  (Mazes at Pimperne, West Ashton, Cotswold Downs, Southwark, and Tothill Fields. Editor adds note *re* maze on Putney Heath.)
Aubrey, J. "History of Surrey," Ed. 1719, Vol. V, p. 80.
  (Suggestion of Scandinavian origin of mazes.)
Stukeley, W. "Itinerarium Curiosum," 1776, pp. 31, 97.
  (Discussion of origin of mazes.)
Roberts, P. "Cambrian Popular Antiquities," 1815, p. 212.
  ("City of Troy" in Wales.)
Cymmrodorion Society, Transactions of, 1822, pp. 67-9.
  ("Idrison" on Caer Troiau. Refers to solar theory.)
Tyack, G. S. Art. "Mazes" in W. Andrews' "Ecclesiastical Curiosities," 1897.
Johnson, W. "Folk-Memory," 1908.
228

(ii) Particular Localities

DE LA PRYME, A. (1671–1704). "Diary." Ed. Surtees Society, 1870.
　　(Alkborough and Appleby.)

Churchwardens' Accounts, Louth, 1544.
　　(Louth.)

HUTCHINS, J. "History and Antiq. of the County of Dorset," 1774, Vol. I, p. 101 (Pimperne); Vol. II, p. 468 (Leigh).

HUTCHINS, J. 3rd ed., 1861, pp. 292–3.
　　(Saffron Walden, Somerton, Tadmarton Heath, Hereford Beacon, Hilton, and Breamore. Figs. of mazes at Pimperne, Sneinton, and Clifton, Notts.)

"Annalia Dubrensia," 1636, reprinted by A. B. Grosart, 1877.
　　(Cotswold Hills, near Chipping Campden.)

CAMDEN, W. "Britannia." Ed. by GOUGH, 1789. Plate opposite p. 288.
　　(Saffron Walden, Sneinton, and Clifton.)

HOARE, Sir R. C. "Ancient Wilts," 1812–21, Vol. I, p. 238.
　　(Breamore.)

WILLIAMS-FREEMAN, J. P. "Field Archaeology, Hants."
　　(Breamore.)

ACKERMANN'S "Repository of Arts," Vol. XIII, 1815, p. 193.
　　(Hull.)

HATFIELD, S. "Terra incognita of Lincolnshire," 1816.
　　(Alkborough.)

ALLEN, T. "History of Lincolnshire," 1834, Vol. II, p. 219.
　　(Appleby.)

WRIGHT, T. "Hist. and Topog. of the County of Essex," 1835, Vol. II, p. 124.
　　(Comberton.)

BRAYBROOKE, Lord. "Audley End and Saffron Walden," 1836, *esp.* MS. insertion of 1859 in Saffron Walden Museum.
　　(Saffron Walden.)

Trollope, E. *Op. cit.* 1858.
    (Sneinton, Wing, Ripon, Boughton Green, and many
    others.)
Gordon, E. O. "Prehistoric London," 1914.
    (Greenwich, or Blackheath.)
Notes and Queries.
    3 ser., X, 1866, p. 283. Barkley, C. W. (Comberton
    and Leigh.) Also in 4 ser., II, 1868.
    3 ser., X, 1866, p. 283. J. F.
    (Alkborough, Holderness, and Sneinton.)
    8 ser., IV, 1893, p. 96. Venables, E., and others.
    (Kent.)
    9 ser., V, 1900, p. 445. Page, J. T.
    (Boughton Green.)
    10 ser., X, 1908, p. 96. Harland-Oxley, W. E.
    (Tothill Fields.)
    12 ser., IV, 1918, p. 160. Austin, G.
    (Egton and Goathland.)
The Times, April 18, 1870.
    (St. Martha's Hill, Guildford.)
The Times, April 5, 1920.
    (Juliberry's Grave, Godmersham.)
Barnes, W., in *Dorset Nat. Hist. and Antiq'n. Field Club
    Proceedings*, Vol. IV, 1882.
    (Leigh, Dorset.)
Ferguson, R. S. "A Labyrinth on Rockliffe Marsh," in
    *Cumberland and West'd Antiq'n and Arch'l. Society
    Transactions*, Vol. VIII, 1883–4, p. 69.
    (Burgh and Rockcliffe.)
*Assoc'd Arch'l. Societies of Northampton, York, etc., Pro-
    ceedings*, Vols. XIX–XX, 1887–8.
    (Alkborough.)
Maynard, G. N. "The Labyrinths or Mazes at Saffron
    Walden," in *Essex Field Club Proceedings*, 1889.
Shore, T. W., and Nisbett, H. C. "Ancient Hampshire
    Mazes," in *Hampshire Field Club Proceedings*, Vol. III,
    Pt. III, 1896, p. 257.
    (Breamore and Winchester.)
Hill, A. D., in *Wilts Arch'l. and Nat. Hist. Magazine*, 1897, p. 98.
    (Breamore and West Ashton.)

TREVES, Sir F. "Highways and Byways in Dorset," 1906.
(Leigh.)
ALLCROFT, A. H. "Earthwork of England," 1908, p. 602.
(Asenby.)
Cambs and Hunts Arch'l. Society Proceedings, Vol. III,
1914, p. 224.
(Hilton.)
IRONS, E. A. "The Turf Maze at Wing," in *Rutland
Arch'l. and Nat. Hist. Society Transactions*, Vol. XIII,
1915.
(Wing.)
The following kindly supplied the writer with recent infor-
mation regarding the mazes at the localities indicated:
E. J. BULL, Esq., Carlisle (Rockcliffe Marshes); J. C.
DENTON, Esq., Cambridge (Comberton); D. H.
GEDDIE, Esq., F.R.Hist.S., Borough Librarian,
Grimsby (Horncastle); O. W. GODWIN, Esq., Troy
Farm, Somerton, Banbury (Somerton); Rev. F. J. W.
TAVERNER, M.A., Wing, Oakham (Wing); Rev. J. J.
WALKER,B.A.,Boughton,Northants (Boughton Green);
Rev. GEO. YORKE, Alkborough, Lincs (Alkborough).

VIII. STONE LABYRINTHS

(For Rock Engravings, *see* "Miscellaneous")

WORM, O. "Danicorum Monumentorum Libri Sex," 1651,
p. 213.
(Denmark.)
RUDBECK, O. "Atlantica," 1695-8, Tab. 35, Fig. 134.
(Sweden.)
VON BAER, C. E., in *Bull. Hist. Phil. de l'Acad. de St. Peters-
bourg*, Vol. I.
ASPELIN, J. R. "Steinlabyrinthe in Finnland," in *Zeitschrift
für Ethnologie*, Vol. IX, 1877, p. 439. (Also *Virchow*,
p. 441, and *Friedel*, p. 470.)
KRAUSE, E. "Die Trojaburgen Nordeuropas," 1893.

IX. THE LABYRINTH IN NON-EUROPEAN COUNTRIES

(i) AMERICAN INDIANS

COTTON, H. S. "Is the House of Tchuhu the Minoan Labyrinth?" in *Science* (New York), N.S. XLV, June 29, 1917, p. 667.

FEWKES, J. W. "A Fictitious Ruin in the Gila Valley, Arizona," in *American Anthropologist*, N.S. IX, 1907, p. 510.

FEWKES, J. W., in *Smithsonian Miscellaneous Collections*, 1920, Vol. 72, No. 1, pp. 47–64.
(Pictograph from Mesa Verde.)

(ii) INDIA

BELLEW, H. W. "From the Indus to the Tigris," 1873–4.
(Circular figures on ground, which may be allied to labyrinth designs.)

(iii) ZULUS

Folk Lore, Vol. 23, 1912. Review of "Some Zulu Customs and Folk-lore," by L. H. SAMUELSON.
(Reference to maze figures on the ground.)

X. MISCELLANEOUS

HOMER. "Iliad," xviii. 590, etc.
(Ariadne's Dance.)

PLINY. "Hist. Nat.," xxxvi. 85.
(Maze Games.)

VIRGIL. "Aeneid," v. 545–603.
(Troy Game.)

SUETONIUS. "Nero," vii.
(Troy Game.)

PALLAS, P. S. "Reise durch verschiedene Provinzen des russischen Reichs," 1778, Vol. III.
(Siberian Crane Dance.)

STRUTT, J. "Sports and Pastimes of the People of England," 1830, p. 317.

NEIDHART VON REUENTHAL, ed. MORITZ-HAUPT, 1858, pp. 154–186.
(Troy-Aldei and Troyerlais.)

BENNDORF, O. "Das Alter des Trojaspiels," in W. REICHEL's "Über Homerische Waffen," 1894, pp. 133–9.
(Troy Game.)

Folk Lore, Vol. 24, 1913. Presidential Address of W. CROOKE, p. 34.
(Magic Ceremonies.)

Folk Lore, Vol. 29, 1918. "Collectanea," pp. 238–47.
(Serbian Troy Dances.)

Notes and Queries.
4 ser., V, 1870.
(Troy Game in England.)
5 ser., I, 1874, p. 104.
("Labyrinth of St. Bernard," Mt. Carmel.)
8 ser., IV, 1893, p. 96, and V, 1894, pp. 37, 96, 351.
("Troy-town" place-names and Troia Nova.)

GORDON, E. O. "Prehistoric London," 1914.
(London as New Troy.)

LAMBERTUS ARDENSIS. "Historia Comitum Ardensium et Guisnensium, A.D. 800–1200," in "Reliquiae Manuscriptorum" of Petrus de Ludewig, 1727, Bk. IV, ch. 127, p. 549.
(Labyrinthine building in French Flanders.)

Fonds Latin. MS. No. 13013. Ninth-century "Comput" of St. Germain.
(Labyrinth figure.)

HENRY OF CLAIRVAUX, in *Hoveden's Chronicle*, under year 1178.
(Reference to Labyrinth. ? Metaphorical.)

BROMPTON, J. "Chronicon," under year 1151, in Sir R. TWYSDEN's "Historiae Anglicanae Scriptores X," 1652.
(Rosamond's Bower.)

HIGDEN, R. "Polychronicon," 1381–94. Ed. C.
BABINGTON, 1886. Bk. VIII, ch. 26.
(Rosamond's Coffer.)

LANG, A. "Magic and Religion," 1901.
(Prehistoric Rock Engravings.)

TATE, G. "The Ancient British Sculptured Rocks of Northumberland, etc.," in *Berwickshire Naturalists' Club Proceedings*, Vol. V, 1864, p. 137, etc.
(Labyrinthoid figures on rocks.)

LUKIS, F. C., in *Journal of British Arch'l. Assn.*, Vol. III,
1848, pp. 269–79.
(Engraved stones on Gav'r Innis, Brittany.)

BICKNELL, C. "A Guide to the Prehistoric Rock Engravings
in the Italian Maritime Alps." *See* figure reproduced in
C. BUCKNALL's paper in *Bristol Nat. Society Proceedings*,
1912, Plate II, Fig. 3.
(Labyrinthoid figure.)

LAW, E. "Masterpieces of the Royal Gallery of Hampton
Court," 1904.
(Maze by TINTORETTO and alleged portrait of "Fair
Rosamond.")

EARP, F. R. "Descriptive Catalogue of Pictures in the
Fitzwilliam Museum," 1902, p. 14, Fig. 133.
(Painting of man with labyrinth.)

DUNBAR, E. D. "Social Life in Former Days," 1865, 1st
series.
(Labyrinth design on Towels.)

BERTHELOT, M., in *La Grande Encyclopédie*, Art. "Labyrinthe,"
final section.
(Labyrinth figure used by Alchemists.)

DURAND, J. *Op. cit.* 1857, p. 127.
(Labyrinth painted on wood.)

ALCIATI, A. "Emblemata," 1531, etc.
(Labyrinth Emblems.)

CATS, J. "Emblèmes touchant les Amours et les Mœurs,"
1618, etc.
(Labyrinth Emblems.)

PARADIN, C. "Devises Héroïques et Emblèmes," 1621, etc.
(Labyrinth Emblems.)

QUARLES, F. "Emblems," 1635, etc.
    (Labyrinth Emblems.)
    Also many other Emblem books.
MOLLET, J. W. "Dictionary of Words used in Art and Archaeology," 1883. Art. "Minotaur."
    (Labyrinth as heraldic crest.)
NORDSTROM, S., in *Svenska Fornminnes föreningens Tidskrift*, Vol. III, 1887, p. 227.
    (Labyrinth designs on bells.)
MASON, G. "An Essay on Design in Gardening," 1795.
    (Appendix on Bowers.)
BRAND'S "Popular Antiquities." Ed. W. C. HAZLITT, 1905.
    (Art. on "St. Julian.")
WRIGHT, J. "The English Dialect Dictionary," 1902. Vol. III, p. 389.
    ("Julian's Bower" variants.)
MEILLET, A., in *French Quarterly*, Vol. II, No. 1, 1920.
    (Etymology of "Labyrinth.")
HAVARD, H. "Dictionnaire de l'Ameublement," etc., 1887–90. Art. "Labyrinthe."
    (Game of "Labyrinthe.")
German Engraving, with verses, *circ.* 1630. Brit. Mus. 1750, c. 1/28.
Belgian Lithographs of Toy Mazes. "Les Labyrinthes" and "Jardin Chinois," *circ.* 1872. Brit. Mus. "Misc. Collections," 1881, c. 3, 69–71.
Patent Specifications. (Toy Mazes.)
    ARNOT, J. M. No. 14764, August 1, 1894.
    BRENTANO, A. No. 6204, April 11, 1889.
    BRIDGE, H. No. 2613, February 2, 1906.
    CUTHBERT, R. A., and BEVITT, W. No. 7381, March 26, 1898.
    NIX, S. D. No. 16092, September 22, 1891.
    PROCTOR, J. No. 9428, April 23, 1898.

INDEX

242

243

245

A CATALOGUE OF SELECTED DOVER BOOKS
IN ALL FIELDS OF INTEREST

A CATALOGUE OF SELECTED DOVER BOOKS
IN ALL FIELDS OF INTEREST

AMERICA'S OLD MASTERS, James T. Flexner. Four men emerged unexpectedly from provincial 18th century America to leadership in European art: Benjamin West, J. S. Copley, C. R. Peale, Gilbert Stuart. Brilliant coverage of lives and contributions. Revised, 1967 edition. 69 plates. 365pp. of text.

21806-6 Paperbound $3.00

FIRST FLOWERS OF OUR WILDERNESS: AMERICAN PAINTING, THE COLONIAL PERIOD, James T. Flexner. Painters, and regional painting traditions from earliest Colonial times up to the emergence of Copley, West and Peale Sr., Foster, Gustavus Hesselius, Feke, John Smibert and many anonymous painters in the primitive manner. Engaging presentation, with 162 illustrations. xxii + 368pp.

22180-6 Paperbound $3.50

THE LIGHT OF DISTANT SKIES: AMERICAN PAINTING, 1760-1835, James T. Flexner. The great generation of early American painters goes to Europe to learn and to teach: West, Copley, Gilbert Stuart and others. Allston, Trumbull, Morse; also contemporary American painters—primitives, derivatives, academics—who remained in America. 102 illustrations. xiii + 306pp. 22179-2 Paperbound $3.50

A HISTORY OF THE RISE AND PROGRESS OF THE ARTS OF DESIGN IN THE UNITED STATES, William Dunlap. Much the richest mine of information on early American painters, sculptors, architects, engravers, miniaturists, etc. The only source of information for scores of artists, the major primary source for many others. Unabridged reprint of rare original 1834 edition, with new introduction by James T. Flexner, and 394 new illustrations. Edited by Rita Weiss. 6⅝ x 9⅝.

21695-0, 21696-9, 21697-7 Three volumes, Paperbound $13.50

EPOCHS OF CHINESE AND JAPANESE ART, Ernest F. Fenollosa. From primitive Chinese art to the 20th century, thorough history, explanation of every important art period and form, including Japanese woodcuts; main stress on China and Japan, but Tibet, Korea also included. Still unexcelled for its detailed, rich coverage of cultural background, aesthetic elements, diffusion studies, particularly of the historical period. 2nd, 1913 edition. 242 illustrations. lii + 439pp. of text.

20364-6, 20365-4 Two volumes, Paperbound $6.00

THE GENTLE ART OF MAKING ENEMIES, James A. M. Whistler. Greatest wit of his day deflates Oscar Wilde, Ruskin, Swinburne; strikes back at inane critics, exhibitions, art journalism; aesthetics of impressionist revolution in most striking form. Highly readable classic by great painter. Reproduction of edition designed by Whistler. Introduction by Alfred Werner. xxxvi + 334pp.

21875-9 Paperbound $3.00

VISUAL ILLUSIONS: THEIR CAUSES, CHARACTERISTICS, AND APPLICATIONS, Matthew Luckiesh. Thorough description and discussion of optical illusion, geometric and perspective, particularly; size and shape distortions, illusions of color, of motion; natural illusions; use of illusion in art and magic, industry, etc. Most useful today with op art, also for classical art. Scores of effects illustrated. Introduction by William H. Ittleson. 100 illustrations. xxi + 252pp.
21530-X Paperbound $2.00

A HANDBOOK OF ANATOMY FOR ART STUDENTS, Arthur Thomson. Thorough, virtually exhaustive coverage of skeletal structure, musculature, etc. Full text, supplemented by anatomical diagrams and drawings and by photographs of undraped figures. Unique in its comparison of male and female forms, pointing out differences of contour, texture, form. 211 figures, 40 drawings, 86 photographs. xx + 459pp. 5⅜ x 8⅜.
21163-0 Paperbound $3.50

150 MASTERPIECES OF DRAWING, Selected by Anthony Toney. Full page reproductions of drawings from the early 16th to the end of the 18th century, all beautifully reproduced: Rembrandt, Michelangelo, Dürer, Fragonard, Urs, Graf, Wouwerman, many others. First-rate browsing book, model book for artists. xviii + 150pp. 8⅜ x 11¼.
21032-4 Paperbound $2.50

THE LATER WORK OF AUBREY BEARDSLEY, Aubrey Beardsley. Exotic, erotic, ironic masterpieces in full maturity: Comedy Ballet, Venus and Tannhauser, Pierrot, Lysistrata, Rape of the Lock, Savoy material, Ali Baba, Volpone, etc. This material revolutionized the art world, and is still powerful, fresh, brilliant. With *The Early Work*, all Beardsley's finest work. 174 plates, 2 in color. xiv + 176pp. 8⅛ x 11.
21817-1 Paperbound $3.00

DRAWINGS OF REMBRANDT, Rembrandt van Rijn. Complete reproduction of fabulously rare edition by Lippmann and Hofstede de Groot, completely reedited, updated, improved by Prof. Seymour Slive, Fogg Museum. Portraits, Biblical sketches, landscapes, Oriental types, nudes, episodes from classical mythology—All Rembrandt's fertile genius. Also selection of drawings by his pupils and followers. "Stunning volumes," *Saturday Review*. 550 illustrations. lxxviii + 552pp. 9⅛ x 12¼.
21485-0, 21486-9 Two volumes, Paperbound $10.00

THE DISASTERS OF WAR, Francisco Goya. One of the masterpieces of Western civilization—83 etchings that record Goya's shattering, bitter reaction to the Napoleonic war that swept through Spain after the insurrection of 1808 and to war in general. Reprint of the first edition, with three additional plates from Boston's Museum of Fine Arts. All plates facsimile size. Introduction by Philip Hofer, Fogg Museum. v + 97pp. 9⅜ x 8¼.
21872-4 Paperbound $2.00

GRAPHIC WORKS OF ODILON REDON. Largest collection of Redon's graphic works ever assembled: 172 lithographs, 28 etchings and engravings, 9 drawings. These include some of his most famous works. All the plates from *Odilon Redon: oeuvre graphique complet*, plus additional plates. New introduction and caption translations by Alfred Werner. 209 illustrations. xxvii + 209pp. 9⅛ x 12¼.
21966-8 Paperbound $4.00

DESIGN BY ACCIDENT; A BOOK OF "ACCIDENTAL EFFECTS" FOR ARTISTS AND DESIGNERS, James F. O'Brien. Create your own unique, striking, imaginative effects by "controlled accident" interaction of materials: paints and lacquers, oil and water based paints, splatter, crackling materials, shatter, similar items. Everything you do will be different; first book on this limitless art, so useful to both fine artist and commercial artist. Full instructions. 192 plates showing "accidents," 8 in color. viii + 215pp. 8⅜ x 11¼. 21942-9 Paperbound $3.50

THE BOOK OF SIGNS, Rudolf Koch. Famed German type designer draws 493 beautiful symbols: religious, mystical, alchemical, imperial, property marks, runes, etc. Remarkable fusion of traditional and modern. Good for suggestions of timelessness, smartness, modernity. Text. vi + 104pp. 6⅛ x 9¼. 20162-7 Paperbound $1.25

HISTORY OF INDIAN AND INDONESIAN ART, Ananda K. Coomaraswamy. An unabridged republication of one of the finest books by a great scholar in Eastern art. Rich in descriptive material, history, social backgrounds; Sunga reliefs, Rajput paintings, Gupta temples, Burmese frescoes, textiles, jewelry, sculpture, etc. 400 photos. viii + 423pp. 6⅜ x 9¾. 21436-2 Paperbound $5.00

PRIMITIVE ART, Franz Boas. America's foremost anthropologist surveys textiles, ceramics, woodcarving, basketry, metalwork, etc.; patterns, technology, creation of symbols, style origins. All areas of world, but very full on Northwest Coast Indians. More than 350 illustrations of baskets, boxes, totem poles, weapons, etc. 378 pp. 20025-6 Paperbound $3.00

THE GENTLEMAN AND CABINET MAKER'S DIRECTOR, Thomas Chippendale. Full reprint (third edition, 1762) of most influential furniture book of all time, by master cabinetmaker. 200 plates, illustrating chairs, sofas, mirrors, tables, cabinets, plus 24 photographs of surviving pieces. Biographical introduction by N. Bienenstock. vi + 249pp. 9⅞ x 12¾. 21601-2 Paperbound $4.00

AMERICAN ANTIQUE FURNITURE, Edgar G. Miller, Jr. The basic coverage of all American furniture before 1840. Individual chapters cover type of furniture—clocks, tables, sideboards, etc.—chronologically, with inexhaustible wealth of data. More than 2100 photographs, all identified, commented on. Essential to all early American collectors. Introduction by H. E. Keyes. vi + 1106pp. 7⅞ x 10¾. 21599-7, 21600-4 Two volumes, Paperbound $11.00

PENNSYLVANIA DUTCH AMERICAN FOLK ART, Henry J. Kauffman. 279 photos, 28 drawings of tulipware, Fraktur script, painted tinware, toys, flowered furniture, quilts, samplers, hex signs, house interiors, etc. Full descriptive text. Excellent for tourist, rewarding for designer, collector. Map. 146pp. 7⅞ x 10¾. 21205-X Paperbound $2.50

EARLY NEW ENGLAND GRAVESTONE RUBBINGS, Edmund V. Gillon, Jr. 43 photographs, 226 carefully reproduced rubbings show heavily symbolic, sometimes macabre early gravestones, up to early 19th century. Remarkable early American primitive art, occasionally strikingly beautiful; always powerful. Text. xxvi + 207pp. 8⅜ x 11¼. 21380-3 Paperbound $3.50

CATALOGUE OF DOVER BOOKS

ALPHABETS AND ORNAMENTS, Ernst Lehner. Well-known pictorial source for decorative alphabets, script examples, cartouches, frames, decorative title pages, calligraphic initials, borders, similar material. 14th to 19th century, mostly European. Useful in almost any graphic arts designing, varied styles. 750 illustrations. 256pp. 7 x 10.   21905-4 Paperbound $4.00

PAINTING: A CREATIVE APPROACH, Norman Colquhoun. For the beginner simple guide provides an instructive approach to painting: major stumbling blocks for beginner; overcoming them, technical points; paints and pigments; oil painting; watercolor and other media and color. New section on "plastic" paints. Glossary. Formerly *Paint Your Own Pictures*. 221pp.   22000-1 Paperbound $1.75

THE ENJOYMENT AND USE OF COLOR, Walter Sargent. Explanation of the relations between colors themselves and between colors in nature and art, including hundreds of little-known facts about color values, intensities, effects of high and low illumination, complementary colors. Many practical hints for painters, references to great masters. 7 color plates, 29 illustrations. x + 274pp.
20944-X Paperbound $2.75

THE NOTEBOOKS OF LEONARDO DA VINCI, compiled and edited by Jean Paul Richter. 1566 extracts from original manuscripts reveal the full range of Leonardo's versatile genius: all his writings on painting, sculpture, architecture, anatomy, astronomy, geography, topography, physiology, mining, music, etc., in both Italian and English, with 186 plates of manuscript pages and more than 500 additional drawings. Includes studies for the Last Supper, the lost Sforza monument, and other works. Total of xlvii + 866pp. 7⅞ x 10¾.
22572-0, 22573-9 Two volumes, Paperbound $10.00

MONTGOMERY WARD CATALOGUE OF 1895. Tea gowns, yards of flannel and pillow-case lace, stereoscopes, books of gospel hymns, the New Improved Singer Sewing Machine, side saddles, milk skimmers, straight-edged razors, high-button shoes, spittoons, and on and on . . . listing some 25,000 items, practically all illustrated. Essential to the shoppers of the 1890's, it is our truest record of the spirit of the period. Unaltered reprint of Issue No. 57, Spring and Summer 1895. Introduction by Boris Emmet. Innumerable illustrations. xiii + 624pp. 8½ x 11⅝.
22377-9 Paperbound $6.95

THE CRYSTAL PALACE EXHIBITION ILLUSTRATED CATALOGUE (LONDON, 1851). One of the wonders of the modern world—the Crystal Palace Exhibition in which all the nations of the civilized world exhibited their achievements in the arts and sciences—presented in an equally important illustrated catalogue. More than 1700 items pictured with accompanying text—ceramics, textiles, cast-iron work, carpets, pianos, sleds, razors, wall-papers, billiard tables, beehives, silverware and hundreds of other artifacts—represent the focal point of Victorian culture in the Western World. Probably the largest collection of Victorian decorative art ever assembled—indispensable for antiquarians and designers. Unabridged republication of the Art-Journal Catalogue of the Great Exhibition of 1851, with all terminal essays. New introduction by John Gloag, F.S.A. xxxiv + 426pp. 9 x 12.
22503-8 Paperbound $5.00

A HISTORY OF COSTUME, Carl Köhler. Definitive history, based on surviving pieces of clothing primarily, and paintings, statues, etc. secondarily. Highly readable text, supplemented by 594 illustrations of costumes of the ancient Mediterranean peoples, Greece and Rome, the Teutonic prehistoric period; costumes of the Middle Ages, Renaissance, Baroque, 18th and 19th centuries. Clear, measured patterns are provided for many clothing articles. Approach is practical throughout. Enlarged by Emma von Sichart. 464pp. 21030-8 Paperbound $3.50.

ORIENTAL RUGS, ANTIQUE AND MODERN, Walter A. Hawley. A complete and authoritative treatise on the Oriental rug—where they are made, by whom and how, designs and symbols, characteristics in detail of the six major groups, how to distinguish them and how to buy them. Detailed technical data is provided on periods, weaves, warps, wefts, textures, sides, ends and knots, although no technical background is required for an understanding. 11 color plates, 80 halftones, 4 maps. vi + 320pp. 6⅛ x 9⅛. 22366-3 Paperbound $5.00

TEN BOOKS ON ARCHITECTURE, Vitruvius. By any standards the most important book on architecture ever written. Early Roman discussion of aesthetics of building, construction methods, orders, sites, and every other aspect of architecture has inspired, instructed architecture for about 2,000 years. Stands behind Palladio, Michelangelo, Bramante, Wren, countless others. Definitive Morris H. Morgan translation. 68 illustrations. xii + 331pp. 20645-9 Paperbound $3.00

THE FOUR BOOKS OF ARCHITECTURE, Andrea Palladio. Translated into every major Western European language in the two centuries following its publication in 1570, this has been one of the most influential books in the history of architecture. Complete reprint of the 1738 Isaac Ware edition. New introduction by Adolf Placzek, Columbia Univ. 216 plates. xxii + 110pp. of text. 9½ x 12¾. 21308-0 Clothbound $10.00

STICKS AND STONES: A STUDY OF AMERICAN ARCHITECTURE AND CIVILIZATION, Lewis Mumford.One of the great classics of American cultural history. American architecture from the medieval-inspired earliest forms to the early 20th century; evolution of structure and style, and reciprocal influences on environment. 21 photographic illustrations. 238pp. 20202-X Paperbound $2.00

THE AMERICAN BUILDER'S COMPANION, Asher Benjamin. The most widely used early 19th century architectural style and source book, for colonial up into Greek Revival periods. Extensive development of geometry of carpentering, construction of sashes, frames, doors, stairs; plans and elevations of domestic and other buildings. Hundreds of thousands of houses were built according to this book, now invaluable to historians, architects, restorers, etc. 1827 edition. 59 plates. 114pp. 7⅞ x 10¾. 22236-5 Paperbound $3.50

DUTCH HOUSES IN THE HUDSON VALLEY BEFORE 1776, Helen Wilkinson Reynolds. The standard survey of the Dutch colonial house and outbuildings, with constructional features, decoration, and local history associated with individual homesteads. Introduction by Franklin D. Roosevelt. Map. 150 illustrations. 469pp. 6⅝ x 9¼. 21469-9 Paperbound

THE ARCHITECTURE OF COUNTRY HOUSES, Andrew J. Downing. Together with Vaux's *Villas and Cottages* this is the basic book for Hudson River Gothic architecture of the middle Victorian period. Full, sound discussions of general aspects of housing, architecture, style, decoration, furnishing, together with scores of detailed house plans, illustrations of specific buildings, accompanied by full text. Perhaps the most influential single American architectural book. 1850 edition. Introduction by J. Stewart Johnson. 321 figures, 34 architectural designs. xvi + 560pp.

22003-6 Paperbound $4.00

LOST EXAMPLES OF COLONIAL ARCHITECTURE, John Mead Howells. Full-page photographs of buildings that have disappeared or been so altered as to be denatured, including many designed by major early American architects. 245 plates. xvii + 248pp. 7⅞ x 10¾.

21143-6 Paperbound $3.50

DOMESTIC ARCHITECTURE OF THE AMERICAN COLONIES AND OF THE EARLY REPUBLIC, Fiske Kimball. Foremost architect and restorer of Williamsburg and Monticello covers nearly 200 homes between 1620-1825. Architectural details, construction, style features, special fixtures, floor plans, etc. Generally considered finest work in its area. 219 illustrations of houses, doorways, windows, capital mantels. xx + 314pp. 7⅞ x 10¾.

21743-4 Paperbound $4.00

EARLY AMERICAN ROOMS: 1650-1858, edited by Russell Hawes Kettell. Tour of 12 rooms, each representative of a different era in American history and each furnished, decorated, designed and occupied in the style of the era. 72 plans and elevations, 8-page color section, etc., show fabrics, wall papers, arrangements, etc. Full descriptive text. xvii + 200pp. of text. 8⅜ x 11¼.

21633-0 Paperbound $5.00

THE FITZWILLIAM VIRGINAL BOOK, edited by J. Fuller Maitland and W. B. Squire. Full modern printing of famous early 17th-century ms. volume of 300 works by Morley, Byrd, Bull, Gibbons, etc. For piano or other modern keyboard instrument; easy to read format. xxxvi + 938pp. 8⅜ x 11.

21068-5, 21069-3 Two volumes, Paperbound $10.00

KEYBOARD MUSIC, Johann Sebastian Bach. Bach Gesellschaft edition. A rich selection of Bach's masterpieces for the harpsichord: the six English Suites, six French Suites, the six Partitas (Clavierübung part I), the Goldberg Variations (Clavierübung part IV), the fifteen Two-Part Inventions and the fifteen Three-Part Sinfonias. Clearly reproduced on large sheets with ample margins; eminently playable. vi + 312pp. 8⅛ x 11.

22360-4 Paperbound $5.00

THE MUSIC OF BACH: AN INTRODUCTION, Charles Sanford Terry. A fine, nontechnical introduction to Bach's music, both instrumental and vocal. Covers organ music, chamber music, passion music, other types. Analyzes themes, developments, innovations. x + 114pp.

21075-8 Paperbound $1.50

BEETHOVEN AND HIS NINE SYMPHONIES, Sir George Grove. Noted British musicologist provides best history, analysis, commentary on symphonies. Very thorough, rigorously accurate; necessary to both advanced student and amateur music lover. 436 musical passages. vii + 407 pp.

20334-4 Paperbound $2.75

JOHANN SEBASTIAN BACH, Philipp Spitta. One of the great classics of musicology, this definitive analysis of Bach's music (and life) has never been surpassed. Lucid, nontechnical analyses of hundreds of pieces (30 pages devoted to St. Matthew Passion, 26 to B Minor Mass). Also includes major analysis of 18th-century music. 450 musical examples. 40-page musical supplement. Total of xx + 1799pp.

(EUK) 22278-0, 22279-9 Two volumes, Clothbound $17.50

MOZART AND HIS PIANO CONCERTOS, Cuthbert Girdlestone. The only full-length study of an important area of Mozart's creativity. Provides detailed analyses of all 23 concertos, traces inspirational sources. 417 musical examples. Second edition. 509pp.

21271-8 Paperbound $3.50

THE PERFECT WAGNERITE: A COMMENTARY ON THE NIBLUNG'S RING, George Bernard Shaw. Brilliant and still relevant criticism in remarkable essays on Wagner's Ring cycle, Shaw's ideas on political and social ideology behind the plots, role of Leitmotifs, vocal requisites, etc. Prefaces. xxi + 136pp.

(USO) 21707-8 Paperbound $1.50

DON GIOVANNI, W. A. Mozart. Complete libretto, modern English translation; biographies of composer and librettist; accounts of early performances and critical reaction. Lavishly illustrated. All the material you need to understand and appreciate this great work. Dover Opera Guide and Libretto Series; translated and introduced by Ellen Bleiler. 92 illustrations. 209pp.

21134-7 Paperbound $2.00

BASIC ELECTRICITY, U. S. Bureau of Naval Personel. Originally a training course, best non-technical coverage of basic theory of electricity and its applications. Fundamental concepts, batteries, circuits, conductors and wiring techniques, AC and DC, inductance and capacitance, generators, motors, transformers, magnetic amplifiers, synchros, servomechanisms, etc. Also covers blue-prints, electrical diagrams, etc. Many questions, with answers. 349 illustrations. x + 448pp. 6½ x 9¼.

20973-3 Paperbound $3.50

REPRODUCTION OF SOUND, Edgar Villchur. Thorough coverage for laymen of high fidelity systems, reproducing systems in general, needles, amplifiers, preamps, loudspeakers, feedback, explaining physical background. "A rare talent for making technicalities vividly comprehensible," R. Darrell, *High Fidelity*. 69 figures. iv + 92pp.

21515-6 Paperbound $1.25

HEAR ME TALKIN' TO YA: THE STORY OF JAZZ AS TOLD BY THE MEN WHO MADE IT, Nat Shapiro and Nat Hentoff. Louis Armstrong, Fats Waller, Jo Jones, Clarence Williams, Billy Holiday, Duke Ellington, Jelly Roll Morton and dozens of other jazz greats tell how it was in Chicago's South Side, New Orleans, depression Harlem and the modern West Coast as jazz was born and grew. xvi + 429pp.

21726-4 Paperbound $3.00

FABLES OF AESOP, translated by Sir Roger L'Estrange. A reproduction of the very rare 1931 Paris edition; a selection of the most interesting fables, together with 50 imaginative drawings by Alexander Calder. v + 128pp. 6½x9¼.

21780-9 Paperbound $1.50

AGAINST THE GRAIN (A REBOURS), Joris K. Huysmans. Filled with weird images, evidences of a bizarre imagination, exotic experiments with hallucinatory drugs, rich tastes and smells and the diversions of its sybarite hero Duc Jean des Esseintes, this classic novel pushed 19th-century literary decadence to its limits. Full unabridged edition. Do not confuse this with abridged editions generally sold. Introduction by Havelock Ellis. xlix + 206pp. 22190-3 Paperbound $2.00

VARIORUM SHAKESPEARE: HAMLET. Edited by Horace H. Furness; a landmark of American scholarship. Exhaustive footnotes and appendices treat all doubtful words and phrases, as well as suggested critical emendations throughout the play's history. First volume contains editor's own text, collated with all Quartos and Folios. Second volume contains full first Quarto, translations of Shakespeare's sources (Belleforest, and Saxo Grammaticus), Der Bestrafte Brudermord, and many essays on critical and historical points of interest by major authorities of past and present. Includes details of staging and costuming over the years. By far the best edition available for serious students of Shakespeare. Total of xx + 905pp. 21004-9, 21005-7, 2 volumes, Paperbound $7.00

A LIFE OF WILLIAM SHAKESPEARE, Sir Sidney Lee. This is the standard life of Shakespeare, summarizing everything known about Shakespeare and his plays. Incredibly rich in material, broad in coverage, clear and judicious, it has served thousands as the best introduction to Shakespeare. 1931 edition. 9 plates. xxix + 792pp. (USO) 21967-4 Paperbound $3.75

MASTERS OF THE DRAMA, John Gassner. Most comprehensive history of the drama in print, covering every tradition from Greeks to modern Europe and America, including India, Far East, etc. Covers more than 800 dramatists, 2000 plays, with biographical material, plot summaries, theatre history, criticism, etc. "Best of its kind in English," *New Republic.* 77 illustrations. xxii + 890pp. 20100-7 Clothbound $8.50

THE EVOLUTION OF THE ENGLISH LANGUAGE, George McKnight. The growth of English, from the 14th century to the present. Unusual, non-technical account presents basic information in very interesting form: sound shifts, change in grammar and syntax, vocabulary growth, similar topics. Abundantly illustrated with quotations. Formerly *Modern English in the Making.* xii + 590pp. 21932-1 Paperbound $3.50

AN ETYMOLOGICAL DICTIONARY OF MODERN ENGLISH, Ernest Weekley. Fullest, richest work of its sort, by foremost British lexicographer. Detailed word histories, including many colloquial and archaic words; extensive quotations. Do not confuse this with the Concise Etymological Dictionary, which is much abridged. Total of xxvii + 830pp. 6½ x 9¼. 21873-2, 21874-0 Two volumes, Paperbound $7.90

FLATLAND: A ROMANCE OF MANY DIMENSIONS, E. A. Abbott. Classic of science-fiction explores ramifications of life in a two-dimensional world, and what happens when a three-dimensional being intrudes. Amusing reading, but also useful as introduction to thought about hyperspace. Introduction by Banesh Hoffmann. 16 illustrations. xx + 103pp. 20001-9 Paperbound $1.00

POEMS OF ANNE BRADSTREET, edited with an introduction by Robert Hutchinson. A new selection of poems by America's first poet and perhaps the first significant woman poet in the English language. 48 poems display her development in works of considerable variety—love poems, domestic poems, religious meditations, formal elegies, "quaternions," etc. Notes, bibliography. viii + 222pp.

22160-1 Paperbound $2.50

THREE GOTHIC NOVELS: THE CASTLE OF OTRANTO BY HORACE WALPOLE; VATHEK BY WILLIAM BECKFORD; THE VAMPYRE BY JOHN POLIDORI, WITH FRAGMENT OF A NOVEL BY LORD BYRON, edited by E. F. Bleiler. The first Gothic novel, by Walpole; the finest Oriental tale in English, by Beckford; powerful Romantic supernatural story in versions by Polidori and Byron. All extremely important in history of literature; all still exciting, packed with supernatural thrills, ghosts, haunted castles, magic, etc. xl + 291pp.

21232-7 Paperbound· $2.50

THE BEST TALES OF HOFFMANN, E. T. A. Hoffmann. 10 of Hoffmann's most important stories, in modern re-editings of standard translations: Nutcracker and the King of Mice, Signor Formica, Automata, The Sandman, Rath Krespel, The Golden Flowerpot, Master Martin the Cooper, The Mines of Falun, The King's Betrothed, A New Year's Eve Adventure. 7 illustrations by Hoffmann. Edited by E. F. Bleiler. xxxix + 419pp.

21793-0 Paperbound $3.00

GHOST AND HORROR STORIES OF AMBROSE BIERCE, Ambrose Bierce. 23 strikingly modern stories of the horrors latent in the human mind: The Eyes of the Panther, The Damned Thing, An Occurrence at Owl Creek Bridge, An Inhabitant of Carcosa, etc., plus the dream-essay, Visions of the Night. Edited by E. F. Bleiler. xxii + 199pp.

20767-6 Paperbound $1.50

BEST GHOST STORIES OF J. S. LeFANU, J. Sheridan LeFanu. Finest stories by Victorian master often considered greatest supernatural writer of all. Carmilla, Green Tea, The Haunted Baronet, The Familiar, and 12 others. Most never before available in the U. S. A. Edited by E. F. Bleiler. 8 illustrations from Victorian publications. xvii + 467pp.

20415-4 Paperbound $3.00

MATHEMATICAL FOUNDATIONS OF INFORMATION THEORY, A. I. Khinchin. Comprehensive introduction to work of Shannon, McMillan, Feinstein and Khinchin, placing these investigations on a rigorous mathematical basis. Covers entropy concept in probability theory, uniqueness theorem, Shannon's inequality, ergodic sources, the E property, martingale concept, noise, Feinstein's fundamental lemma, Shanon's first and second theorems. Translated by R. A. Silverman and M. D. Friedman. iii + 120pp.

60434-9 Paperbound $1.75

SEVEN SCIENCE FICTION NOVELS, H. G. Wells. The standard collection of the great novels. Complete, unabridged. *First Men in the Moon, Island of Dr. Moreau, War of the Worlds, Food of the Gods, Invisible Man, Time Machine, In the Days of the Comet.* Not only science fiction fans, but every educated person owes it to himself to read these novels. 1015pp. (USO) 20264-X Clothbound $6.00

LAST AND FIRST MEN AND STAR MAKER, TWO SCIENCE FICTION NOVELS, Olaf Stapledon. Greatest future histories in science fiction. In the first, human intelligence is the "hero," through strange paths of evolution, interplanetary invasions, incredible technologies, near extinctions and reemergences. Star Maker describes the quest of a band of star rovers for intelligence itself, through time and space: weird inhuman civilizations, crustacean minds, symbiotic worlds, etc. Complete, unabridged. v + 438pp. (USO) 21962-3 Paperbound $2.50

THREE PROPHETIC NOVELS, H. G. WELLS. Stages of a consistently planned future for mankind. *When the Sleeper Wakes,* and *A Story of the Days to Come,* anticipate *Brave New World* and *1984,* in the 21st Century; *The Time Machine,* only complete version in print, shows farther future and the end of mankind. All show Wells's greatest gifts as storyteller and novelist. Edited by E. F. Bleiler. x + 335pp. (USO) 20605-X Paperbound $2.50

THE DEVIL'S DICTIONARY, Ambrose Bierce. America's own Oscar Wilde—Ambrose Bierce—offers his barbed iconoclastic wisdom in over 1,000 definitions hailed by H. L. Mencken as "some of the most gorgeous witticisms in the English language." 145pp. 20487-1 Paperbound $1.25

MAX AND MORITZ, Wilhelm Busch. Great children's classic, father of comic strip, of two bad boys, Max and Moritz. Also Ker and Plunk (Plisch und Plumm), Cat and Mouse, Deceitful Henry, Ice-Peter, The Boy and the Pipe, and five other pieces. Original German, with English translation. Edited by H. Arthur Klein; translations by various hands and H. Arthur Klein. vi + 216pp.
20181-3 Paperbound $2.00

PIGS IS PIGS AND OTHER FAVORITES, Ellis Parker Butler. The title story is one of the best humor short stories, as Mike Flannery obfuscates biology and English. Also included, That Pup of Murchison's, The Great American Pie Company, and Perkins of Portland. 14 illustrations. v + 109pp. 21532-6 Paperbound $1.25

THE PETERKIN PAPERS, Lucretia P. Hale. It takes genius to be as stupidly mad as the Peterkins, as they decide to become wise, celebrate the "Fourth," keep a cow, and otherwise strain the resources of the Lady from Philadelphia. Basic book of American humor. 153 illustrations. 219pp. 20794-3 Paperbound $1.50

PERRAULT'S FAIRY TALES, translated by A. E. Johnson and S. R. Littlewood, with 34 full-page illustrations by Gustave Doré. All the original Perrault stories—Cinderella, Sleeping Beauty, Bluebeard, Little Red Riding Hood, Puss in Boots, Tom Thumb, etc.—with their witty verse morals and the magnificent illustrations of Doré. One of the five or six great books of European fairy tales. viii + 117pp. 8⅛ x 11. 22311-6 Paperbound $2.00

OLD HUNGARIAN FAIRY TALES, Baroness Orczy. Favorites translated and adapted by author of the *Scarlet Pimpernel.* Eight fairy tales include "The Suitors of Princess Fire-Fly," "The Twin Hunchbacks," "Mr. Cuttlefish's Love Story," and "The Enchanted Cat." This little volume of magic and adventure will captivate children as it has for generations. 90 drawings by Montagu Barstow. 96pp.
22293-4 Paperbound $1.95

THE RED FAIRY BOOK, Andrew Lang. Lang's color fairy books have long been children's favorites. This volume includes Rapunzel, Jack and the Bean-stalk and 35 other stories, familiar and unfamiliar. 4 plates, 93 illustrations x + 367pp.

21673-X Paperbound $2.50

THE BLUE FAIRY BOOK, Andrew Lang. Lang's tales come from all countries and all times. Here are 37 tales from Grimm, the Arabian Nights, Greek Mythology, and other fascinating sources. 8 plates, 130 illustrations. xi + 390pp.

21437-0 Paperbound $2.50

HOUSEHOLD STORIES BY THE BROTHERS GRIMM. Classic English-language edition of the well-known tales — Rumpelstiltskin, Snow White, Hansel and Gretel, The Twelve Brothers, Faithful John, Rapunzel, Tom Thumb (52 stories in all). Translated into simple, straightforward English by Lucy Crane. Ornamented with headpieces, vignettes, elaborate decorative initials and a dozen full-page illustrations by Walter Crane. x + 269pp. 21080-4 Paperbound $2.00

THE MERRY ADVENTURES OF ROBIN HOOD, Howard Pyle. The finest modern versions of the traditional ballads and tales about the great English outlaw. Howard Pyle's complete prose version, with every word, every illustration of the first edition. Do not confuse this facsimile of the original (1883) with modern editions that change text or illustrations. 23 plates plus many page decorations. xxii + 296pp.

22043-5 Paperbound $2.50

THE STORY OF KING ARTHUR AND HIS KNIGHTS, Howard Pyle. The finest children's version of the life of King Arthur; brilliantly retold by Pyle, with 48 of his most imaginative illustrations. xviii + 313pp. 6⅛ x 9¼.

21445-1 Paperbound $2.50

THE WONDERFUL WIZARD OF OZ, L. Frank Baum. America's finest children's book in facsimile of first edition with all Denslow illustrations in full color. The edition a child should have. Introduction by Martin Gardner. 23 color plates, scores of drawings. iv + 267pp. 20691-2 Paperbound $2.50

THE MARVELOUS LAND OF OZ, L. Frank Baum. The second Oz book, every bit as imaginative as the Wizard. The hero is a boy named Tip, but the Scarecrow and the Tin Woodman are back, as is the Oz magic. 16 color plates, 120 drawings by John R. Neill. 287pp. 20692-0 Paperbound $2.50

THE MAGICAL MONARCH OF MO, L. Frank Baum. Remarkable adventures in a land even stranger than Oz. The best of Baum's books not in the Oz series. 15 color plates and dozens of drawings by Frank Verbeck. xviii + 237pp.

21892-9 Paperbound $2.25

THE BAD CHILD'S BOOK OF BEASTS, MORE BEASTS FOR WORSE CHILDREN, A MORAL ALPHABET, Hilaire Belloc. Three complete humor classics in one volume. Be kind to the frog, and do not call him names . . . and 28 other whimsical animals. Familiar favorites and some not so well known. Illustrated by Basil Blackwell. 156pp. (USO) 20749-8 Paperbound $1.50

EAST O' THE SUN AND WEST O' THE MOON, George W. Dasent. Considered the best of all translations of these Norwegian folk tales, this collection has been enjoyed by generations of children (and folklorists too). Includes True and Untrue, Why the Sea is Salt, East O' the Sun and West O' the Moon, Why the Bear is Stumpy-Tailed, Boots and the Troll, The Cock and the Hen, Rich Peter the Pedlar, and 52 more. The only edition with all 59 tales. 77 illustrations by Erik Werenskiold and Theodor Kittelsen. xv + 418pp. 22521-6 Paperbound $3.50

GOOPS AND HOW TO BE THEM, Gelett Burgess. Classic of tongue-in-cheek humor, masquerading as etiquette book. 87 verses, twice as many cartoons, show mischievous Goops as they demonstrate to children virtues of table manners, neatness, courtesy, etc. Favorite for generations. viii + 88pp. 6½ x 9¼.
22233-0 Paperbound $1.25

ALICE'S ADVENTURES UNDER GROUND, Lewis Carroll. The first version, quite different from the final Alice in Wonderland, printed out by Carroll himself with his own illustrations. Complete facsimile of the "million dollar" manuscript Carroll gave to Alice Liddell in 1864. Introduction by Martin Gardner. viii + 96pp. Title and dedication pages in color. 21482-6 Paperbound $1.25

THE BROWNIES, THEIR BOOK, Palmer Cox. Small as mice, cunning as foxes, exuberant and full of mischief, the Brownies go to the zoo, toy shop, seashore, circus, etc., in 24 verse adventures and 266 illustrations. Long a favorite, since their first appearance in St. Nicholas Magazine. xi + 144pp. 6⅝ x 9¼.
21265-3 Paperbound $1.75

SONGS OF CHILDHOOD, Walter De La Mare. Published (under the pseudonym Walter Ramal) when De La Mare was only 29, this charming collection has long been a favorite children's book. A facsimile of the first edition in paper, the 47 poems capture the simplicity of the nursery rhyme and the ballad, including such lyrics as I Met Eve, Tartary, The Silver Penny. vii + 106pp. (USO) 21972-0 Paperbound $1.25

THE COMPLETE NONSENSE OF EDWARD LEAR, Edward Lear. The finest 19th-century humorist-cartoonist in full: all nonsense limericks, zany alphabets, Owl and Pussycat, songs, nonsense botany, and more than 500 illustrations by Lear himself. Edited by Holbrook Jackson. xxix + 287pp. (USO) 20167-8 Paperbound $2.00

BILLY WHISKERS: THE AUTOBIOGRAPHY OF A GOAT, Frances Trego Montgomery. A favorite of children since the early 20th century, here are the escapades of that rambunctious, irresistible and mischievous goat—Billy Whiskers. Much in the spirit of Peck's Bad Boy, this is a book that children never tire of reading or hearing. All the original familiar illustrations by W. H. Fry are included: 6 color plates, 18 black and white drawings. 159pp. 22345-0 Paperbound $2.00

MOTHER GOOSE MELODIES. Faithful republication of the fabulously rare Munroe and Francis "copyright 1833" Boston edition—the most important Mother Goose collection, usually referred to as the "original." Familiar rhymes plus many rare ones, with wonderful old woodcut illustrations. Edited by E. F. Bleiler. 128pp. 4½ x 6⅜. 22577-1 Paperbound $1.00

Two Little Savages; Being the Adventures of Two Boys Who Lived as Indians and What They Learned, Ernest Thompson Seton. Great classic of nature and boyhood provides a vast range of woodlore in most palatable form, a genuinely entertaining story. Two farm boys build a teepee in woods and live in it for a month, working out Indian solutions to living problems, star lore, birds and animals, plants, etc. 293 illustrations. vii + 286pp.

20985-7 Paperbound $2.50

Peter Piper's Practical Principles of Plain & Perfect Pronunciation. Alliterative jingles and tongue-twisters of surprising charm, that made their first appearance in America about 1830. Republished in full with the spirited woodcut illustrations from this earliest American edition. 32pp. 4½ x 6⅜.

22560-7 Paperbound $1.00

Science Experiments and Amusements for Children, Charles Vivian. 73 easy experiments, requiring only materials found at home or easily available, such as candles, coins, steel wool, etc.; illustrate basic phenomena like vacuum, simple chemical reaction, etc. All safe. Modern, well-planned. Formerly *Science Games for Children*. 102 photos, numerous drawings. 96pp. 6⅛ x 9¼.

21856-2 Paperbound $1.25

An Introduction to Chess Moves and Tactics Simply Explained, Leonard Barden. Informal intermediate introduction, quite strong in explaining reasons for moves. Covers basic material, tactics, important openings, traps, positional play in middle game, end game. Attempts to isolate patterns and recurrent configurations. Formerly *Chess*. 58 figures. 102pp. (USO) 21210-6 Paperbound $1.25

Lasker's Manual of Chess, Dr. Emanuel Lasker. Lasker was not only one of the five great World Champions, he was also one of the ablest expositors, theorists, and analysts. In many ways, his Manual, permeated with his philosophy of battle, filled with keen insights, is one of the greatest works ever written on chess. Filled with analyzed games by the great players. A single-volume library that will profit almost any chess player, beginner or master. 308 diagrams. xli x 349pp.

20640-8 Paperbound $2.75

The Master Book of Mathematical Recreations, Fred Schuh. In opinion of many the finest work ever prepared on mathematical puzzles, stunts, recreations; exhaustively thorough explanations of mathematics involved, analysis of effects, citation of puzzles and games. Mathematics involved is elementary. Translated by F. Göbel. 194 figures. xxiv + 430pp. 22134-2 Paperbound $3.50

Mathematics, Magic and Mystery, Martin Gardner. Puzzle editor for Scientific American explains mathematics behind various mystifying tricks: card tricks, stage "mind reading," coin and match tricks, counting out games, geometric dissections, etc. Probability sets, theory of numbers clearly explained. Also provides more than 400 tricks, guaranteed to work, that you can do. 135 illustrations. xii + 176pp.

20335-2 Paperbound $1.75

MATHEMATICAL PUZZLES FOR BEGINNERS AND ENTHUSIASTS, Geoffrey Mott-Smith. 189 puzzles from easy to difficult—involving arithmetic, logic, algebra, properties of digits, probability, etc.—for enjoyment and mental stimulus. Explanation of mathematical principles behind the puzzles. 135 illustrations. viii + 248pp.
20198-8 Paperbound $1.75

PAPER FOLDING FOR BEGINNERS, William D. Murray and Francis J. Rigney. Easiest book on the market, clearest instructions on making interesting, beautiful origami. Sail boats, cups, roosters, frogs that move legs, bonbon boxes, standing birds, etc. 40 projects; more than 275 diagrams and photographs. 94pp.
20713-7 Paperbound $1.00

TRICKS AND GAMES ON THE POOL TABLE, Fred Herrmann. 79 tricks and games— some solitaires, some for two or more players, some competitive games—to entertain you between formal games. Mystifying shots and throws, unusual caroms, tricks involving such props as cork, coins, a hat, etc. Formerly *Fun on the Pool Table*. 77 figures. 95pp.
21814-7 Paperbound $1.00

HAND SHADOWS TO BE THROWN UPON THE WALL: A SERIES OF NOVEL AND AMUSING FIGURES FORMED BY THE HAND, Henry Bursill. Delightful picturebook from great-grandfather's day shows how to make 18 different hand shadows: a bird that flies, duck that quacks, dog that wags his tail, camel, goose, deer, boy, turtle, etc. Only book of its sort. vi + 33pp. 6½ x 9¼. 21779-5 Paperbound $1.00

WHITTLING AND WOODCARVING, E. J. Tangerman. 18th printing of best book on market. "If you can cut a potato you can carve" toys and puzzles, chains, chessmen, caricatures, masks, frames, woodcut blocks, surface patterns, much more. Information on tools, woods, techniques. Also goes into serious wood sculpture from Middle Ages to present, East and West. 464 photos, figures. x + 293pp.
20965-2 Paperbound $2.00

HISTORY OF PHILOSOPHY, Julián Marias. Possibly the clearest, most easily followed, best planned, most useful one-volume history of philosophy on the market; neither skimpy nor overfull. Full details on system of every major philosopher and dozens of less important thinkers from pre-Socratics up to Existentialism and later. Strong on many European figures usually omitted. Has gone through dozens of editions in Europe. 1966 edition, translated by Stanley Appelbaum and Clarence Strowbridge. xviii + 505pp. 21739-6 Paperbound $3.50

YOGA: A SCIENTIFIC EVALUATION, Kovoor T. Behanan. Scientific but non-technical study of physiological results of yoga exercises; done under auspices of Yale U. Relations to Indian thought, to psychoanalysis, etc. 16 photos. xxiii + 270pp.
20505-3 Paperbound $2.50

Prices subject to change without notice.
Available at your book dealer or write for free catalogue to Dept. GI, Dover Publications, Inc., 180 Varick St., N. Y., N. Y. 10014. Dover publishes more than 150 books each year on science, elementary and advanced mathematics, biology, music, art, literary history, social sciences and other areas.